Pogroms

Pogroms

A Documentary History

Edited by

EUGENE M. AVRUTIN AND ELISSA BEMPORAD

OXFORD
UNIVERSITY PRESS

OXFORD
UNIVERSITY PRESS

Oxford University Press is a department of the University of Oxford. It furthers
the University's objective of excellence in research, scholarship, and education
by publishing worldwide. Oxford is a registered trade mark of Oxford University
Press in the UK and certain other countries.

Published in the United States of America by Oxford University Press
198 Madison Avenue, New York, NY 10016, United States of America.

Library of Congress Cataloging-in-Publication Data
Names: Avrutin, Eugene M., editor, author. | Bemporad, Elissa, editor, author.
Title: Pogroms : a documentary history / Eugene M. Avrutin and Elissa Bemporad.
Description: New York : Oxford University Press, [2021] |
Includes bibliographical references and index.
Identifiers: LCCN 2021015017 (print) | LCCN 2021015018 (ebook) |
ISBN 9780190060084 (hardback) | ISBN 9780190060091 (paperback) |
ISBN 9780190060114 (epub)
Subjects: LCSH: Pogroms—Russia—History—Sources. |
Pogroms—Europe, Eastern—History—Sources. |
Jews—Persecutions—Russia—History—Sources. |
Jews—Persecutions—Europe, Eastern—History—Sources. |
Antisemitism—Russia—History—Sources. |
Antisemitism—Europe, Eastern—History—Sources.
Classification: LCC DS134.84 .P64 2021 (print) | LCC DS134.84 (ebook) |
DDC 947/.004924—dc23
LC record available at https://lccn.loc.gov/2021015017
LC ebook record available at https://lccn.loc.gov/2021015018

DOI: 10.1093/oso/9780190060084.001.0001

1 3 5 7 9 8 6 4 2

Paperback printed by LSC communications, United States of America
Hardback printed by Bridgeport National Bindery, Inc., United States of America

In memory of David Shneer
(1972–2020)

Contents

Acknowledgments

The initial idea for this volume emerged from a series of conversations between the editors about the relationship between Jewish history and violence, and about the pogrom conundrum in Russia and East Central Europe in modern times. These conversations materialized into facts. In May 2019, we organized a conference at the Center for Jewish History to commemorate the centennial of the 1919 wave of anti-Jewish violence unleashed by the Russian Civil War. A distinguished group of scholars came together to discuss the pogroms through the lenses of the specific geopolitical context where the violence erupted, as well as in a comparative framework in relation to anti-Black violence. We also explored the power of literary responses to anti-Jewish violence and reassessed the role that pogroms play in Jewish memory and history. The conference was followed by an inspiring workshop where we discussed drafts of the chapters and our vision for the documentary collection. We are truly grateful to the superb contributors, to Nancy Toff of Oxford University Press (OUP), and to Julie Chervinsky and Olga Golovanova of the Blavatnik Archive Foundation for their wisdom, suggestions, and good humor. The Blavatnik Archive Foundation, the Leonid Nevzlin Research Center for Russian and East European Jewry at the Hebrew University of Jerusalem, and the Center for Jewish History provided financial and organizational resources without which we would not have been able to convene the workshop.

We are indebted to David Mazower, bibliographer and editorial director at the Yiddish Book Center, for knowing everything about Yiddish sources, and to Chana Pollack, archivist at the *Forward*, for locating a precious image from the archives. We thank the *Forward* for granting us permission to publish the image in the book. Our heartfelt thanks go out to Robert Weinberg, Valerie Kivelson, and Samuel Kassow for offering insightful comments on our introductory essay, as well as Kevin Mumford for his assistance with the comparative dimension. We are grateful to Leyzer Burko, Anna Cichopek-Gajraj, Glenn Dynner, Asia Lev, Harriet Murav, Eugenia Tietz-Sokolskaya, Daniel Unowsky, and Polly Zavadivker for translating the primary sources. Diana Jaher, Diamond Dadej, and Joshua Woolf-Senoff provided timely research assistance over a span of many years. Therese Malhame skillfully copyedited the volume. We would like to say a warm thank you to Nancy Toff, our editor at OUP, for believing in this project, handling the complicated administrative arrangements, and answering our numerous queries. Thanks also to Nancy's colleague Isabelle Prince at OUP for guiding this book to publication.

The research and writing of this book have been made possible by the generous support of different institutions. First of all, we are delighted to express our appreciation to the Blavatnik Archive Foundation for awarding us a generous grant to support the publication of this documentary collection, as well as for granting us permission to reprint the visual materials. Further financial support came from the Tobor Family Endowment, the Research Board of the University of Illinois, and the PSC-CUNY Research Award Program and the Research Foundation of the City University of New York.

This book is dedicated to the memory of our colleague David Shneer, whose untimely passing in November 2020 has deprived the fields of East European, Russian, and Jewish history of his wisdom and creativity.

Pogroms

An Introduction

Eugene M. Avrutin and Elissa Bemporad

April 26, 1881, was a warm and pleasant Sunday afternoon in Kiev (Kyiv). Crowds of people spent the day strolling around public squares and bazaars when a skirmish broke out between Jewish and Christian children. It took no time for a mob of youths and neighborhood thugs, armed with hammers and bludgeons, to gather around. Shouting, "Beat the Yids who killed our tsar," the rioters threw rocks at Jewish homes. A pogrom had devastated Elisavetgrad several days earlier. Troops—on high alert that day and expecting more trouble—struggled to contain the violence. At least three Jews died in the mayhem and nearly 190 people (not all Jews) were injured. Rioters ransacked shops, taverns, and prayer houses. A special correspondent for the Anglo-Jewish newspaper, the *Jewish World*, traveled to Kiev to investigate. "Looking closely at the shops, traces of the recent campaign are only too apparent," the journalist observed. "The well-to-do have all new doors, new window sashes, and many of them newly painted signboards. The less prosperous are more readily noted. Windows still broken; sashes and signs battered in; plaster hanging down; and, more significant still, nothing whatever inside the shop but broken wood and splintered furniture."[1]

At the turn of the twentieth century, an upsurge of explosive pogroms caused much pain and suffering in the eastern borderlands of Europe, the territories under consideration in our book. Jews were not the only ethnic group swept up in the violence, but they usually bore the brunt of the ill-treatment. In the summer of 1885, Romanian peasant rioters attacked Jewish property and caused physical harm to women and children, resulting in the expulsion of around 130 Jews from a village. In the Habsburg Empire, in 1898, the governor of Galicia declared a state of emergency in the aftermath of some 400 anti-Jewish riots. The Russian Empire was the site of some of the world's most fatal and meticulously documented pogroms, many of which occurred in cities such as Kishinev, Kiev, and Elisavetgrad, which suffered

---

[1] Natan M. Meir, *Kiev Jewish Metropolis: A History, 1859–1914* (Bloomington: Indiana University Press, 2010), 51–57; and *Jewish World*, July 15, 1881, 5 (Document 1.9 in this book). For an analysis of British society's responses toward anti-Jewish violence, see Sam Johnson, *Pogroms, Peasants, Jews: Britain and Eastern Europe's "Jewish Question," 1867–1925* (New York: Palgrave Macmillan, 2011), 41–66.

Eugene M. Avrutin and Elissa Bemporad, *Pogroms* In: *Pogroms*. Edited by: Eugene M. Avrutin and Elissa Bemporad, Oxford University Press. © Oxford University Press 2021. DOI: 10.1093/oso/9780190060084.003.0001

repeated outbreaks, with the scope and breadth of the violence in Odessa standing second to none.[2]

World War I and the Russian Civil War (1918–1921) represented a turning point in the history of the pogroms. The brutality reached its peak during the ruthless conflict to gain political and territorial control that followed the 1917 Bolshevik Revolution. The forces at war included the Red Army, which fought on behalf of Bolshevik power, and faced the White movement, a coalition of anticommunist forces, that tried to take over postrevolutionary Russia. Under the leadership of the Directory of the Ukrainian People's Republic, Ukrainian troops also faced the Bolsheviks in a desperate struggle for independence. As part of the Polish–Soviet War, Polish troops fought against the Red Army as they advanced eastward on behalf of the Second Polish Republic. The combatants also included a diverse group of peasant bands in Ukraine, Belarus, and central Russia. Although they disassociated themselves from the ideology of the other combatants, the peasant bands consistently resisted the Red Army and its grain requisition policies to feed its troops.

The territories affected by war and revolution, in particular the western borderlands of the Russian Empire, saw an exponential rise in the scale of violence. More than 1,500 pogroms took place in a continuum of unprecedented brutality, with the epicenter in present-day Ukraine. The figures of fatalities and wounded, of orphaned children and raped women, together with the extent of damage to property, reached staggering proportions, which were overshadowed only by the Holocaust some twenty years later. The pogrom that took place in February 1919, in the city of Proskurov (Proskuriv, now Khmelnytsky), in the region of Podolia, when more than 1,500 Jews were killed in less than four hours, became the symbol of the scope and breadth of the violence of this period.

The term "pogrom" has cast a dark shadow on Jewish life. It has stood as a metonym for Jewish pain and suffering across the arc of a century. Gruesome images— as depicted in photographs, postcards, and artwork—offer a stark reminder of the traumatic impact of pogrom violence on Jewish communities. One of the challenges of analyzing pogroms is in coming to terms with the frequency, diversity, and dynamism of the events that we include under this heading. Scholars have used the term to label anti-Jewish violence that took place in Odessa in 1871, in the southwestern borderlands after the assassination of Tsar Alexander II in 1881, in Łódź in 1892, in Kishinev and Gomel in 1903, during the revolutionary uprisings of 1905–1906, amid the years of war and revolution, and in different areas of Central and Eastern Europe during the 1930s and 1940s. As a leading scholar of anti-Jewish violence summarized the problem, "Virtually the only common feature of these events

---

[2] For a wide-ranging exploration of these and other similar episodes of anti-Jewish violence, see the essays in Robert Nemes and Daniel Unowsky, eds., *Sites of European Antisemitism in the Age of Mass Politics, 1880–1918* (Waltham, MA: Brandeis University Press, 2014); John D. Klier and Shlomo Lambroza, eds., *Pogroms: Anti-Jewish Violence in Modern Russian History* (Cambridge: Cambridge University Press, 1992); and Christhard Hoffmann, Werner Bergmann, and Helmut Walser Smith, eds., *Exclusionary Violence: Antisemitic Riots in Modern German History* (Ann Arbor: University of Michigan Press, 2002).

"After a Pogrom." Drawing of a ravaged room. The artist P. I. Geller depicts three dead women. A dead child lies on top of the woman in the center. An old man—perhaps the grandfather—is holding the child in agony and bewilderment.
Courtesy of the Blavatnik Archive.

was that Jews were among the victims, although they were not always the primary target."[3]

What, then, was a pogrom, and more important, what do we gain from analyzing a series of distinct historical events under this common rubric? Much like the term "violence," which has been used to describe everything from the routine to the extreme, from the lawful to the illicit, and from the structural to the symbolic, scholars have used the term "pogrom" to refer to acts that have occurred in different times and regions around the world.[4] No less significant are the many myths and half-truths that have clouded scholarly and popular understandings of pogrom violence over the years. Russia may have been remembered as the birthplace of pogroms, and Jews may have been the most visible victims, but there was nothing peculiarly Russian or Jewish about pogroms.[5] Russia was neither the first nor the only place where ethnic riots took place, and Jews were by no means the only ethnic group

[3] John D. Klier, *Russians, Jews, and the Pogroms of 1881–1882* (Cambridge: Cambridge University Press, 2011), 59.

[4] For an insightful discussion, see David Engel, "What's in a Pogrom?," in *Anti-Jewish Violence: Rethinking the Pogrom in East European History*, ed. Jonathan Dekel-Chen, David Gaunt, Natan M. Meir, and Israel Bartal (Bloomington: Indiana University Press, 2011), 21. On the problem of defining the term "violence," see Laura Engelstein, "Weapons of the Weak (Apologies to James Scott): Violence in Russian History," *Kritika: Explorations in Russian and Eurasian History* 4, no. 3 (2003): 678–79.

[5] Hans Rogger, "Conclusion and Overview," in Klier and Lambroza, *Pogroms*, 314–72.

targeted by rioters. In our book, the term "pogrom" characterizes mob attacks or deadly ethnic riots that were usually, but not always, carried out in urban settings. To capture the complexity of the phenomena, "pogrom" refers to a constellation of violent events, ranging from spontaneous ethnic riots (resulting in bodily injury, looting or destruction of property, and death) to genocidal violence (the deliberate killing of an entire group of people).[6]

From the end of the nineteenth century onward, pogroms have presented a distinct challenge of interpretation: the daunting task of grappling with the role of anti-Jewish violence in the writing of Jewish, Russian, and Eastern European history and culture. How could pogroms erupt in so many places seemingly simultaneously? What were their underlying causes? Why did government and police officials fail to suppress the violence? What role, if any, did state actors and army officials play in instigating pogroms? The first generation of revisionist historians, working in the 1980s and the early 1990s, pushed aside the tendency to view anti-Jewish violence through the prism of conspiratorial theory, or the alleged role that the imperial Russian government played in organizing and perpetrating pogrom violence. In their judicious explanations, the revisionist scholars considered a broad range of factors that fueled ethnoreligious strife: the strains of uneven economic development, fierce antisemitic press campaigns, demographic fears, and a rootless, hard-drinking, working-class culture.[7]

Yet the conspiratorial theory of pogroms continues to live on in the popular imagination, despite the publication of a stream of books drawing on new sources and new approaches to the study of anti-Jewish violence. To this day, the notion that state officials played an important role in condoning, if not organizing, popular violence against Jews continues to be propagated in novels and films, in classroom discussions and lecture halls, and in scholarly books.[8] The second, updated edition of the *Oxford English Dictionary* adds to the misconception by defining "pogrom" as an "organized massacre" that is "officially tolerated" from above.[9] It is our hope that the publication of *Pogroms: A Documentary History* will correct this view for a new generation of readers and will broaden our understanding of the complexity of the phenomena.

Above all, pogroms broke out in borderland regions where ethnicity played a formative role in ordering and dividing diverse communities. The eastern borderlands of Europe, the historic home of the Russian and Habsburg Empires, were populated

[6] For a balanced explanation of the terms "ethnic riot," "pogrom," and "genocide," see Donald L. Horowitz, *The Deadly Ethnic Riot* (Berkeley: University of California Press, 2001), 17–23.

[7] The collection of essays edited by Klier and Lambroza, *Pogroms: Anti-Jewish Violence in Modern Russian History*, decisively dispels the idea that the Russian government was complicit in fomenting and instigating anti-Jewish violence.

[8] In an otherwise superb book, Alan E. Steinweis argues that Russian pogroms "were characterized by grassroots antisemitic violence that was condoned, if not organized, by the authorities." See Steinweis's *Kristallnacht 1938* (Cambridge, MA: Harvard University Press, 2009), 2.

[9] Sam Johnson, "Uses and Abuses: 'Pogrom' in the Anglo-American Imagination, 1881–1919," in *Jews in the East European Borderlands: Essays in Honor of John D. Klier*, ed. Eugene M. Avrutin and Harriet Murav (Boston: Academic Studies Press, 2012), 149–50. On the development of the conspiratorial myth of pogroms, see Klier, *Russians, Jews, and the Pogroms*, 384–414.

הנודרים

"The Wanderers." Between 1881 and 1914, around 1.5 million Jews immigrated to the United States. An additional 500,000 Jews left Russia for Palestine, Argentina, and many other destinations across the globe. Some scholars and contemporary observers attributed pogroms as the most important catalyst for Jewish emigration. The theory that the pogroms of 1881 served as a watershed moment has been discredited. Pogroms increased the number of refugees, but most Jewish families who experienced pogroms could not afford the expenses associated with overseas travel. The Jews who emigrated did so for a variety of economic, social, and demographic reasons.

Courtesy of the Blavatnik Archive.

by diverse nationalities, languages, cultural traditions, and spiritual and polit-ical movements. For long stretches of time, Jews, Poles, Ukrainians, Romanians, Russians, Germans, and Greeks inhabited a shared world. Most neighbors had a good sense of each other's daily rhythms and life-cycle rituals. They walked the same streets, bought goods and produce from the same neighborhood markets, drank beer and vodka in the same taverns, and occasionally dwelled in the same apartment buildings. This is not to imply that social relations between neighbors were always amicable or peaceful. In the borderlands, it was not uncommon for re-ligious prejudices, including vicious rumors of Jews kidnapping and slaughtering Christian children for their blood, to erupt into violent conflicts during religious festival periods, when Easter traditionally coincides with Passover; or for rowdy gatherings, verbal altercations, and neighborhood fistfights to escalate into some-thing more sinister and uncontrollable. Authorities generally did what they could to protect private property and maintain a just social order. Then, as now, the last thing that government and police officials wanted to deal with was an explosive riot that raged out of control.[10]

Before the outbreak of World War I, Jewish communities in the Russian and Habsburg Empires experienced three cycles of anti-Jewish violence: in 1881–1884, in 1898, and in 1903–1906. On March 1, 1881, a member of the executive com-mittee of a revolutionary political group known as the People's Will threw a bomb that fatally wounded Tsar Alexander II of Russia. Rumors circulated that the new tsar, Alexander III (1845–1894), had issued a decree to beat Jews as punishment for his father's murder. The outbreak of the Elisavetgrad pogrom on April 15 and the waves of anti-Jewish violence that followed were largely spontaneous events. Nearly 250 pogroms—some in large urban settings, others in market towns and railway depots in rural districts—devastated the southwestern borderlands. Rioters inflicted violence to humiliate, deride, and plunder, but generally avoided inflicting physical harm. Fifty people died in the pogroms of 1881 and 1882, and half of them were Jews.[11]

The 1881 pogroms took place during a religiously charged season of the calendar year, when a mundane fistfight or clash could escalate into a riot. Violence against Jews echoed highly ritualized confrontations, while the atmosphere resembled the enor-mously popular festivities associated with carnival. Crowds of people—including men, women, and children—watched rioters cause mayhem, without usually causing bodily harm to Jews. Provincial administrators scrambled to establish precautionary meas-ures to prevent rioting and looting. They circulated public announcements, warning that anyone caught disturbing the peace would be promptly prosecuted with the full

---

[10] On the problem of coexistence, see David Frick, "Jews in Public Places: Further Chapters in the Jewish-Christian Encounter in Seventeenth-Century Vilna," *Polin* 22 (2010): 215–48. On the challenges of European states in exerting control over anti-Jewish violence, see Helmut Walser Smith, *The Continuities of German History: Nation, Religion, and Race across the Long Nineteenth Century* (Cambridge: Cambridge University Press, 2008), 117, 158–62.

[11] Klier, *Russians, Jews, and the Pogroms*, 84.

force of the law. Still, damage to Jewish property was considerable. Journalistic accounts and contemporary judicial reports chronicled how pogrom perpetrators ripped featherbeds, broke furniture, stoned windows, and looted drinking establishments with impunity. Newspapers worldwide published disturbing descriptions of the pogroms, including occasional references to the rape of Jewish women.

Anti-Jewish violence—especially the highly volatile disturbances associated with pogroms—proved difficult to contain. The presence of police in small communities was largely ineffective in maintaining social stability, not least because of the limited numbers. In Habsburg Galicia, the pogroms occurred in a corner of the empire marked by the pains of uneven economic development. Violence broke out in towns and villages where Jews owned a disproportionate number of restaurants, shops, taverns, and stores. The 1898 riots, fueled by baseless rumors and sensational Catholic propaganda, constituted the most lethal outbreak of anti-Jewish violence in the Habsburg Empire before World War I. The riots raged for nearly four months, resulting in more than five thousand arrests.[12]

The bloodshed that the Jewish communities experienced in tsarist Russia between 1903 and 1906 was far more volatile and deadly than the anti-Jewish violence in the 1880s or in 1898. Kishinev, a city on the Romanian border, plagued by poverty, endemic corruption, and lawlessness, was the site of one of the world's well-known pogroms. Almost twice as many Jews died on April 6–7, 1903, as in the anti-Jewish riots of 1881–1884. The atrocities ranged from murder and torture to bodily mutilation and gang rape. The lack of effective action by officials encouraged mob violence. At least two hundred rioters, composed mainly of rowdy youths and neighborhood drunks, ransacked liquor stores, Jewish shops, and apartment buildings, stealing all they could carry. After some forty-eight hours of rioting, the number of deaths totaled forty-nine and those jailed around nine hundred. The damage to property was estimated at 3 million rubles, with seven hundred houses burned and six hundred shops looted. Newspapers all around the world published sensational stories of the pogrom. A wealth of postcards and photographs circulated across the Atlantic, chronicling the pogrom's carnage.[13]

In the aftermath of Bloody Sunday (January 9, 1905, when troops set off months of revolutionary protests by firing on a demonstration of unarmed workers), anti-Jewish violence devastated small mining settlements as well as important commercial centers. The pogroms of 1905 were part of a much wider pattern of social conflict in the empire, including unprecedented labor and student unrest and a surge in crime.[14] Masses of labor migrants, including criminals, adventurers,

---

[12] Daniel Unowsky, *The Plunder: The 1898 Anti-Jewish Riots in Habsburg Galicia* (Stanford, CA: Stanford University Press, 2018). See also Keely Stauter-Halsted, "Jews as Middleman Minorities in Rural Poland: Understanding the Galician Pogroms of 1898," in *Antisemitism and Its Opponents in Modern Poland*, ed. Robert Blobaum (Ithaca, NY: Cornell University Press, 2005), 39–59.

[13] Steven J. Zipperstein, *Pogrom: Kishinev and the Tilt of History* (New York: Liverlight, 2018).

[14] On crime, see Joan Neuberger, *Hooliganism: Crime, Culture, and Power in St. Petersburg, 1900–1914* (Berkeley: University of California Press, 1993), 71–110; Roshanna P. Sylvester, *Tales of Old Odessa: Crime and Civility in a City of Thieves* (DeKalb: Northern Illinois University Press, 2005); and Ilya Gerasimov, *Plebian*

and Jews from the northwestern Pale of Settlement, traveled south to the industrial heartland looking for work. The newcomers lived in squat huts and company housing, often in primitive conditions. By day, they worked in mines, steel mills, and artisanal workshops. By night and on holidays and weekends, they spent their time socializing: drinking liquor to excess in taverns and cheap diners; playing cards in gambling dens; and organizing mass fights or brawls for entertainment. This highly transient population, known for its rough working-class lifestyle, was prone to violent outbursts, many of which were directed against Jews.[15] Between October 1905 and September 1906, according to conservative estimates, nearly 660 pogroms broke out in the Pale of Settlement, resulting in more than 3,100 Jewish deaths, at least one-fourth of whom were women, with the damage to Jewish property, estimated at a staggering 57 million rubles, decimating entire neighborhoods. Other riots broke out beyond the Pale of Settlement in cities such as Tver with small Jewish communities. In these instances, students and professionals were the main source of the rioters' fury.[16]

Who participated in the riots? Why were Jews targeted disproportionately for abuse? What motivated town residents to commit violent acts against their Jewish neighbors? As soon as a pogrom took a life of one of its own, group boundaries and ethnic loyalties crystallized. The populations that saw themselves as superior applied force on the basis of group membership.[17] Anti-Jewish violence was almost always a highly patterned and ritualized affair. Christians hung crosses and icons on the windows and doors of their shops and homes to safeguard against vandalism. Legacies of past events, moreover, became deeply ingrained in popular memory, with each episode lessening social constraints and providing a model for future disturbances. Hundreds, sometimes thousands, of people—including neighborhood youths, workers, revolutionaries, right-wing activists, professional criminals, railroad workers, and rowdy students—participated in pogrom-related activities. Although local police officials, military commanders, and troops usually did not plan pogroms, their actions proved largely incapable of stopping the rioters' rage. In some instances, they looked the other way. On other occasions, they looted homes, shops, and businesses with batons and whips in hand. It was not uncommon for peasants from nearby villages to load carts with bundles, bags, and boxes filled with Jewish belongings. As centralized authority collapsed amid war, revolution, and counterrevolution, state actors struggled to control the deadly outbreaks of anti-Jewish violence.

Modernity: Social Practices, Illegality, and the Urban Poor in Russia, 1905–1917 (Rochester, NY: University of Rochester Press, 2018).

[15] Charters Wynn, *Workers, Strikes, and Pogroms: The Donbass-Dnepr Bend in Late Imperial Russia, 1870–1905* (Princeton, NJ: Princeton University Press, 1992).
[16] Shlomo Lambroza, "Jewish Responses to Pogroms in Late Imperial Russia," in *Living with Antisemitism*, ed. Jehuda Reinharz (Hanover, NH: Brandeis University Press, 1987), 268; and Samuel D. Kassow, *Students, Professors, and the State in Tsarist Russia* (Berkeley: University of California Press, 1989), 274–75.
[17] On ethnic boundaries and riots, see Horowitz, *Deadly Ethnic Riot*, 43–70.

At a time of national emergency, Jews became easy targets for abuse. In the 1880s Russian officials blamed Jews for exploiting the peasant population. Some went so far as to argue that Jews' hostilities against Christians were deeply ingrained in the Jewish national psyche. Journalists on both sides of the political spectrum publicized these views widely, lamenting that Jews possessed characteristics that would not allow them to assimilate. "What the Jews were, so they shall remain," the conservative *Novoe vremia* (New Times) opined following the pogrom in Elisavetgrad in March 1881. Many other newspapers, including the *Tserkovnoobshchestvennyi vestnik* (Church Society Gazette), circulated vicious rumors about Jews as relentless exploiters: "Jewish profiteers really do suck the blood from the poor peasants and use unconscionable tricks to drive them to ruin. The greed of the Jews, one must say, has no limits and constitutes, as it were, a special and specific affinity of the Israelite race." Even the liberal *Golos* (Voice) felt that "the Semitic race, for all its aptitudes, possesses many qualities which make it far from a sympathetic object for Russians."[18]

But the problem with Jews was not solely economic. By the turn of the twentieth century, right-wing groups made Jews easy scapegoats for the internal political difficulties and increasingly desperate living conditions that plagued the empire. A highly charged racial ideology set the tone for discriminatory attitudes and actions. The developments surrounding the 1905 revolution did much to link race with mass politics and anti-Jewish violence. In times of social and political unrest, newspapers and periodicals disseminated crude, racist images to educated elites and the semiliterate public. The figure of the Jew, standing at the very center of an insidious plot against the Russian nation, was featured prominently in the press. Cartoons in right-wing newspapers and satirical publications depicted Russian national symbols, contrasting them with ugly representations of internal enemies (usually Jews) intent on subverting the Russian nation.[19] The Black Hundreds— a paramilitary group associated with the Union of the Russian People—operated extortion schemes of Jewish communities with threats of violence and pogroms; participated in assassination attempts of Jews and leftist politicians and journalists; attacked and robbed Jews on the streets; and circulated antisemitic newspapers and leaflets.[20]

Against this backdrop, it is tempting to make the argument that a deep-rooted ethnic hatred against Jews was largely responsible for unleashing pogrom violence. The documentary evidence compiled in our book takes into consideration the role that antisemitism played in fomenting anti-Jewish violence, but it also presents a variety of other forces at work. In the last decades of the nineteenth century and the

---

[18] Quoted in Klier, *Russians, Jews, and the Pogroms*, 139, 141.

[19] Robert Weinberg, "The Russian Right Responds to 1905: Visual Depictions of Jews in Postrevolutionary Russia," in *The Revolution of 1905 and Russia's Jews*, ed. Stefani Hoffman and Ezra Mendelsohn (Philadelphia: University of Pennsylvania Press, 2008), 53–69; and Stephen M. Norris, "*Pliuvium's* Unholy Trinity: Russian Nationhood, Anti-Semitism, and the Public Sphere after 1905," *Experiment* 19 (2013): 87–116.

[20] Jacob Langer, "Corruption and the Counterrevolution: The Rise and Fall of the Black Hundred" (PhD diss., Duke University, 2007), 56–114, 193–96.

In the aftermath of the 1905 revolution, extreme right-wing political parties relied on cheap newspapers and journals to galvanize popular support. Crude images and cartoons frequently asserted that Jews rejected the core values of Russian autocracy. Graphic artists often depicted Jews in unflattering terms as the chief source of Russia's problems.
Pliuvium, no. 18 (1907).

first decade of the twentieth century, pogroms broke out in moments of intense political crisis and economic turbulence. The people who engaged in pogrom violence were no doubt influenced by the mass mobilization of antisemitism—by the vulgar images of Jews reproduced in cheap newspapers and brochures and by the public protests, festivals, and rallies that popularized baseless conspiracy theories of Jews drinking Christian blood or inciting revolutionary activities—but they rarely justified their actions with references to formal ideology.[21] Almost always,

---

[21] Hillel Kieval, "Afterword: European Antisemitism: The Search for a Pattern," in Nemes and Unowsky, *Sites of European Antisemitism*, 259–60.

physical violence against Jews was shaped by a complex mixture of social and political factors, rather than solely by long-standing ethnic resentments.

World War I and the Russian Civil War marked a fundamental shift in the distinguishing features of pogrom violence. Unlike previous pogroms, which were largely spontaneous attacks, the violence during this period emerged under the auspices of organized military activity carried out by different troops and armies. The pogroms often turned into full-blown military actions. The vast population dislocations caused by World War I and the civil war make it almost impossible to retrace the precise impact of violence on the Jewish demographics of each city and town and to determine the exact casualty figures. Perhaps as many as 100,000 Jews were murdered. Many others died as a result of the catastrophic health and sanitary conditions unleashed by the conflict. Epidemics may have been the cause of no fewer deaths than the pogroms proper.[22] According to some sources, combining direct and indirect casualties, approximately 10 percent of the Jewish population in Ukraine—which became the epicenter of the violence—perished as a result of the pogroms.[23] The Russian Red Cross Committee to Aid Victims of Pogroms estimated that between 1917 and 1920, one million Jews in Ukraine suffered from pogroms and their consequences.[24]

In contrast to earlier waves, where the deadliest pogroms were largely confined to cities, in the 1918–1921 period, shtetls or small market towns experienced the brunt of the violence. Jews constituted about half or a significant proportion of the population in shtetls. During the civil war, pogroms often spread to cities from nearby towns, which became the stronghold of Ukrainian military groups and peasant insurgent units fighting against the Red Army. The central commanders of the different armies issued official proclamations condemning the pogroms and gave orders restraining attacks on Jews in cities. But they refrained from doing so in shtetls, spurred by the realization that in the absence of a firm ideological conviction, the pogroms and the ensuing looting might be beneficial to consolidate military power. The unwillingness to restrain or deter violence against Jews resulted in the complete obliteration of many smaller Jewish settlements.

The behavior of the different troops and members of peasant bands who partook in the pogroms varied not only from month to month but also from place to place. Some soldiers and peasants engaged in anti-Jewish violence were drawn by the appeal of plunder and extortion; others by religiously based antisemitism; and still others by stereotypes of Jews as capitalist exploiters of the downtrodden proletariat.

---

[22] According to the historian Jacob Lestschinsky, as many as 100,000 Jews died due to epidemics, primarily typhus. He also noted that by 1928, 18.8 percent of the Jewish population living in former war zones were still praying for deliverance. Jacob Lestschinsky, *La situation économique des juifs depuis la guerre mondiale* (Paris: Rousseau, 1934), 47, 49.

[23] State Archive of Kyiv Oblast (DAKO), f. R-3050, op. 2, d. 4, l. 1, "Report on the Activity of the Kiev Region Section of the Evobkom."

[24] DAKO, f. R-3050, op. 1, d. 162, ll. 7-7ob. These numbers were also used by the Jewish Section of the People's Commissariat for Nationalities; see Lidia B. Miliakova, ed., *Kniga pogromov: Pogromy na Ukraine, v Belorussii i evropeiskoi chasti Rossii v period Grazhdanskoi voiny, 1918–1922 gg. Sbornik dokumentov* (Moscow: ROSSPEN, 2007), 807–8, 817–19.

The soldiers who had experienced the violence of World War I and participated in the campaigns to expel Jews, who were often branded as a dangerous enemy group that sabotaged the war effort, adjusted more easily to killing civilian populations. When the soldiers were less familiar with and confused by the norms and customs the violence should follow, they turned to officers for approval, and received some guidance as to whether to target men only or Jewish women and girls as well. With the acquiescence of their superiors, soldiers engaged in murder, rape, and systematic plunder.

To be sure, paramilitarism contributed a great deal to mass Jewish terror. But the brutality of the pogroms of the civil war, which in many instances turned genocidal, was also the consequence of neighbors killing neighbors. In the aftermath of World War I, and in the context of the extreme socioeconomic calamity and famine, new forms of violence narrowed inhibitions to murdering and to witnessing murder. This period marked an important turning point in the way neighboring populations committed violence against one another. Those who participated in the pogroms were often peasants and fellow town dwellers, or neighbors, who had known each other for decades. As in pre-revolutionary times, the violence in 1919 built on memories of previous pogroms, with perpetrators and victims playing well-known roles and sharing preexisting knowledge of highly ritualized ethnic confrontations.

Victims referred to the new wave of anti-Jewish violence by using the familiar term "pogrom." But many witness accounts emphasized the unprecedented nature of the brutality, unparalleled even in the history of anti-Jewish pogroms— comparing the violence to the Armenian genocide. Although the term "genocide" had not been coined yet, information about the extermination of the Armenian population by the Young Turks in the context of the collapsing Ottoman Empire during World War I was widely available. Others preferred the Yiddish term *khurbn*, or destruction, in lieu of "pogrom." Perpetrators too built their actions on memories of previous waves of anti-Jewish violence. In launching the attack against the Jewish population of Proskurov, on February 15, 1919, shouts of "Yids, we will remind you of the times of Gonta and Khmelnytsky!" echoed through the city streets.[25] The massacres of Jews perpetrated by Bohdan Khmelnytsky and Ivan Gonta in the seventeenth and eighteenth centuries were connected to the pogroms of the civil war via an established culture of anti-Jewish violence.

Marked by indiscriminate killing, systematic propaganda, and mass rape, the pogroms of the civil war warrant historians to consider them within the framework of genocidal violence. Like other instances of genocidal violence in modern times, the pogroms of the civil war were not centrally orchestrated by state power, which had collapsed, but rather coincided with the downfall of empires. A case in point is the paramilitary attacks carried out by bandits roaming the countryside. Nikifor Grigor'ev (a former tsarist officer-cum-Ukrainian-nationalist sympathizer) sided with the Bolsheviks at one point, only to turn against the Red Army

[25] Institute for Jewish Research Archives (YIVO), Tcherikower Collection, RG 80, folder 358, p. 32710.

to carry out lethal attacks, murdering some 3,400 Jews in fifty-two locations over the course of eighteen days in May 1919.[26] Another example is the violent pogroms that coincided with the armies' withdrawal, for which the documentary evidence is particularly revealing. Rabbi Yechezkel Abramsky witnessed the pogrom that took place in Minsk in the summer of 1920, which was perpetrated by the retreating Polish troops. "I walk through the ruined streets, without the strength to keep my head up, buried under the burden of destruction, freshly spilled blood and cries of orphans ... theft and murder in every section of the city and in every neighborhood touched by the Polish army, I doubt that the world will ever believe that such horrendous crimes were committed by human beings ... people elegantly dressed with European manners."[27]

More than in previous pogroms, and not unlike other genocidal contexts, women played an active role in perpetrating and promoting the violence. In their eagerness to seize the property pillaged by their husbands during the attacks on the Jewish population, women emboldened violence and even murder. In some cases, Russian and Ukrainian women were encouraged to actively participate in the violence. As a result of their more intimate interactions with their neighbors, they were called on to put an end to buying from and selling to the Jews, in the hope that the boycott would promote ethnic cleansing.

The pervasiveness of rape became one of the discriminating features of the genocidal violence of the civil war. Often carried out in public, in the presence of parents, relatives, and neighbors, rape became a common feature of the pogroms, significantly exceeding the incidence of sexual violence of previous pogroms. If rape had become more common during the 1903–1906 wave of anti-Jewish violence, it typically was not at the center of the pogrom script. During the years 1918–1921, it was an essential weapon of war used to terrorize the Jewish civilian population. The troops involved in the conflict, as well as locals and neighbors, employed sexual violence to punish Jews for allegedly acting as agents of the Red Army, for antagonizing the national cause, or for controlling the production of bread or salt in the midst of the extreme scarcity of war.

Propaganda was widely used to justify the treatment of Jews as a biological and political enemy. Purported Jewish support for the Soviet cause loomed large as a motive to carry out extreme violence against Jewish communities. All actors involved in the military conflicts—from the Whites and the Ukrainian nationalists to the German and Polish armies—equated the Bolsheviks and the Jews, labeling Bolshevism a quintessentially Jewish doctrine. The White and the Polish armies in particular made extensive use of modern technologies of transportation and communication such as the railroad and print media to encourage anti-Jewish violence incorporating racial discourse. They yielded a sophisticated array of antisemitic

---

[26] Brendan McGeever, *Antisemitism and the Russian Revolution* (Cambridge: Cambridge University Press, 2019), 95–96.

[27] Central Scientific Archives of the Academy of Sciences of Belarus (TsNANANB), f. 72, op. 1, d. 4, l. 67.

posters, leaflets, and publications that depicted Bolshevism as an alien force imposed by Jews on Russia or Poland. Justifying anti-Jewish violence as a response to the Jewish tendency to side with the Bolsheviks became prevalent in the reports from the apostolic nuncio in Warsaw to the Vatican in Rome, something that might have given some legitimacy to the accusation of Judeo-Bolshevism in Western Europe as well.[28]

Ukrainian forces also employed anti-Bolshevik propaganda that identified the Reds with Jews. They built on the widespread notion that the revolution represented the Jewish attempt to seize political power, an idea that had caught on during the early 1900s. An example of this kind of propaganda was the so-called Chomskii trial, a staged military trial of a young Jewish man who was arrested in the summer of 1919 by the Ukrainian forces and falsely accused of being a Bolshevik leader in the struggle against Ukrainian independence. The trial served as a public ratification of the connection between Jews and Bolshevism. The historian Elias Tcherikower, who did so much to collect and record the materials about the pogroms of this period, compared the trial to the 1894 Dreyfus affair in France and to the 1913 Beilis trial in tsarist Russia, and described it as the pinnacle of the regime of Symon Petliura, the president of the Ukrainian People's Republic and the leader of the Ukrainian army.[29]

Most of the territories shaken by the civil war eventually came under the control of the Soviet Union, which officially—albeit not always successfully—enforced a ban on antisemitism as well as on any kind of collective violence against Jews. Elsewhere in Eastern Europe, pogroms waned but did not disappear. During the interwar period, instances of collective violence targeting Jews persisted in independent Poland, in particular after 1935, and occasionally took place in Romania. The rise of aggressive anti-Jewish policies by growing right-wing organizations and publications, and the worldwide economic crisis of the 1930s, served as fertile ground for the violence. The first large-scale pogrom in Poland following the years of the Polish–Soviet War took place during the summer of 1935, when hundreds of locals attacked Jews and Jewish property in the city of Grodno. Writing shortly after the events, the *Jewish Telegraphic Agency* lamented that local police authorities and military from the town's garrison refused to intervene and protect the Jewish population.[30] Two Jews were killed in the riots and several were wounded.[31]

Prominent activists and institutions lost no time in raising awareness of the injustices. In the spring and summer of 1881, after the eruption of mob violence in the southwestern borderlands of the Russian Empire, communal leaders in Britain and the United States organized monetary drives, public demonstrations, and

[28] Archivio Apostolico Vaticano, Nunziatura Apostolica in Varsavia, b. 218, 144–47, Conversazioni del governo polacco sugli ebrei.

[29] Elias Tcherikower, ed., *In der tkufe fun revolutsye: memuarn, materyaln, dokumentn* (Berlin: Yidisher literarisher farlag, 1924), 211.

[30] "Grodno Police Refused to Protect Jews," *Jewish Telegraphic Agency*, July 1935, 1, 8.

[31] Jeffrey Koerber, *Borderland Generation: Soviet and Polish Jews under Hitler* (Syracuse, NY: Syracuse University Press, 2020), 85–87.

КТО И КАКЪ УПРАВЛЯЕТЪ РУССКИМЪ НАРОДОМЪ.

PAR QUI ET COMMENT EST GOUVERNÉ LE PEUPLE RUSSE.

WHO AND HOW RULES THE RUSSIAN PEOPLE.

VON WEM UND WIE DAS RUSSISCHE VOLK REGIERT WIRD

A black-and-white anti-Bolshevik cartoon depicts Leon Trotsky, the leader of the Red Army, in deeply negative and antisemitic colors. His larger-than-life terrifying figure wearing a Red Army uniform is carrying a massive rifle. His huge hands are dripping in blood, as he takes over the Kremlin and supervises the killing of the enemies of the Bolshevik Revolution. Workers and an Orthodox priest are among those who are being murdered by Red Army soldiers. A sea of skulls flows from the Kremlin's walls. The caption above Trotsky's head reads in German, French, English, and Russian, "Who and How Rules the Russian People." The poster is one of many examples that expose the identification between Jews and Bolshevism.

Courtesy of the Institute for Jewish Research Archives (YIVO), New York.

diplomatic missions to thwart what they perceived as human rights abuse.[32] In 1903, as the sensational news spread of the Kishinev massacre, the American community launched events to collect funds to aid the victims. Prominent theaters and philanthropic organizations, with the support of leading Jewish institutions, as well as the Chinese and Christian communities in New York and San Francisco, staged benefit performances. The Academy of Music in Brooklyn sponsored a three-day performance, with speeches delivered in English, Yiddish, and Chinese. Tens of thousands of people showed up at meetings to protest what President Grover Cleveland described as "something intensely horrible," the "wholesale murder of unoffending, defenseless men, women, and children, who have been tacitly or expressly assured of safety under the protection of a professedly civilized Government."[33] In London, some ten thousand people gathered to express solidarity with the Jewish victims in Kishinev.[34] Similar efforts on the part of the Jewish communities to document pogrom violence, collect data and witness accounts, and establish humanitarian and philanthropic aid organizations remained a common denominator during the different waves of pogroms.

At the height of the pogrom violence, in September 1919, the *New York Times* published an ominous article warning that, in light of the unprecedented killings, six million Jews in Ukraine were in danger.[35] Two months later, Jewish leaders in New York City organized a march in protest of the massacres, with twenty-five thousand participants. The demonstration culminated in a mass meeting at Carnegie Hall. Similar demonstrations were organized elsewhere in North America and Canada.[36] Stores in cities across America closed in protest of the Jewish massacres in Ukraine.[37] In New York City the Ladies Waist and Dressmakers Union organized a march of mourning and refrained from working to protest the "slaughter in Ukraine and in other countries, where pogroms are carried out against our sisters and brothers from across the ocean."[38] On the other side of the globe, the Bolsheviks reacted ambivalently. Although Lenin famously condemned anti-Jewish violence as a "counterrevolutionary activity," he stopped short of labeling pogroms as crimes against the Jewish people. The Soviet regime nonetheless organized public protests against anti-Jewish violence and even carried out public executions of perpetrators.[39]

Despite the international outcry, the violence of the civil war was largely forgotten. Several reasons exist for this striking marginalization. Foreign policy played

---

[32] Klier, *Russians, Jews, and the Pogroms*, 236–45.

[33] Quoted in Philip Ernest Schoenberg, "The American Reaction to the Kishinev Pogrom of 1903," *American Jewish Historical Quarterly* 63, no. 3 (1974): 270.

[34] Faith Hillis, *Utopia's Discontents: Russian Emigres and the Quest for Freedom, 1830–1930* (New York: Oxford University Press, 2021), 92.

[35] *New York Times*, September 8, 1919, 6.

[36] YIVO, Elias Tcherikower Collection, RG 80, file 136, p. 11119.

[37] "As an Expresssion of Grief and Protest," *Forverts*, November 22, 1919, 9.

[38] "Veyst un dresmeyker troyer parad," *Forverts*, November 23, 1919, 9.

[39] YIVO, Tcherikower Collection, RG 80, file 540, pp. 46376 and 46374.

a key role. During the 1919–1920 Paris Peace Conference meetings that followed World War I, the victorious France, England, and the United States focused their attention almost exclusively on their new allies in Eastern Europe, namely, independent Poland and, to a lesser extent, Romania, where pogroms took place but were less extreme. The pogroms in Ukraine, now under Soviet rule, became demoted in the ensuing political debates, and their memory and history obfuscated precisely at the time when various organizations were busy collecting documents on anti-Jewish violence, some of which are published in our book.

The Soviet Union too played an important role in overshadowing the history of the pogroms of the Russian Civil War. This violence represented a dogmatic problem for the Bolsheviks, who imposed on the events a simplistic ideological interpretation of counterrevolutionary forces fighting against revolutionary forces. In fact, members of all social classes, including workers, perpetrated the violence and targeted Jews of all classes, including workers. As a result, over the course of the 1930s in particular, the Soviets tended to universalize the victims of the pogroms. The memory of the civil war pogroms was slighted in favor of the pogroms of 1881–1882 and 1903–1906, which the Soviets described as violence orchestrated by the evil tsarist regime. Finally, the genocide of European Jewry some twenty years later facilitated the oblivion of the pogroms of the civil war. The majority of those who experienced the violence and remained in the territories of the former Pale of Settlement were killed during the 1941 German invasion of the Soviet Union, and with them the memory of the genocidal violence of the civil war.

The perception of Jews as powerless victims of violence, tragically devoid of agency, encumbers the cultural memory of the pogroms. One of the first to harshly criticize the notion of powerlessness was Hayim Nahman Bialik (1873–1934) in his poetic response to the 1903 Kishinev pogrom. Bialik's widely read poem, "In the City of Killing," was part of an outpouring of creative responses, including songs, jokes, plays, poetry, and fiction, that confronted the enormity of the destruction. The poet resorted to criticism as a call to action, in the hope that Jews would resist, or at least reject, the shame of husbands and fathers who hid while their mothers, wives, and daughters were raped. Subsequent literary accounts of the pogroms in Hebrew and Yiddish tried to come to terms with the violence. Some writers produced forms of documentary fiction that also engaged with notions of Jewish revenge against the pogromists.

Significantly, Bialik's condemnation of Jewish passivity helped kindle the rise of the self-defense movement, one of the most compelling responses to protect the Jewish population from attacks. During the early 1900s, and then in interwar Poland, the Jewish socialist party Bund and the labor Zionist organization Poalei Zion were most active in forming self-defense militias to resist the violence, at times successfully, and occasionally in cooperation with their non-Jewish neighbors. In October 1905, in Vilna, the Bund dispatched self-defense units to guard local synagogues and protect religious Jews during the Sabbath and Jewish holidays, as elderly grandmothers blessed the Bundist fighters. In 1906, the Bund had managed to put together an arsenal of five hundred revolvers.[40] Jewish women too joined self-defense units, many of them smuggling weapons and carrying out acts of revenge against pogrom agitators.[41]

The violence endured by the Jewish population from 1914 to 1921 encouraged many to join the Red Army to defend their communities. If the Red Army shared responsibility in the anti-Jewish violence, Soviet power was alone in condemning pogroms and punishing their own forces for targeting Jews for violence. Thousands of Jewish soldiers, moreover, who had served in the tsarist army created military divisions or joined self-defense units. Jewish armed formations in Odessa reached an almost legendary status as they successfully prevented pogroms when the city changed hands eight times from 1917 to 1921.[42] In general, the scarcity of arms had an impact on the number of Jews who participated in the struggle for self-defense. In Zlatopol, Kiev province, pogrom survivors who wished to join the self-defense units pleaded for weapons with the Red Army, "Give fathers and mothers the possibility of arming themselves, so as to die honorably at least."[43] In December 1922, the *New York Times* reported that 500,000 Jews had joined the battle to put an end to the pogroms. The journalist celebrated the accomplishment by noting that "for the first time since the days recorded in the Bible, the Jewish people have a large army, capable of protecting the lives and interests of 5 million of their race living in Russia."[44]

The almost complete annihilation of Jewish life in Eastern Europe during the Holocaust weighs heavily on the narrative of Jewish history, shaping the memory of Jewish responses to pogroms and skewing both the victims' agency and the complexity of neighborly relations. Times of extreme violence could give rise to greater cooperation between Jews and their neighbors. During the 1930s pogroms in Poland, for instance, members of the Polish Socialist Party (PPS) joined the Bund participating in self-defense units or helped out by infiltrating Polish communities and warning the Bund about upcoming pogroms.[45] The apparent irreconcilability of victim and perpetrator has muddled the memory of the thousands of Jews who fought back against the pogroms in self-defense. It has also forced historians to overlook those instances in which Jews supported the forces that carried out the pogroms, or even partook in the pogroms, as peripheral as these cases may have been.

---

[40] Shlomo Lambroza, "Jewish Self-Defense During the Russian Pogroms of 1903–1906," *Jewish Journal of Sociology* 23, no. 2 (1981): 123–35, quote on 126.

[41] Deborah Hertz, "Manya Shochat and Her Travelling Guns: Jewish Radical Women from Pogrom Self-Defense to the First Kibbutzim," in *Jews and Leftist Politics: Judaism, Israel, Antisemitism, and Gender*, ed. Jack Jacobs (Cambridge: Cambridge University Press, 2017), 214–15.

[42] On Jewish self-defense units in Odessa, see Mihaly Kalman, "Hero Shtetls: Jewish Armed Self-Defense from the Pale to Palestine, 1917–1970" (PhD diss., Harvard University, 2017), esp. chap. 4, 234–309.

[43] Elias Heifetz, *The Slaughter of the Jews in the Ukraine in 1919* (New York: Thomas Seltzer, 1921), 130.

[44] "South Russia's Jews Raise Strong Army," *New York Times*, December 20, 1922, 3.

[45] Celia Stopnicka Heller, *On the Edge of Destruction: Jews of Poland between the Two World Wars* (Detroit, MI: Wayne State University Press: 1994), 290.

Map of the southwestern provinces of the Russian Empire. Home to some of the largest and oldest Jewish communities, the territories of the provinces of Volynia (Volhynia), Podolia, and Kiev (Kyiv) were hit the hardest during the military conflicts of 1914–1921. The Jewish population of the hundreds of small towns located in the war zone between the rivers Dnister (Dniester) and Dnipro (Dnieper) bore the brunt of the violence, as they experienced forced evacuation, looting, rape, and murder. Whether they acted on behalf of a specific political program, drew inspiration from anti-Jewish stereotypes, or were encouraged by the desperate economic crisis, disciplined soldiers perpetrated the violence. The military, lacking the spontaneity associated with previous pogroms, pursued far-reaching, systemic, and highly destructive antisemitic measures. When civilians engaged in anti-Jewish violence, they replicated military-organized violence, and indiscriminately targeted men, women, and children for terror. As a result of the shift in tactics, the Jewish population of entire towns was completely decimated, with whole families massacred and children killed in front of their parents.

Map drawn by Suleyman Sarihan, Slavic and East European Library at the University of Illinois, with the assistance of Merrily Shaw, Russian, East European, and Eurasian Center at the University of Illinois.

Pogrom violence served as a convenient instrument to punish and terrorize Jewish communities—fulfilling a function similar to what lynching did to Black Americans. But in contrast to the American South, where violence broke down in a neat black–white divide, the boundaries between perpetrator and victim were not always evident in the borderlands of Eastern Europe. As surprising as it may seem, Jews themselves were not immune to looting and taking part in anti-Jewish violence based on perceptions of class allegiance. In some rare instances, as part of the pogroms of 1905, Jews grabbed items from shops or taverns owned by fellow Jews. During World War I and the Russian Civil War, in the midst of a complete breakdown of civil society, what was once a rare phenomenon became somewhat more widespread. Some Jews supported and participated in the White, anti-Bolshevik movement, even after the Volunteer Army began to perpetrate deadly pogroms, while others joined peasant bands roaming the countryside, helping identify the wealthier members of the Jewish community who were targeted for plunder or murder.

Given the extraordinary violence that overwhelmed the Jewish communities of Europe during World War II, particularly the exterminatory rhetoric and practices of "total ethnic war" launched in German-occupied Eastern Europe, some scholars resist applying the term "pogrom" to the collective violence against Jews from 1939 through 1945. Other historians do not share this view. They use "pogrom" to describe the massacres that coincided with Operation Barbarossa, or Germany's attack on the Soviet Union. In June and July of 1941, Germans and their collaborators used the same repertoire of techniques, including uninhibited looting, rape, and murder carried out in public, in the midst of an urban crowd, which had become widespread during the violence of World War I and the civil war. The parallels between the two time periods are striking. From June 25 to 27, 1941, a group of Lithuanian nationalists beat to death with crowbars several dozen Jewish men in the city of Kaunas (Kovno), in the neighborhood of the Lietukis garage, in the "first public pogrom in Lithuania."[46] Both scholars and survivors have referred to massacres such as those carried out in Romania (Jasi, 1941), Poland (Jedwbne, 1941), and Western Ukraine (Lviv, 1941) as "pogroms."[47] Building on the memory of anti-Jewish violence, some survivors used the term "pogrom" for mass executions in the midst of the Holocaust. On March 2, 1942, when the Germans and their collaborators massacred five thousand Jews in the Minsk ghetto, the twenty-two-year-old ghetto inmate Raisa Abramovna got word of the killings at the site of the "Pit," or *Yama*, and referred to them as a pogrom. The fear of further "pogroms" encouraged her to search for hiding places within the ghetto and eventually to flee and join the Soviet partisans.[48]

Most of the German-sponsored, large-scale, anti-Jewish killing operations were perpetrated during the early months of World War II on the Eastern Front, in the cities and towns of today's Eastern Poland, Lithuania, Western Belarus, and Western Ukraine. These were territories that had been annexed by the Soviet Union following the 1939 nonaggression pact with Nazi Germany, which underwent a systematic and brutal Sovietization campaign. As soon as the Soviets left, in the first few days of the German occupation, a staggering wave of pogroms occurred in the

[46] Rūta Vanagaitė and Efraim Zuroff, *Our People: Discovering Lithuania's Hidden Holocaust* (Lanham, MD: Rowman and Littlefield, 2020), 59–60.

[47] On Jedwabne, see Jan T. Gross, *Neighbors: The Destruction of the Jewish Community in Jedwabne, Poland* (Princeton, NJ: Princeton University Press, 2001), and Jason Wittenberg and Jeffrey Kopstein, *Intimate Violence: Anti-Jewish Pogroms on the Eve of the Holocaust* (Ithaca, NY: Cornell University Press, 2018), 57–64. On the massacres in Lviv, see John Paul Himka, "The Lviv Pogrom of 1941: The Germans, Ukrainian Nationalists, and the Carnival Crowd," *Canadian Slavonic Papers* 53, no. 2–4 (2011): 209–43.

[48] United States Holocaust Memorial Museum (USHMM), RG-50.477*0774, Oral history, Transcript of interview with Raisa Abramovna Livshitz, October 16, 1991.

areas.[49] Many Eastern Europeans came to see the German occupation as a "liberation" from a mythical overpowering Jewish Bolshevism.[50]

The end of World War II triggered a renewed spike in pogroms. In Poland, anti-Jewish violence coincided with the desperate context of refugees returning to half-destroyed cities that lacked food and other essentials. The transition from the war years to postwar communism throughout East-Central Europe led to renewed outbursts of punitive public violence against Jews. The returning Jews who had survived the war and demanded their property back, in particular their homes, were met with hostility and often violence.[51] Their Christian neighbors had moved into their homes and taken their things, and feared that if the Jews came back, they would have to return everything that they had stolen. On the streets of Kiev, in the fall of 1945, a pogrom caused havoc when thirty-six of the one hundred victims in the attacks were hospitalized and five were murdered.[52] The violence also affected a number of non-Jewish civilians "who looked like Jews." Apparently, the local police did not intervene until a few days later. In response to the Kiev pogrom, some Jews openly protested in disbelief, "It is a disgrace... that a Jewish pogrom occurred here in Kiev under the Soviets... after our victory over German fascism.... It will be written in the history of our revolution that the first Jewish pogrom since the collapse of tsarism occurred... in the 28th year since the October revolution."[53]

Across the eastern borderlands of Europe, pogroms transformed Jewish lives and relationships in enduring ways. The stories of human suffering and disaster—many of which are documented in this volume, from multiple perspectives—are a profound testament of the world that Jews and their multiethnic neighbors made and inhabited.[54] In some cases, pogroms wiped out of existence entire communities. More generally, they were part of a larger story of destruction, ethnic purification, and coexistence that played out over a span of some six decades in the region. Bringing together archival and published sources—many for the first time in English translation—*Pogroms* surveys the complex history of pogroms in nine case studies. The documents assembled here include eyewitness testimony, oral histories, diary excerpts, literary works, trial records, and press coverage. They also include

[49] On anti-Jewish violence in Western Ukraine, see Wendy Lower, "Pogroms, Mob Violence, and Genocide in Western Ukraine, Summer 1941: Varied Histories, Explanations, and Comparisons," *Journal of Genocide Research* 13, no. 3 (2011): 217–46.

[50] See Oleksandr Melnyk, "Stalinist Justice as a Site of Memory: Anti-Jewish Violence in Kyiv's Podil District in September 1941 through the Prism of Soviet Investigative Documents," *Jahrbücher für Geschichte Osteuropas* 61, no. 2 (2013): 223–48.

[51] Péter Apor, Tamás Kende, Michala Lônčíková, and Valentin Săndulescu, "Post–World War II Anti-Semitic Pogroms in East and East Central Europe: Collective Violence and Popular Culture," *European Review of History: Revue europeenne d'histoire* 26, no. 6 (2019): 913–27.

[52] "NKGB USSR Communiques about the Events in Kiev, September 1945," in Mitsel, *Evrei Ukrainy v 1943–1953gg: Ocherki dokumentirovannoi istorii* (Kyiv: Dukh i litera, 2004), 63–69; and "NKVD Ukrainy: V secretariat TsK KP(b)U ob intsidente v Kieve 4 sentiabria 1945," in Kostyrchenko, *Gosudarstvennyi antisemitizm v SSSR ot nachala do kulminatsii, 1938–1953* (Moscow: Materik, 2005), 62–63.

[53] "Byvshie frontoviki-evrei: I. V. Stalinu, L. L. Berii, P. N. Pospelov o potvorstve ukrainskikh vlastei antisemitizmu, Sentiabr, 1945," in Kostyrchenko, *Gosudarstvennyi antisemitizm v SSSR*, 65–71.

[54] For an insightful reading of the meaning of violence in Jewish history, see Adam Teller, "Revisiting Baron's 'Lachrymose Conception': The Meaning of Violence in Jewish History," *AJS Review* 38, no. 2 (2014): 431–39.

memos and field reports authored by army officials, investigative commissions, humanitarian organizations, and government officials.

Our book treats the history of pogroms not so much as discrete events, with clear origins and outcomes, but as a messy historical process. We devote much space to exploring the motivations, policy directives, and reactions of the most powerful decision-makers to those officials and their accomplices operating in the provinces. Our goal is to understand anti-Jewish violence from a top-down perspective and also from below, in all its complexity and intimacy. We probe the experiences and emotions of the exploited and the marginal—the men, women, and children caught up in the maelstrom of physical violence and suffering—showcasing the voices of ordinary lives, relationships, and activities that rarely appear in historical studies of pogroms. To that end, we invite our readers to explore pogroms in dynamic terms, where violence, ethnic categories, human experiences, power relations, and social and cultural processes interact in subtle, often ambiguous ways.

1

Pogroms in Russia's Borderlands, 1881–1884

Eugene M. Avrutin

On April 15, 1881, approximately six weeks after the assassination of Tsar Alexander II (1818–1881), a fight broke out in a tavern in Elisavetgrad, Kherson province. The proprietor of the tavern, the Jew Shulim Grichevskii, and one of his customers, a Ukrainian townsman, got into a heated argument. As the spat escalated, a crowd of curious onlookers gathered around. A police sergeant urged everyone to disperse, but the mob of men, some of whom were visibly drunk and agitated, paid no attention to the entreaties. Shouting, "The Yids are beating our people!" they proceeded to throw large rocks into Jewish shop windows. Jewish shopkeepers used crowbars and axes to defend themselves. Tensions simmered to a boil when Jews allegedly fired revolvers at the rioters from one of the synagogues. Over the course of two days, the rioters attacked 418 Jewish homes and demolished 290 Jewish shops and stalls. Peasants from nearby villages joined in the looting. The governor called for reinforcements to patrol the city and the surrounding villages, warning that anyone caught with stolen merchandise would be promptly arrested. The unrest finally died down on the morning of April 17, after a night of heavy rain and cold wind. Out of the 601 people arrested, most of whom were local townsmen and urban laborers, 480 individuals were brought to trial; only a small number were convicted.[1]

The Elisavetgrad pogrom was the first of more than 250 anti-Jewish riots that erupted in the Russian Empire between 1881 and 1884. Some of the disturbances lasted only a couple of hours, and others took two or more days to subside. In most instances the pogroms originated in large urban centers, rippling outward to neighboring market towns along railroads, rivers, roads, and other paths of transportation. The vast majority of the violence was concentrated in the southern and southwestern provinces (present-day Ukraine). A handful of minor episodes broke out in the northwestern territories (present-day Lithuania and Belarus).[2] Three noticeable

---

[1] Grigorii Ia. Krasnyi-Admoni, ed., *Materialy dlia istorii antievreiskikh pogromov v Rossii*, vol. 2 (Petrograd: Gosudarstvennoe izdatel'stvo, 1923), 28–29, 31.

[2] For an analysis of the geographical pattern of anti-Jewish violence, see I. Michael Aronson, *Troubled Waters: The Origins of the 1881 Anti-Jewish Pogroms in Russia* (Pittsburgh: University of Pittsburgh Press, 1990), 108–24. For an examination of anti-Jewish violence in the northwest provinces, see Darius Staliūnas, *Enemies for a Day: Antisemitism and Anti-Jewish Violence in Lithuania under the Tsars* (Budapest: CEU Press, 2015), 85–127; and Claire Le Foll, "The Missing Pogroms of Belorussia, 1881–1882: Conditions and Motives of an Absence of

Eugene M. Avrutin, *Pogroms in Russia's Borderlands, 1881–1884* In: *Pogroms*. Edited by: Eugene M. Avrutin and Elissa Bemporad, Oxford University Press. © Oxford University Press 2021. DOI: 10.1093/oso/9780190060084.003.0002

"The Assault of a Jew in the Presence of the Military at Kiev." The Jewish question in the Russian Empire, including the 1881–1882 pogroms, received broad coverage in the British press. The *Illustrated London News*, among many other periodicals, usually reported that the police and the military were careless in allowing the violence against Jews to get out of hand. Occasionally, journalists suggested that the police and military had permitted pogroms to occur under their special protection.
Illustrated London News, June 4, 1881, 549

waves of pogroms took place in 1881: in Elisavetgrad and Kherson (April 15–21); Kiev, Tavrida, and Ekaterinoslav (April 26–May 10); and Poltava and Chernigov (June 30–August 16). Additional pogroms followed in Warsaw (December 13, 1881) and Balta (March 29–30, 1882), with two isolated outbreaks occurring in Ekaterinoslav in 1883 and Nizhnii Novgorod in 1884.

In their extensive explanations, tsarist officials blamed the eruption of pogroms on revolutionary elements and on Jews' economic manipulation of the peasantry. Authorities argued that the exploitation practices, allegedly carried out in all areas of trade and commerce, made Jews an object of hatred of the local population. Liberal journalists and Jewish communal leaders rejected this interpretation. They felt that "dark and mysterious" forces were behind what they considered to be the most notorious antisemitic conspiracy in modern times. Writing at the turn of the twentieth century in his highly influential history of Jews in Russia and Poland, S. M. Dubnov argued that men in Russia's most powerful governing circles masterminded the riots that spread quickly and uncontrollably from the epicenter to dozens of adjacent

Violence," in *Anti-Jewish Violence: Rethinking the Pogrom in East European History*, ed. Jonathan Dekel-Chen, David Gaunt, Natan M. Meir, and Israel Bartal (Bloomington: Indiana University Press, 2011), 159–73.

Sites of pogroms in the Russian Empire, April 15 to August 16, 1881.

towns. The pogroms were carefully "prepared and engineered," Dubnov observed, and "everywhere they followed the same routine, characterized by the well-organized 'activity' of the mob and the deliberate inactivity of the authorities."[3]

For well over five decades, Dubnov's writings—based on the power of conspiratorial theories—shaped widely held interpretations of the origins and proliferation of pogrom violence. Revisionist scholars, considering a broad range of materials, including newly declassified archival documents, have established that Russian officials, including at the provincial level, did not conspire to stir up violence against Jews. Local

[3] S. M. Dubnow, *History of the Jews in Russia and Poland, from the Earliest Times until the Present Day*, trans. I. Friedlander, 3 vols. (Philadelphia: The Jewish Publication Society of America, 1918), 2:248–49.

police units, in most cases ill-prepared and seriously understaffed, did what they could to take precautions, punish the perpetrators, and maintain order and civility. This does not mean that authorities did not harbor resentment or that they were always successful in implementing measures that successfully prevented rioting. The pogroms, which devastated Jewish communities and contributed to a national emergency in the imperial borderlands lasting approximately two years, had many causes. These include:

1. *Political shock caused by the assassination of Tsar Alexander II.* On March 1, 1881, the tsar's death plunged the autocracy into political crisis. That several Jews belonged to the organization responsible for the tsar's murder sparked conspiratorial fears that the Jewish population was behind many of the misfortunes afflicting the empire.
2. *Social dislocations due to the uneven economic modernization of the empire.* In the pivotal months preceding the outbreak of the pogrom violence in April 1881, the southwestern provinces, the site of pogroms, underwent an economic boom, while many other regions of the empire experienced industrial depression and near-famine conditions. The rapid expansion of metallurgy and mining in the industrial heartland attracted a steady stream of labor migrants. The mass of this ethnically diverse, uneducated, and transient population was especially prone to heavy drinking and violent behavior, much of which was directed toward Jews.
3. *The circulation of rumors.* Rumormongering was an important aspect of pogrom violence. Almost all the riots were accompanied by false rumors that the tsar had authorized the attacks on the Jews; that Jewish property could be seized with impunity; and that Jews deserved to be beaten for their ruthless economic manipulation of the Christian population. Newspapers across the political spectrum reported on the pogroms, explaining their origins and offering distinct proposals for solving the Jewish Question.[4] Jews were often faulted for taking advantage of the laboring classes and participating in the nascent revolutionary movement. They were also seen as the chief source of the impoverishment of the Christian population. Journalists writing for conservative newspapers such as *Novoe vremia* (New Times) and *Novorossiiskii telegraf* (The Novorossiisk Telegraph) did not advocate violence against Jews. But they managed to stir up emotions by publishing baseless, inflammatory reports. Some articles accused Jews of "beating the Russian population with the ruble" and "sucking the juice from the inhabitants among whom they live."[5] Other articles helped spread fears by hinting of impending rioting. Still others agitated for popular vengeance by publishing fantastic claims that the tsar had issued an explicit order instructing the Christian population to beat Jews.
4. *The role of the religious calendar in providing the occasion for anti-Jewish violence.* In some places such as Elisavetgrad and Balta, riots broke out at

[4] For a wide-ranging exploration of the Jewish Question in the mass circulation press, see John D. Klier, *Imperial Russia's Jewish Question, 1855–1881* (Cambridge: Cambridge University Press, 1995); and Klier, *Russians, Jews and the Pogroms of 1881–1882* (Cambridge: Cambridge University Press, 2011), 128–50.
[5] Aronson, *Troubled Waters*, 72.

Eastertide, a ritually charged time of the Christian religious calendar, which often coincided with Passover. In 1881–1882, as in Kishinev in 1903 and many other instances of anti-Jewish violence, rumors of Jews kidnapping and slaughtering Christian children for their blood (the ritual murder charge) became a prominent feature of pogroms.[6] The religious festival period, with its large, boisterous crowds, provided the occasion for drinking, as well as the sporadic squabble and fistfight that always had the potential for evolving into a full-blown riot. Petty disputes over unpaid bills, broken glasses and dishes, or the amount of liquor served or consumed often helped ignite the rioting. The 1881–1882 pogroms displayed forms that echoed highly ritualized confrontations, while the atmosphere resembled the popular festivities associated with carnival. Crowds often gathered around the spectacle to observe the looting and destruction of Jewish property.

In the aftermath of the pogroms, Tsar Alexander III (1845–1894) used the events of 1881 and 1882 to strengthen the state by pursuing ruthless authoritarian policies. Russification meant the subjugation of non-Russian nationalities to the ideal Russian national character.[7] To prevent future outbreaks, on May 2, 1882, the government pursued policies that stood in stark contrast to the tolerance of Tsar Alexander II's reign. The minister of the interior, Count Nikolai Pavlovich Ignat'ev, issued a series of temporary legislative measures—known as the May Laws—designed to reduce Jewish power over the Christian population. Ignat'ev shared the widely held view that the economic harmfulness of the Jewish population was the primary cause of the pogrom violence. The May Laws made life frustratingly difficult for Jewish communities all across the Pale of Settlement. In an effort to draw distinct boundaries between Jews and non-Jews, the legislation restricted the Jewish population from residing outside urban settlements (i.e., cities and towns) and carrying on trade on Sundays and the twelve major feasts of the Orthodox Church. Thousands of individuals were expelled from non-urban settlements. Furthermore, the tsarist state established quotas on the admission of Jewish students to educational institutions. The *numerus clausus* emerged directly out of the public discussion among officials of the most productive ways to limit Jews' harmful activities.[8]

Jews who experienced, or were threatened by, pogroms responded in a number of ways. Jewish communal notables wrote telegrams and petitions to provincial governors, calling for protection, heightened security, and special precautions. Some Jews took matters into their own hands by arming themselves with handguns or organizing self-defense units (though the effectiveness of these strategies paled

---

[6] On the role of the ritual murder accusation in Eastern Europe and the metaphors of blood drinking as a rallying cry in sparking anti-Jewish violence, see Eugene M. Avrutin, Jonathan Dekel-Chen, and Robert Weinberg, eds., *Ritual Murder in Russia, Eastern Europe, and Beyond: New Histories of an Old Accusation* (Bloomington: Indiana University Press, 2017), 5–6.

[7] Richard S. Wortman, *Scenarios of Power: Myth and Ceremony in Russian Monarchy*, vol. 2 (Princeton, NJ: Princeton University Press, 2000), 237–38.

[8] Benjamin Nathans, *Beyond the Pale: The Jewish Encounter with Late Imperial Russia* (Berkeley: University of California Press, 2004), 257–82.

"Your Money, Jew, or Your Life!" Jews often fought back against Christian rioters. In 1881 and 1882, Jewish communities tended to organize self-defense groups informally. Authorities viewed Jewish armed patrols with alarm, fearing that Jews armed with firearms and clubs would only intensify pogrom violence.
Harper's Weekly, February 11, 1882

in comparison to the more organized efforts in Kishinev in 1903, the revolution of 1905, and beyond). Some Jewish families fled to neighboring urban centers such as Odessa that maintained well-established charitable institutions and communal networks. Thousands of Jewish refugees crossed the lightly guarded imperial frontier to neighboring border towns such as Brody and Podvolochisk in Galicia and as far as Königsberg in Prussia. The refugee crisis and gruesome accounts of the pogrom violence, including rape, pillage, and murder, were widely reported in the international press, on both sides of the Atlantic. As the sensational news spread,

"The Flight of the Jews from Podolia Province." The pogrom crisis of 1881 caused thousands of Jews to pack their bags and look for shelter in neighboring towns. Some Jews decided to leave the empire by flocking across the Russo-Austrian border. The town of Brody, located in eastern Galicia, became a magnet for Jewish refugees and international relief efforts.

A sketch by G. Broling, *Illustrirte Zeitung*, no. 2029, May 20, 1882, 399

prominent activists and organizations lost no time in organizing public campaigns to protest the pogroms.[9]

The imperial government's reactionary response to the pogrom crisis, including the smear campaign in the conservative press, played an important role in undermining confidence in the ability of Jews to integrate into Russian society. A small circle of Jewish intellectuals reached the conclusion that the political impact of the anti-Jewish violence constituted an immediate threat to the established way of life. As a result, a political movement was born that promoted the creation of a radically new environment based on two distinct revolutionary ideologies: the mass migration of Jews to Ottoman Palestine inspired by Zionist ideas, and a militant internationalism grounded in Marxist thought.[10] Significantly, the pogroms did not reverse the entrance of Jews into Russia's civil society, but the events marked an important turning point by creating a blueprint for future waves of pogrom violence that rocked the empire in the last decades of the old regime and beyond.

[9] Klier, *Russians, Jews and the Pogroms*, 236–39, 255–57.
[10] Jonathan Frankel, *Prophecy and Politics: Socialism, Nationalism, and the Russian Jews, 1862–1917* (Cambridge: Cambridge University Press, 1981), 49–132.

Document 1.1. Pogrom in Smela, Kiev Province

On the order of the minister of internal affairs, Count P. I. Kutaisov was appointed to write a detailed analysis on the hostilities between Jews and Christians and their social causes. In the summer of 1881, Kutaisov traveled widely in southern Russia, met with Jewish delegations, communal leaders, and well-to-do merchants. Based on his own research, as well as detailed memoranda he received from the Jewish communities, Kutaisov penned the first official report on the origins and causes of pogrom violence. Kutaisov believed that Jews were economic exploiters, but he opposed popular violence against Jews and generally blamed local officials for their incompetence in handling the pogroms. Kutaisov's report, focusing on the events in Smela on May 3–4, 1881, offers a sober characterization of the realities of the time.

A sense of alarm began to pervade the Jewish population of Kiev province almost immediately after the unrest in Elisavetgrad. After the Kiev pogrom, as news rapidly spread throughout the province, Jews everywhere were in a state of panic. There were persistent rumors that in Kiev Jews had been beaten with the authorities' permission and that the troops had offered only weak resistance to the rampaging crowd. Among all the places in Kiev province that suffered the most from the anti-Jewish movement, the town of Smela, in Cherkasskii district, is of particular importance. Smela, with a population nearing fifteen thousand, half of whom are Jews, is quite significant to the area, both in its trade volume and in the number of factories located within and around it. The Kiev pogrom caused such a terrible panic there that in order to bring about calm Count Bobrinskii was forced to ask the governor-general to dispatch troops. In his opinion, this was especially necessary because alarming rumors of an upcoming beating of the Jews were circulating not just in Smela, but also in Korsun, Shpola, and other areas along the Fastov railroad, the location of the largest number of factories as well as the largest number of railway shops. This request was granted. Three companies of the Bender infantry regiment were dispatched there, which, as it turned out later, was insufficient for such a densely populated area that houses, in addition to permanent residents, guest workers at the factories, who number two to four thousand people.

It is very important to note that the rioting in Kiev coincided with the arrival of workers from adjacent provinces who come every year in April to assist with repairs, work in the fields, and other jobs. These workers, who had seen the rioting in Kiev and likely even participated in it, spread word of extremely unrealistic details about it in Smela and its environs. The local administration, meanwhile, was unable to counter the false interpretations of the anti-Jewish movement by Christians, because its staff was in quite a pitiful state at the time. The police chief for Cherkasskii district back then was a person nearly mentally ill from drinking (currently confined to a hospital for the mentally ill), and his deputy was suffering from tuberculosis and had therefore been unable to perform his duties for several months by that time. The only representatives of administrative authority during this troubled time were the local police chief and several police officers, who were the only people who could prevent the spread of the ridiculous rumors and, in reassuring the people, explain to them the real meaning of the anti-Jewish movement and the government's attitude toward it. But it is understandable that given a plethora of other duties borne by the police, the aforementioned representatives of the administration were unable to perform this task, so even the Bender regiment commander, Colonel Golubev, who arrived in Smela with the three companies, quickly noticed the almost complete absence of police officers and reported this as early as April 29, 1881, to the Kiev military district chief of staff, requesting his assistance with augmenting the police forces. This petition was granted, and the district police chief was replaced with a new person on May 2, that is, the day before the destruction in Smela.

On May 3, a two-week fair began in Smela, which brought in many peasants from the surrounding areas. During the fair, a Jew, a local meat seller, bought a cow from one peasant for 42 rubles, but while he was getting out the money to pay him, another peasant came up and offered 45 rubles for it. Thus, prevented from purchasing the cow, the Jew began cursing the Russian and hit both peasants, the buyer and seller, with a stick. This quarrel attracted a crowd of Christians and Jews at the fair, between whom a general fight broke out, which quickly transformed, as a result of the Christians' advantage in numbers, into an open attack on the Jews and their homes. In response to the call of "we're under attack!" crowds of workers from the factories began pouring in, and almost instantaneously the mere market-square fight turned into wholesale carnage. The troops summoned by the alarm would pass in tight formation along the streets and disperse the crowd wherever they could, but the crowd, running away from one spot, would quickly gather in another, with yells of "beat the Jews!" The troops tried as much as possible to track down and disperse the rioters, but the order to disperse had no effect: the ever-growing crowd raged more and more, breaking glass and doors, destroying Jewish homes, and in some places engaging in bitter fights with Jews armed with clubs and stakes, who had also gathered in huge numbers. Given how few of them there were, the troops could do nothing: it was not them coming after the people, but rather the people holding them under a kind of siege. In fact, the raging crowd did not stop at curses and disobedience and started to throw rocks and firewood at them, such that even Colonel Golubev was hit in the shoulder by a log.

Seeing that admonitions had completely failed and that his demands were not being obeyed, Colonel Golubev decided to turn to more active measures and announced that if the crowd did not disperse, he would be forced to shoot. But the people did not pay this threat any mind. Then he ordered that two volleys of blanks be fired into the air. This measure only elicited jeers and cries of "you won't dare shoot," as a result of which Colonel Golubev ordered four rifles to be loaded with live ammunition and fired into the crowd; two were killed by these shots, and one woman was wounded lightly in the foot. The shots did not have the expected effect: the people did not disperse and did not calm down at all. On the contrary, the crowd became only more enraged, and from every side came curses and yells that Christian blood was being shed for the Yids. This was around two in the afternoon. Seeing how tough the situation was and the complete impossibility of restoring order given the small number of troops at his disposal, Colonel Golubev decided to send a telegram about it to the chief of staff for the Kiev military district, Major General Cherkesov, requesting immediate reinforcements. At the same time, news was received that a violent fight had broken out between Jews and Christians in the suburb of Kovalevka, populated primarily by Jews; this report still further galvanized the crowd, which was by then breaking into Jewish homes and obliterating, looting, and destroying everything inside.

Colonel Golubev's position, meanwhile, was becoming more and more critical. His limited force was completely exhausted, and he could clearly see that given the current state of affairs there was nothing he could do. Along with everything else, he also had to make sure that the rampaging crowd was kept away from the people he had arrested, as well as from his barracks, warehouses, and so on. Given this situation, around eight in the evening he decided to return his men, who had not eaten anything all day, to the barracks and at the same time send a repeat telegram to Major General Cherkesov requesting reinforcements. It was as though the crowd was waiting for exactly those orders and in a rage, no longer held back by anything, it set to beating the Jews and destroying their homes and property, and only nightfall stopped this terrible rampage. All the Jewish homes on Volovaia, Politseiskaia, Serebriannaia, Mostovaia, Kievskaia, Muchnaia, Vladimirskaia, Lvovskaia, Naberezhnaia, Bazarnaia, Kovalevka, Zhitomirskaia, and Furmanskaia Streets, in the Jewish quarter, and on Evreiskii and Zamalanyi Lanes were destroyed, their windows, doors, and shutters broken, the walls in some torn down, fireplaces and chimneys destroyed, floors torn up, and all the property that had been in the houses and was thrown into the street was spoiled, torn up, and broken, with the feathers and down dumped out of the pillows and blankets.

In the morning on May 4, once again a large number of workers flowed in from the nearby factories and the Fastov railroad shops, plus peasants from nearby areas came with their wives on carts, and the looting and destruction of previously untouched Jewish shops began in Smela. The craftsmen brought hammers and crowbars, which they used to break the locks, shutters, and doors of the shops. The crowd began throwing the goods out into the street; meanwhile, the peasants and their wives rushed to them, loaded up their carts with Jewish property, and immediately took it out of town. According to eyewitnesses, in some cases the same peasant was able to load up his wagon twice and run the looted property back to his village. The rampaging crowd brought sugarloaves out from the shops and immediately broke them apart, threw bolts of cloth into the mud or barrels of kerosene, or ripped them to pieces; in shops selling ready-made clothing, the goods were ripped apart and the pieces thrown into the street; some would change into new clothing and boots right there in the shops. The troops, posted that day on certain streets to block the crowd's path to the other quarters of the town that had not yet been touched, held back the Jews itching to defend their property by gathering up to three thousand of them in a square and surrounding them. In general, early in the day the troops, faced with a crowd that had grown to seven thousand to eight thousand, could not take particularly active measures to stop the rioting.

It was not until five in the evening, when another five companies of the Bender regiment and a hundred Cossacks arrived, that they went on the offensive and began dispersing the people, during which time they made around three hundred arrests. The arrests were indiscriminate: they would detain anyone they caught in the street, since the rampage involved practically everyone; the detainees were taken to a square that was surrounded by troops. Colonel Golubev, along with officers and the local police chief, arrived at the square, and at the former's orders, punishment was immediately dispensed. Four loads of canes were brought, and those at fault for the rioting were subjected to corporal punishment; when there were not enough canes, whips were used. Among those punished here at the square for the looting of Jewish property were several women (four or five); these details were reported to me, by the way, by the local court investigator Prince Orbelianii, who was present during the punishment. It is difficult to determine who exactly was subjected to corporal punishment, because the local police chief, who was trying to compile a list of those punished, was constantly called away from his place to perform other job duties and was only able to collect fragmentary information on this matter. In addition to the women punished on the square, according to Colonel Golubev himself, several other women charged with looting were subjected to punishment in the courtyard of his house.

The Jews included in the police chief's list were subjected to corporal punishment for attacking Christians with sticks and other weapons. The total number punished was three hundred people, but who exactly was punished still remains unknown, since the majority of those lashed were released immediately after punishment, and among the participants in the riots only those few listed in the enclosed report were subjected to legal prosecution. The number of lashes varied: some claim that it was set by Colonel Golubev between twenty and two hundred lashes, while others claim fifty to three hundred.

During the rioting, some worker swung a hammer at the Bender regiment staff captain Sukhalskii; in his defense, the officer shot at him with his revolver. Many suspected that the worker was a Finn, Eklend, who is currently in the hospital and was whipped after being wounded. Eklend was so drunk that he does not remember who wounded him or when, and similarly does not remember when he was punished, citing complete drunkenness, but according to court investigator Spardo, he has bruises on his backside that bear witness to his being whipped.

The local police, in the form of the police chief and two officers, and the judicial authorities completely melted into the background during the entire course of the rioting, handing all their power over to the regimental commander, who arrested, released, and punished people and separated the guilty from the innocent at his own discretion, basing his actions, the talk goes, on the fact that when leaving Kiev he received just one order: "Do everything to pacify the region as God would direct his soul to do." During May 3 and May 4, Smela witnessed the following deaths: two people from gunshots and four from the crowd; thirty-five were wounded, including one woman wounded by a bullet when the troops opened fire. As for the number of Jewish homes destroyed and looted, and the amount of damages they sustained, the figure is set at 150,000 to 200,000 rubles, and there are up to eight hundred Jews (landlords and tenants) who suffered as a result of the pogrom. Even though Jewish victims significantly exaggerate their losses, according to people with no interest in this affair, such as Count Bobrinskii, the cited figure is quite close to reality, and the amount of losses was indeed quite large.

The governor and local deputy prosecutor arrived in Smela on May 5, but by that day the rioting had already ceased. All that was left to do was to complete the sorting, commenced the previous day, of detainees who were to be subjected to legal prosecution. On the same day, as I was told by the deputy chief of the gendarme department, Captain Rudov, another forty people were whipped again by Colonel Golubev's orders, and, finally, certain persons who had been visibly directing the crowd were arrested and handed over to the court investigator.

The town of Smela hosts quite a lot of trade, which will undoubtedly be affected by the rioting, but one must furthermore note that the pogrom primarily came down on the poorest residents: the rich Jews had time to transport out some of their goods in advance and hide their valuables, whereas among the poor, indeed, many were left only with what they had on them when they fled to the street. A committee was formed in Smela to provide aid to the victims, and Count V. A. Bobrinskii gave a one-time gift of 3,000 rubles and allocated 100 rubles daily for an unlimited time for bread and provisions to be handed out to those most affected. By June 10, the committee had raised around 10,000 rubles, which is being used to cover expenses to provide the poorest residents with bread and meat, and after that financial aid will be given out to those most affected.

News of the riots in Smela quickly spread throughout its environs, assisted by the peasants flowing in from the nearby villages for the fair on Sunday. As early as the morning of Monday, May 4, local peasants, even well-to-do peasants, in the villages of Konstantinovka, Budki, Balakleia, Malo-Staroselee, Malaia Smilianka, Grechkovka, Iablonovka, Berezniaki, Zalevka, Pleskalka, Stepanovka, and Dubeevka, began gathering in groups and discussing that they should treat the Jews just as they had been treated in Smela. These gatherings took place, for the most part, in taverns, and the peasants would at first pay for their vodka and then, after having some to drink, demand it by force. The Jewish tavern keepers would, of course, put up a fight and not hand over vodka without payment; then the peasants, in turn, would respond by destroying first the tavern, and then the remaining Jewish homes in the village. That was the general nature of the unrest in all the villages listed above. Particular cruelty manifested itself in the village of Berezniaki, where up to fifty local peasant elders took part in the looting and beating of Jews, including even the village head. In that village, several Jewish homes were destroyed, the tavern was torn down completely, and the unconsumed vodka was drained out of the barrels. Indeed, the enraged crowd there engaged in various forms of savagery. For example, one retired soldier threw a Jewish boy who had been fleeing the pogrom into the river after taking away what he was carrying (the boy, however, did not drown); an entire crowd attacked the house of the landlord and, having destroyed and looted everything inside and not found the landlord himself, grabbed his father, an old man of over eighty years, attacked him furiously, beat him, demanding money, and finally finished him off with an axe to the head.

[. . .]

Coming now to addressing the question of the causes that gave rise to the rioting in Smela and its environs, I must say that they primarily comprise: (1) the hatred of the Christians toward the Jewish people; and (2) the rumors regarding the unrest in Elisavetgrad and Kiev, which were perversely interpreted by the local population. The substantial significance of the first element in this case is confirmed by a very compelling fact: the pogrom in Smela affected only Jewish homes, only Jewish property was looted, the violence was directed exclusively at Jews. It is quite difficult to imagine that outsiders had prepared this movement, and especially that it was done by members of the socialist revolutionary party, who would have, naturally, directed the people's movement not just against the Jewish population, but also, according to their agenda, against the landowners and factory owners. But there was no such movement, and the crowd did not touch anything belonging to the local Christian population or to Count Bobrinskii. Even if there were some among the crowd who did not appear to belong to the local population, it may well be that they appeared there from Kiev or other places during the rioting. No indication exists that such persons prepared the anti-Jewish movement. I presume that these were merely workers who had arrived looking for work and the local population had not yet, so to speak, given them a good look. Lately there had been some indication that a movement may be forming among the peasants concerning land, but even if we allow that signs of it had appeared in some areas in Kiev province, there is nonetheless no link between it and the anti-Jewish movement. Besides, even its manifestations are, for the most part, overstated by people interacting with peasants, as can be easily seen in the report from Zehten, a member of the Kiev province Peasant Affairs Department who had investigated this issue under orders from the Kiev governor. The riots in Elisavetgrad and Kiev undoubtedly influenced the development of the anti-Jewish movement in Smela. The workers who had arrived from Kiev had time to relay details of the pogrom effected there, which clearly amplified the sense of alarm among the people and triggered an attack on Jews at the first available excuse. No preventative measures were taken, and who could have taken them, given the police presence there. Even the troops ended up there basically by accident, not at the request of the local administration, but only at Count Bobrinskii's request, so it is quite understandable how the rioting there managed to develop to such a large extent and have such deplorable and grave consequences.

Source: Grigorii Ia. Krasnyi-Admoni, ed., *Materialy dlia istorii antievreiskikh pogromov v Rossii*, vol. 2 (Petrograd: Gosudarstvennoe izdatel'stvo, 1923), 208–19. Translated from the Russian by Eugenia Tietz-Sokolskaya.

Document 1.2. Leaflets Dropped around Kharkov Inviting People to Commit Anti-Jewish Violence

Rioters generally believed in the lawfulness of their actions and that they were misled to commit pogroms. The circulation of false rumors played a particularly important role in agitating anti-Jewish violence and behavior. One means by which rumors spread was by wall posters or leaflets. Anti-Jewish notices such as the one reprinted here appeared few in number, however. Leaflets often created a sense of panic of impending violence and forced the government to send troops to places threatened by pogroms.

Are we really going to perish because of the Yids? Let's gather, brothers, above all to destroy the Jewish row. Even today, or on St. Nicholas's day, hurry, brothers, workers—all together. Don't get scared.

Brothers, let's beat the Yids. Or did you lose heart? Or, is [*sic*] the people not like in Odessa? They've already been beaten everywhere else, but here in Kharkov the beating of the Yids has been held up. Don't believe the announcements, there's no ban on beating Yids. Or are we going to perish for the Yids? That's why there's no bread—they send all the bread abroad. Let's beat the Yids, all together, brothers, let's get going. The police and governor have been bought off by the Yids. We're ready now, brothers, beat the Yids faster, or they'll all leave. Brothers, what's the truth in the world? The governors and others sent several hundred rubles to the Yids in Odessa, but nothing to our people. There are so many without bread in the villages. Workers—all together.

Brothers, beat the Yids. The police have been bought off by the Yids, but there won't be anything for the Yids, brothers, and if they beat us for the Yids, then all the police in Kharkov will be blown up with dynamite—people have already told us. Beat the Yids all together, brothers, get on it.

Kharkov beat the Yids, attack from all ends of the city, don't take anything, make everything into trash.

Source: Grigorii Ia. Krasnyi-Admoni, ed., *Materialy dlia istorii antievreiskikh pogromov v Rossii*, vol. 2 (Petrograd: Gosudarstvennoe isdatel'stvo, 1923), 297. Translated from the Russian by Eugenia Tietz-Sokolskaya.

Document 1.3. Telegram to the Minister of Internal Affairs from Prince Donbukov, Odessa, May 5, 1881

The government's response centered on containing the violence, in hopes of avoiding its recurrence. The Ministry of the Interior established guidelines for governors and governors-general to use precautionary measures to prevent pogroms. Authorities is- sued public warnings that violence against Jews and non-Jews would be prosecuted

with the full force of the law. Under existing emergency legislation, authorities had ex-
tensive powers to punish those charged with disturbing the peace. According to impre-
cise official statistics, officials arrested a minimum of 5,500 people for pogrom-related
activities in 1881 and an additional 700 people in 1882, but only a small portion of
those arrested were punished.

Today, May 4, throughout the day and until 11 o'clock at night, the peace was not disturbed. Isolated attempts to attack taverns were immediately identified and stopped. I personally traveled around the city and found that yesterday's damage was limited to the destruction and looting of about a dozen wooden vendors' stalls in the bazaar, destruction of dishware in several drinking establishments, and the breaking of glass in a small number of houses. Today, as a warning, we made preliminary arrests of about 250 people, including about 80 Jews who were armed with axes and revolvers and were apparently intending to incite rioting. The detainees will be sent to the barge at anchor in the harbor, as were those arrested yesterday. Those seriously wounded in the fighting include one Jew and one Christian; the number of beating victims is high.

Source: Grigorii Ia. Krasnyi-Admoni, ed., *Materialy dlia istorii antievreiskikh pogromov v Rossii*, vol. 2 (Petrograd: Gosudarstvennoe izdatel'stvo, 1923), 33. Translated from the Russian by Eugenia Tietz-Sokolskaya.

Document 1.4. Telegram Sent to the Ministry of the Interior on May 5, 1881, from the Rovno Jewish Community, Volhynia Province

Authorities usually took extensive precautions to prevent mob violence. Jews were
continuously reminded to avoid conflict and to conduct themselves cautiously. But as
soon as a pogrom took on a life of its own, officials could do little to suppress the mob
violence. The regular police force proved largely inadequate in manpower and incom-
petent in training. Fearing assault, Jewish communities formed self-defense units on
occasion. They also wrote appeals for protection directly to authorities in the highest
echelons of power.

The eight-thousand-strong Jewish population of the city of Rovno, Volhynia province, has been left without any protection, besides the local garrison, which is occupied with standing watch, and the police, consisting of a captain, two wardens, and six officers. There is no military force. We fear attack by the workers of the Zhitanskii, Oleksinskii, and Mizochiskii sugar factories, located near the city, as well as the Zdolbunov railroad workers, a total of three thousand people. In addition, five hundred workers will arrive on May 10 to work on the Stepan railway, and extremely alarming rumors are in the air. The storm is near. Among the local Christian population all we hear is that very soon it will reach us. We fear slaughter and looting. We appealed to the governor-general for help, for troops to be deployed to us, if possible, and the response was that there was nothing to fear, and that there is nowhere to get troops. The deployment of troops is possible only in cases specified by law. Since protection is necessary before the storm hits, and fearing the coming holidays on May 9 and May 10, being in a desperate situation, we tearfully beg Your Excellency to look with an eye of mercy upon your defenseless people: please give orders for an immediate deployment to us of at least a hundred Cossacks and an infantry battalion from the closest troop disposition.

Signed by the representatives of the Rovno Jewish community.

Source: Grigorii Ia. Krasnyi-Admoni, ed., *Materialy dlia istorii antievreiskikh pogromov v Rossii*, vol. 2 (Petrograd: Gosudarstvennoe izdatel'stvo, 1923), 33. Translated from the Russian by Eugenia Tietz-Sokolskaya.

Document 1.5. Circular Distributed on May 6, 1881, by E. I. Totleben, the Governor-General of Vilna, to His Subordinates

After the first wave of pogroms broke out in Elisavetgrad in April 1881, officials in various parts of the empire, including the northwest provinces, responded to rumors and threats made against Jews. News of the pogroms alarmed authorities. Governor-General Totleben, as well as other officials in the northwest provinces, sent out detailed instructions to their subordinates to prevent violence. Nevertheless, authorities in Vilna and other nearby towns noted an increase in violence between Jews and Christians, including fistfights, damage to Jewish property, and other minor confrontations. Two large urban anti-Jewish riots broke out in September 1881 in Bal'verzhishki (Balbieriškis) and in August 1882 in Preny (Prienai).

Malicious people, in order to achieve their criminal goals, are spreading false rumors and outrageous incitations, stirring up anxiety and fear among the people, both for their personal safety and the security of their property. Per my responsibility to take care of the public safety for this region, I warn you that I have given the necessary orders for the purposes of protecting the population and its property. In order to avoid the need to take extreme measures, and to eliminate the occurrence of any disorder, I appeal to all law-abiding residents of this province, entrusted to me, with the following requests: (1) to help refute any unjustified, outrageous content of rumors, to the best of their abilities and within their respective spheres of activity; (2) if the malefactors do attempt to instigate anyone to criminal action, to talk sense into everyone convinced by them, and to keep them, by counseling and convincing them where possible, from breaking the law; (3) to cooperate, for their own safety, in the discovery of persons engaged in the dissemination of rumors and instigation; and (4) in the event of ongoing unrest, not to join the crowd out of curiosity, in order to, on the one hand, not obstruct the actions of the police and military authorities aimed at ending the unrest, and on the other, protect oneself from unfortunate consequences that could result if the troops take decisive measures with their weapons. At the same time, I consider it my duty to warn the populace that any congregation, gathering, or congestion of people in squares and streets is prohibited. If despite the demands of authorities, the crowd does not disperse, then, as permitted by law, weapons will be used against those who do not obey, and those who participate in protest and rioting will be immediately arrested and subjected to well-deserved punishment.

Source: Grigorii Ia. Krasnyi-Admoni, ed., *Materialy dlia istorii antievreiskikh pogromov v Rossii*, vol. 2 (Petrograd: Gosudarstvennoe izdatel'stvo, 1923), 38–39. Translated from the Russian by Eugenia Tietz-Sokolskaya.

Document 1.6. Observations Made by a Nameless Doctor

Beginning in the 1860s, railroads connected the southwestern territories with the Black Sea and the interior of the empire. In the western borderlands, militant groups used railroads to spread ethnic unrest. Railway employees and workers took part in pogroms. The pogrom violence usually originated in urban centers and spread in waves to neighboring market towns and villages, along railroads, rivers, and roads. A pogrom could occur in a large town, stop for days or weeks, and then break out in smaller market towns, connected along paths of transportation.

When determining the reasons for the rioting in the south involving the beating of Jews, in my opinion it is sufficient to take note of the map of the southern railways in order to come to the final conclusion that the riots did not result from the exploitation of Jews, but from incitement by dark individuals, in whose interest it was to cause confusion, in this case taking advantage of the peasants' religious antipathy toward the Jews. And indeed: if the beating of the Jews had as its root cause the Jews themselves, that is, exploitation, then it would have been more likely to take place in the villages, settlements, and provincial towns far away from busy points, where, as a given, there are more opportunities for exploitation, than in cities or towns located along the railway line. On the contrary, the riots sprang up almost exclusively in cities, settlements (Golta, Belaia Tserkov), and villages located along the southern railway line, which allow these dark individuals to spend less money and time traveling with the aim of simultaneously inciting Christians in different places, while in order to get to the areas far away from the railway station, one has to waste a lot of time, have a means of transportation, and most important, look respectable. The same can explain the fact that all the cities and towns located inside and outside of the quadrilateral bounded by the Odessa–Kiev, Elisavetgrad–Kharkov, and Fastov railway lines have so far remained free from anti-Jewish violence, and if these riots have appeared in recent days in a few points far from the railway stations (Kanev, Vasilkov), it is very possible that this could have happened at the initiative of the peasants themselves, due to rumors of the successful looting of Jews in Kiev and other places.

Doctor [signature indecipherable]

Source: Grigorii Ia. Krasnyi-Admoni, ed., *Materialy dlia istorii antievreiskikh pogromov v Rossii*, vol. 2 (Petrograd: Gosudarstvennoe izdatel'stvo, 1923), 40–41. Translated from the Russian by Eugenia Tietz-Sokolskaya.

Document 1.7. Secret Memo by the Deputy Chief of the Gendarme Department in Chernigov Province

The Nezhin pogrom in Chernigov province exacted the highest human casualties of any pogrom in 1881 and 1882. At the time of the pogrom, the police had disappeared from the streets. The battalion of troops, called in to pacify the angry mob, proved largely inadequate. On the second day of the pogrom, the rioters, shouting "Beat the Yids," destroyed Jewish property and looted drinking establishments. The Chernigov governor arrived with additional troops, and the pogrom was halted on the morning of July 22. Eleven Christian rioters died. The Jewish community suffered an estimated 150,000 rubles in damages. The secret memo reprinted here was authored shortly after the pogrom broke out in Nezhin on July 20–22, 1881.

On July 20, 1881, at around eight in the evening, a group of boys led by two adults set out from Avdeevka, a suburb of Nezhin, and, singing, headed toward the fairground, saying as they went that they were on their way to beat the Jews. This was made known to the police, but by the time the precinct head and police chief arrived at the scene, the group of boys had been joined by a rather substantial crowd of adults, whom first the precinct head, then the police chief tried to convince to disperse. All their exhortations were in vain, as a result of which they sent for the troops. When the on-call troop of the sixty-sixth reserve battalion arrived at the fairground and began arresting the most apparent instigators, the crowd dispersed to the outskirts of the city and began destroying Jewish homes and taverns there. Small detachments were sent to various parts of the city to try to stem the unrest where possible. One such detachment under an officer's command met with a large crowd, which, not listening to the officer's exhortations, began surrounding the detachment, threatening to take away their rifles, following which, forced to do so by the extreme situation, the officer ordered the troops to shoot, resulting in four killed and one wounded.

After continuing to riot all night, quite a large crowd gathered on the morning of July 21 in the center of the city and began demanding the release of everyone who was arrested during the night. When the crowd's demand was not met, the entire mass of people headed to the market square and began destroying all the shops, houses, and taverns owned by Jews. With the soldiers' help, the police would disperse the rioters wherever possible, but later, when almost everyone had had extra to drink, it became more difficult to handle them. The drunks not only cursed at the police and troops for interceding on the Jews' behalf and killing Christians, but also voiced various threats and finally began throwing broken bottles at the police and took up harness shafts to attack, for which reason soldiers were once again ordered to shoot, resulting in five killed and two wounded. After the fired salvo, some left the square, while the majority remained until dusk, continuing to riot in various places. In addition, I must mention the antics of Peter Ogievskii, the priest of the Spaso-Preobrazhenskaia Church, who, after the salvo was fired and several fell, walked up to the commander of the sixty-sixth reserve battalion, Colonel Nelidov, and loudly, in front of the raging crowd, began upbraiding him for ordering his troops to shoot, which was, given the circumstances at the time, at the very least inappropriate. After that the entire night was peaceful. Then today, at around nine in the morning, small groups again began to destroy the houses still standing, but they were dispersed without much trouble, and when two hussar squadrons arrived in the city, they dispersed everyone completely, and as of now the unrest has ceased. In reporting the foregoing to Your Honor [most likely, to the minister of the interior], I believe it my duty to add that although the unrest is not ongoing this very minute, the populace is seriously enraged that Christian blood was spilled because of Jews, conjecturing that the police and troops have been bought off by the Jews, and spreading the most absurd rumors of Jews and Tatars attacking Christian children, and so forth.

Source: Grigorii Ia. Krasnyi-Admoni, ed., *Materialy dlia istorii antievreiskikh pogromov v Rossii*, vol. 2 (Petrograd: Gosudarstvennoe izdatel'stvo, 1923), 143–54. Translated from the Russian by Eugenia Tietz-Sokolskaya.

Document 1.8. Memo Written on June 9, 1881, by the Ekaterinoslav Governor to the Ministry of the Interior

Most local officials agreed that Jewish economic exploitation was the main source of the antagonistic relationship between Jews and Christians. Russian officials accepted this motive. Almost every non-Jewish contemporary analysis of the pogroms shared the sentiment that Jews' economic misconduct was the essential cause of anti-Jewish violence.

In delving into the causes of the pogrom that took place in this province against the Jews, and in asking oneself why the violence toward them erupted only in Aleksandrovsk and its surrounding area even though the discontent in the minds of the peasants and rumors concerning impending violence against Jews were wide-spread in all parts of Ekaterinoslav province without exception, one must, on the basis of observations made, reach the following conclusions: the same impetuses that drove the populace to attack the Jews in Kiev, Elisavetgrad, and other cities in southern Russia undoubtedly constituted the source of the anti-Jewish movement here as well. The hatred of the Russian people toward Jews is an age-old, historic reality, formed in southern Russia back in the age of the Cossacks, who were eternally at war with the Poles and their accomplices in combatting oppression of the Cossacks and Jews.

These historic traditions were subsequently joined by reasons of a purely economic nature. The population—not just the lower classes, but the upper classes as well—feels that it is under the Jewish yoke; not just small-scale, but even large-scale trade and manufacturing is, for the most part, in the hands of Jews; as for the rural settlements, there trade has been completely taken over by Jews, who, furthermore, by the shiftiness of their character, conduct it using such tricks for rapid profit that Russian merchants absolutely cannot compete with them. A Jew is capable of anything: deceiving a guileless peasant; or bending the laws if they stand in the way of his exploitative activities; or demeaning himself to the point of abandoning human dignity, if there is profit in it. Since the Jew senses his superiority over Russians, his insolence and disdain for everything Russian exceeds all possible limits. All of these qualities understandably render the Jewish race extremely unappealing to Russians and engender hatred toward it. But the most corrosive evil penetrates the people's economic and moral order by way of bootlegging and usurious moneylending—Jews' favorite occupations. In a rural settlement, the appearance of a Jewish boot-legger undermines the economic well-being of the people and severely demoralizes them. Meanwhile, examples of Jewish usury can be appalling: for a few rubles loaned to a peasant at a time of dire need, often the debtor's entire harvest passes into the Jew's hands. The lender entangles his victim in his web so that once indebted, it will be long before a peasant can free himself.

In short, a Jew that comes to live in a settlement sucks out all the population's living juices, and if at the same time he is also the landlord for government-owned or estate property, then the peasants are literally bonded to him. All of this could not, of course, do anything but build up hatred toward Jews among the people, and if that hatred did not erupt until now, it may well be that the instigators of these passions were under orders from persons belonging to a specifically revolutionary party. This conjecture is founded on the following considerations: the causes of hatred against Jews among the people are not new; they also existed previously, but never caused an explosion of popular discontent among the village population. However, in these troubled times it was very convenient for anarchists to take advantage of the people's pent-up hatred toward the Jews for their own shady purposes. They understood very well that the authorities would not permit any vigilantism or violence against Jews and would take stringent measures to quell the riots, and the anarchists could take advantage of this to sow discontent among the people against the authorities, framing them as the protectors of the Jewish race despised by the people. Add to that the conviction that has spread among the peasants—possibly by the same anarchists—that the persecution of Jews was ordered by a decree from the tsar, in which case action to counter it by the authorities could cause among the peasants a very dangerous form of doubt and even greater confusion. Finally, the conjecture that the anti-Jewish movement may have been abetted by shady persons in need of such a movement is also suggested by the fact that it erupted in different places almost simultaneously.

Source: Grigorii Ia. Krasnyi-Admoni, ed., *Materialy dlia istorii antievreiskikh pogromov v Rossii*, vol. 2 (Petrograd: Gosudarstvennoe izdatel'stvo, 1923), 127–28. Translated from the Russian by Eugenia Tietz-Sokolskaya.

Document 1.9. The Russo-Jewish Question

A Special Correspondent of the *Jewish World*

As news of the destruction spread, Russia's stature in the international community dropped. Anti-Russian rallies protested what was regarded as an unprecedented humanitarian emergency. Newspapers all around the world published graphic details of plunder and destruction of property and of Jewish refugees fleeing the mob violence. Disturbing accounts of violence against women and rape claims were published by foreign-language newspapers such as the Jewish World *and the* Times. *The sensational reportage circulated widely around the world.*

In the course of a six hours' drive in and around Kiev, I have managed to visit the principal points where the recent attacks on the Jews were made. Kiev, I think I have already mentioned, lies, as it were, on two sides of an abominably steep hill. The Podol, or Old Town, is in the valley on the Dnieper side, and one of the prettiest sights imaginable is the view of the city and its winding river from the hilltop, its regular streets, with their seemingly tiny houses, their green and red roofs in picturesque contrast, and the prettily built and many-domed churches, all gilding and emerald green, standing out clear above the other buildings against a blue and cloudless sky. The new and fashionable center adjoins Khreshchatyk Street—"place of baptism," as the word signifies—in the declivity on the other side. Driving along this busy thoroughfare, through which the droshkies and little carts drawn by a yoke of oxen are constantly passing and repassing, we turn the corner, thus rounding the hill, and enter Aleksandrovskaia Street, a thoroughly Jewish street. Almost every second shop belongs, as the name and often an inscription in Judeo-German sufficiently indicates, to a Jew. Clothes shops and drapers, fancy warehouses and grocers' stores, tobacconists and refreshment rooms, all are owned by Hebrews. And there they stand, or sit, at the door, just as one may see like any day in London.

Looking closely at the shops, traces of the recent campaign are only too apparent. The well-to-do concerns have all new doors, new window sashes, and many of them newly painted signboards. The less prosperous are more readily noted. Windows still broken; sashes and signs battered in; plaster hanging down; and, more significant still, nothing whatever inside the shop but broken wood and splintered furniture. Even in the depots of those who have found means to pay for the repairs necessary to recommence business, the appearance of activity is delusive. I entered several shops and found in every case that the entire stock was in the window. The rest—well, the rest—is pretty fairly divided, I understand, among the mob and the police. Driving somewhat further, passing scores of Jewish warehouses, we come to the Aleksandrovskii Bazaar, or market—for the word "Bazaar" retains its original Eastern signification. Here, in the Aleksandrovskii Bazaar, the rioting, on the memorable Sunday morning some six weeks ago, first commenced. Here was the starting point of the attack, the rendezvous of the attacking parties.

[. . .]

The fact that no precautions were adopted by the police or military rendered the work of the rioters easy enough. The battering and plundering commenced at a flour depot, three doors from the corner; of course, a depot owned by a Jew. Crashing in the heavy iron doors the sacks were dragged out, the contents strewn about, large quantities carried off, and much entirely wasted. Police and military, always about, came upon the scene, and looked on! More police and military came and helped— to look on! Seeing that there was no attempt made to interfere with them—and as half-a-dozen Cossacks with their whips only could have driven off the rioters—they went on with their work right royally. The wooden [construction] they made short work of. And then they proceeded to every Jewish [shop] and warehouse in the Bazaar, in Aleksandrovskaia Street and in Podol, smashing, breaking, and tearing everything they came across; knocking down every Jew they met; hunting women out of the streets; robbing Hebrews in the open road, and committing—in the words of the advocate Ravitzky—"every disgraceful, criminal act [known to men] was that day and the next committed." Men were injured and females outraged. Women were stripped of their clothing and flogged along the streets under the very eyes of the soldiers and police. And how did the police behave, how [did they] conduct themselves? Let me give the words of Dr. Mandelstamm—to whom I have before referred, and who was an eyewitness of the scene. "At one corner of the [shop] stood the police, at the other the soldiers, under their officers. Between the two—as if to guard them from molestation—the mob, pillaging and robbing; the police calling out, ever and anon, as the wreck of one place was completed, 'Move on, move on,' as if to invite them to the next Jewish place."

And so, the mob went along, escorted on one side by the police and on the other by the military. And thus, without any actual interference, the work of pillage went on till late at night. Soft good depots, grocery stores, candle and soap shops, and brandy cellars were emptied of their contents, and with the latter came the drunken period of the attack. What deeds were committed will never be wholly known. But let the readers of the *Jewish World* note one fact, which has been kept very quiet, five women—two married women and three young girls—were so grossly violated by the mob that they died the next morning. And these were five out of the eight murders in Kiev—a garrison town where 40,000 men are interned—under the very eyes almost of the governor-general of Kiev. The terror in which the Jews passed the night, not knowing what was to be the next item in the program, may be imagined.

Encouraged by the indifference of the authorities, and under the impression that the pillage was permissible, the mob flocked into the town the next morning in larger numbers than before. Then might have been witnessed a rare sight: peasants bringing in their little wagons to remove the Jews' goods; respectable persons in droshkies receiving from the plunderers bundles of soft goods and draperies, whole cones of sugar and bags of groceries, and driving off with them; Cossacks on horseback stuffing under their saddles and police officials under their tunics, velvets and silks, watches and jewelry, handed over to them by the obliging and considerate mob. A characteristic story was told to me this afternoon concerning the things stolen by the soldiers themselves. Dr. [unspecified name], a Jew, who related the circumstances to me himself, is the principal dentist in the town. A colonel of Cossacks, who lost two of his teeth during the rioting, came to him to have them replaced. In the course of conversation, which naturally turned upon the recent disturbances, the officer assured the doctor that so many of his men had brought stolen goods to the barracks that he had been obliged to gather the lot and burn them, fearing the fact that, should they be discovered, his men would be liable to trial by court martial.

Source: *Jewish World*, July 15, 1881, 5.

2

The 1898 Anti-Jewish Violence
in Habsburg Galicia

Daniel Unowsky

In the spring and early summer of 1898, anti-Jewish violence swept across the western and central districts of Habsburg Galicia.[1] Polish-speaking peasants broke into shops and taprooms administered by Jews on the outskirts of small villages. They bashed in windows and knocked down doors with scythes, hatchets, canes, and rocks. They consumed vodka and beer, shattered glasses, destroyed furniture, and ransacked chests of drawers. Attackers beat Jewish men and women with sticks and hit them with rocks. Hundreds of peasants, artisans, shopkeepers, and members of local governing councils looted Jewish-owned businesses lining market squares in towns like Kalwaria, Frysztak, Nowy Sącz, and Stary Sącz. Participants stole flour, vodka, clothes, kitchen utensils, mattresses, and pillows. Some filled baskets, others piled their booty onto carts driven into town for this purpose. By the time the Galician governor Leon Count Piniński announced a state of emergency in the thirty-three westernmost districts of the province on June 28, anti-Jewish attacks had taken place in more than four hundred localities.

The 1898 Galician riots constituted the most serious example of ethnic violence experienced in Austria-Hungary before World War I.[2] Thousands of people took part or cheered on more active participants. Assailants injured scores of Jews, though none were killed. The gendarmes and the army attempted to restore order and, in several incidents, fired on attackers. These security forces killed at least eighteen Christian rioters and bystanders. The authorities charged some 5,170 people—peasants, day laborers, miners, railroad construction workers, village leaders, teachers, and shopkeepers; young men in their late teens and village elders in their sixties and seventies, as well as women of all ages. Of these, at least

---

[1] This essay is based on Daniel Unowsky, *The Plunder: The 1898 Anti-Jewish Riots in Habsburg Galicia* (Stanford, CA: Stanford University Press, 2018).

[2] There is a great deal of scholarship on clashes between Czech and German nationalists in Prague and other areas of Bohemia. See, among others, Nancy Wingfield, *Flag Wars and Stone Saints: How the Bohemian Lands Became Czech* (Cambridge, MA: Harvard University Press, 2007).

Daniel Unowsky, *The 1898 Anti-Jewish Violence in Habsburg Galicia* In: *Pogroms*. Edited by: Eugene M. Avrutin and Elissa Bemporad, Oxford University Press. © Oxford University Press 2021. DOI: 10.1093/oso/9780190060084.003.0003

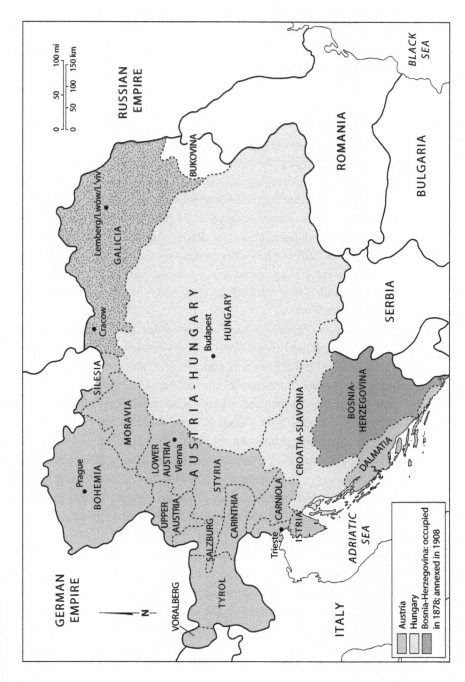

Map of Austria-Hungary, 1867–1914.

GERMAN EMPIRE

RUSSIAN EMPIRE

BLACK SEA

ROMANIA

BULGARIA

SERBIA

ITALY

ADRIATIC SEA

N

VORALBERG

TYROL

SALZBURG

CARINTHIA

UPPER AUSTRIA

LOWER AUSTRIA

Vienna

STYRIA

CARNIOLA

ISTRIA

Trieste

CROATIA-SLAVONIA

DALMATIA

BOSNIA-HERZEGOVINA

A U S T R I A - H U N G A R Y

BOHEMIA

Prague

MORAVIA

SILESIA

Cracow

GALICIA

Lemberg/Lwów/L'viv

BUKOVINA

HUNGARY

Budapest

100 mi
50
0

150 km
100
50
0

Austria
Hungary
Bosnia-Herzegovina: occupied in 1878; annexed in 1908

3,816 were tried and 2,328 sentenced to prison terms lasting from a few days to three years.

Local confrontations between Roman Catholics and Jews took place intermittently before and after the spring and summer of 1898. In these months, however, a number of factors transformed such incidents into a wave of violence that spread from town square to village tavern and drew in ever greater numbers of people as participants in and objects of mass violence.

1. *Economic crisis*. Since the 1850s, large numbers of peasants had lost their hold on the land in the wake of the end of serfdom and the arrival of capitalist agriculture, leading many to seek short-term work in the few large-scale governmental projects (rail, river regulation, and fortress construction). Harvest failures combined with glacial economic development in Galicia to produce terrible consequences in the late 1890s. Crop yields in 1897, in some areas reported as 75 percent lower than the previous year, overpopulation, and parcellation increased the number of rural bankruptcies. Although Jewish businesses in small towns were also devastated, Jews were prominent among those purchasing land. Many Christians in small towns and villages were indebted to Jewish tavern keepers and moneylenders.

2. *A sharpening Jewish–Christian cultural and economic divide*. Economic crisis exacerbated economic and social divisions between Jews (mostly employed in commerce and petty trade; owners and administrators of small businesses and saloons lining the region's market squares); and Christians (overwhelmingly working in the agricultural sectors and inhabiting villages). These divisions were made visible by a deep cultural divide. Christians and Jews living in close proximity in western and central Galicia differed in speech, dress, religious custom, and patterns of daily life. These differences did not equal conflict; however, the notion of essential difference was not an import from larger cities or other parts of Europe. The slow but noticeable growth of Christian commerce in this period also heightened tensions in rural areas between Christians and Jews.

3. *Catholic antisemitism*. In the 1890s, a new and virulent Catholic antisemitism melded traditional anti-Jewish charges (Christ killers, Talmudic immorality, and ritual murder) with modern ones (Jewish prominence in trade, usurious interest rates, and alcohol monopoly). The Catholic Congress held in Kraków in 1893 called for a boycott of the Jews and the separation of Jews and Christians in all aspects of life. New Catholic workers' associations and newspapers like Kraków's popular *Głos Narodu* and *Prawda*, the latter published under the auspices of the Catholic hierarchy and directed toward the Catholic Polish-speaking peasantry, amplified and disseminated these anti-Jewish messages. Weekly sermons from parish pulpits delivered more of the same.

4. *The arrival of mass politics.* The expansion of the parliamentary suffrage in the Austrian half of Austria-Hungary transformed politics. Galicia's new peasant and socialist parties competed vigorously for the votes of village and small-town inhabitants in 1897 and 1898. Near nonstop election campaigning and political agitation by Father Stanisław Stojałowski's Christian People's Party and its rivals blanketed the countryside with anti-Jewish messages that complemented those promoted in Catholic circles: Jewish difference equaled Jewish danger; modernization for the Polish-speaking rural population could only advance with the exclusion of the Jews from their positions of economic prominence.

5. *Rumors and the role of the press.* Rural and urban newspapers documented every attack as well as the spread of increasingly outlandish tales of papal and imperial approval for violence against Jews. These printed accounts then became "evidence" that such rumors were plausible. Those active in spreading news about violence and in gathering crowds to participate in attacks drew on and contributed to these circulating stories. Catholic and partisan publications opposed violence, even as they denounced the Jews and their nefarious activities.

6. *Slow response by the forces of order.* The Galician administration had few gendarmes to rely on to halt the spread of attacks. Some local officials initially dismissed Jewish accounts of rumors of pending violence as Jewish fantasies. The Habsburg Monarchy was a constitutional *Rechtsstaat*, committed to equal protection for all citizens. In this context, however, rumors of official permission quickly gained credence. The deployment of thousands of soldiers and the institution of a state of emergency at the end of June succeeded in bringing an end to the waves of attacks, though a few serious incidents occurred in July in eastern Galicia.

The violence took place in specific settings. Large-scale incidents often began in town squares on market days, religious holidays like Palm Sunday, Corpus Christi, regular Sunday church services, or newly invented "national" festivities such as those organized to celebrate the poet Adam Mickiewicz. Attacks then spread to side streets and eventually the countryside. Those who had traveled to town for special events returned to surrounding villages, bringing home with them their experience of violence as well as rumors that authorities (the pope, politicians, Emperor Franz Joseph) had sanctioned anti-Jewish violence. In other cases, isolated Jewish enclaves between villages proved tempting targets for those riled up by news and stories about violence taking place elsewhere.

People participated for a variety of reasons. Some had experienced economic dislocation and turned their rage on specific Jews viewed as gaining from their losses. Others were regular readers of the rural antisemitic press or attended one or more political rallies at which politicians railed against the Jews. Among the most enthusiastic perpetrators were people with long criminal records, perhaps taking advantage of a sense of chaos. Curious people went along to see if rumored violence would in fact materialize. They then became part of the encouraging crowds urging on plunderers. In many instances, these onlookers later joined in the action.

Populist politicians maneuvered to position themselves as sympathetic to the rioters. They did not advocate violence, but they acknowledged the righteous anger of poor people allegedly kept drunk and ignorant and pushed into bankruptcy by the Jewish enemy. In speeches and publications, they called for a systematic politics of exclusion to replace random and ineffective efforts at violent solutions for the problems of the countryside. Galicia's Social Democratic Party leaders denounced the violence and antisemitism. Yet, on the floor of the parliament in Vienna, the party's most important figure, Ignacy Daszyński, decried the alliance of Jewish saloon keepers and moneylenders with the hated Polish aristocracy. In response to Daszyński and to the violence, Austrian Minister President Franz Anton von Thun und Hohenstein defended the rule of law and its application to the threatened Jewish population, even as he and others in the Austrian and Galician administrations ultimately shared the view that Jews had brought the violence upon themselves.

As the violence subsided, the trials began. For six months, audiences in packed courtrooms in central and western Galicia watched and listened as the accused, prosecutors, witnesses, and defense attorneys sought to define justice. Newspapers printed indictments and excerpted testimony. The trials constituted a seemingly impressive effort on the part of the state to restore order. In some widely publicized cases, however, prosecutors and judges conceded the essence of the main charges made by the antisemitic political forces attempting to gain political profit from the wave of violence and its aftermath. For some Jews, like Emil Byk, a leading liberal politician from the Galician capital, this process reaffirmed the pro-Jewish sentiments of the benevolent emperor and the Vienna government's firm commitment to Jewish equality. For other Jews, like Byk's rival Joseph Bloch, the Vienna-based rabbi, politician, and journalist originally from Galicia, the necessity of the state of emergency and the temporary setting aside of constitutional niceties in order to ensure the safety of the Jewish population was far from comforting.[3] What would happen should the Habsburg authorities be succeeded by others less committed to protecting the Jewish population from the wrath of their neighbors?

---

[3] Byk's views are clearly expressed in the excerpt from his November parliamentary speech quoted in this chapter. For Bloch, see *Dr. Bloch's Österreichische Wochenschrift*, July 29, 1898, 558.

Document 2.1. Pamphlet Widely Disseminated in Western Galicia: *Jewish Secrets*

This pamphlet was originally published as a series of articles in Prawda, *a viciously antisemitic weekly close to the Catholic hierarchy in Kraków. The author, Mateusz Jeż, a priest and catechist at Kraków's St. Anna Church, argued that Christians could not be racists and, therefore, should reject racial antisemitism. Instead, Jeż promoted what he and others termed "asemitism," the complete separation from and rejection of Jews.* Jewish Secrets *was published in early 1898. The print run of five thousand sold out in a few weeks and a second expanded edition followed. The antisemitic peasant-oriented Christian People's Party advertised this pamphlet and made inexpensive copies available at political rallies. Connections between this pamphlet and the earliest anti-Jewish attacks, as well as complaints by Jewish community leaders, led to an investigation and eventual ban on the dissemination of* Jewish Secrets. *In mid- to late June, in several incidents, riot leaders read out passages from this brochure that seemingly exhorted the peasants to rob and attack Jews while preserving Jewish lives. The following excerpt constitutes the core of the section titled "We must defend ourselves!"*

But does anyone among us call out today for a war against the Jews? No! Does anyone demand "the burning of synagogues with sulfur, pitch, and hellfire, to tear down the houses of the Jews, to take their cash, and to drive them out like mad dogs for the glory of God and Christianity?" No; although Martin Luther demanded all of this, though he liked the Jews so much that he was charged with having "vacillating views about the Jews!" In fact, here and there in Galicia in recent times the blood of Jews has flowed, but this is caused by the Jews themselves and at the hands of people who have certainly never heard of antisemitism or at least have not read antisemitic publications. Even those Viennese antisemites, who vex our Jewish friends the most (in part justifiably, since they are not very pleasant to the Poles), even they do not permit themselves to commit any acts of violence or murder against the Jews. Among the Jews of Vienna, it is possible to find at worst some "very frightened" due to the antisemites, but that does not do any harm.

Furthermore, the friends of the Jews (judophiles) insist *antisemitism propagates racial or tribal hatred* against the Jews, and that this is not in accord with Christian religion. The Jew is a person and deserves to live.

That is true, but that is not all. Even though Jews do not consider us as human, but only animals that have human appearance, we still do not refuse them the right to call themselves humans and we acknowledge them as human. If antisemites express racial hatred against the Jews, this is not right. It may be that someone does not like the Jewish nose, or *peyos*, or muddy caftan, or a Christian may not suffer a Jew because he has a different nose, or black or red hair, or he smells different from other people, that is not right. We Christians love people, but we hate their defects.

Kikeriki, a Viennese satirical and antisemitic magazine, produced a series of hideous depictions of plotting Galician Jews triumphing over innocent Christian peasants during and after the riots. Here the Jews say: "In Galicia the 'free play of market forces' has been restored!" while the long arm of the emergency decree silences the helpless Polish peasant.

Kikeriki, July 14, 1898, 2

In Jews we cannot endure their swindling, their perfidy!! It is not racial hatred since surely Jews recognize these qualities as inherent features of their race. [. . .]

However, it is not possible to insist again from Christians that they only have sensitive words, patience, and tender affection for the Jews. No wonder that sometimes a harsher word is spoken. The issue is immediate and vitally important. *It is about the rescue of our property and our national life. It is about saving the Christian religion, whose oldest and worst enemies are the Jews. Either us or the Jews!*

Source: Mateusz Jeż, *Tajemnice Żydowskie* (Kraków, 1898), 76–80. Translated from the Polish by Daniel Unowsky.

Document 2.2. Election Campaign Promotion from *Wieniec Polski*

While the rioting was ongoing and a special June election campaign was heating up for a seat to the Vienna parliament from the universal suffrage curia district centered on the town of Jasło, Wieniec Polski, one of the two main publications of Father Stanisław Stojałowski and his Christian People's Party, printed numerous attacks like this on Jan Stapiński and other leaders of the rival People's Party.

To Brother Voters!

Brothers! In this decisive moment of the elections, remember that we are Christians and that we have an obligation to act together when the Christian cause is at stake.

The Jewish kahal and rabbis are sending to every Jew throughout the countryside the recommendation that they vote only for the peasants who will give their votes to *Stapiński* [of the rival People's Party]. One of these lithographs has fallen into our hands and we can show it to you. This is clear evidence of the betrayal of the people, and whoever now still gives their vote to Stapiński should be pointed out as just as much a traitor to the interests of the people.

Source: *Wieniec Polski*, June 20, 1898. Translated from the Polish by Daniel Unowsky.

Document 2.3. Report from the Kalwaria Zebrzydowska District Captain

On May 25, anti-Jewish violence broke out in the Catholic pilgrimage town of Kalwaria Zebrzydowska during a celebration commemorating the hundredth anniversary of the birthday of Adam Mickiewicz, the important Polish-language poet. On the following day, more serious violence involving hundreds of people was quelled by the intervention of a handful of gendarmes. They fired on the crowd, killing one rioter. The following excerpt is from the report by a local official about the rise of virulent anti-Jewish sentiment in the area.

Some weeks before the Mickiewicz celebration that took place on the twenty-fifth and twenty-sixth of this month [May] the rumor spread in Kalwaria as well as in the surrounding villages that the Jews would be beaten on May 26 of this year.

This rumor disturbed the Israelite inhabitants of Kalwaria, who appeared before the commander of the gendarme post and expressed their fears.

As a result of this, the gendarmes searched for the origins of the rumor, investigated in Kalwaria and in the surrounding villages, and learned from the village elders the news that this rumor was false and that the rural population had only received the invitation to participate in the Mickiewicz celebrations from the Kalwaria committee [organizing the festivities].

Very probably the cause of the outbreak of unrest can be found in the announcement of the Mickiewicz celebrations and the invitation to the rural population to participate. After all, the uneducated folk, with very few exceptions, had no understanding of what poets are, and they also are not capable of understanding the purpose of the announced festivity honoring the poet Mickiewicz, of whom they know almost nothing. In this situation, malicious people gave this announced celebration an entirely different meaning, and because the growing hatred of the rural population against the Jews has been nourished by the antisemitic publications read in the countryside, the tales that the announced celebration really meant the organization of an attack on the Jews found not only believers but also willing listeners. [. . .]

An agent of the Bauman firm appeared to the Kalwaria businessman Leo Kąkol extolling a newly invented remedy for the removal of ink stains, and left with [Kąkol] a few advertising flyers that read as follows:

"The newly invented remedy Statin removes every ink stain."*

Kąkol distributed this advertisement among the population, and the rumor spread that Kąkol was distributing flyers with permission to beat Jews, and three young men came to him [Kąkol] with the request to hand over the flyers.

Source: Central Archives of Historical Records (AGAD), CK MS, box 307, file 3. Translated from the Polish by Daniel Unowsky.

Documents 2.4 and 2.5. Anti-Jewish Flyers

In a few instances, handwritten or cheaply reproduced flyers were placed on Jewish homes, posted at train stations, and so on. The following are two examples. The first is a transcription made by local authorities of a printed flyer placed on Jewish homes in Myślenice at the end of May 1898. The second is a translation from an original handwritten flyer posted on houses in Szczurowa at the end of June 1898.

Flyer 1

Attention: Away with the Jews, with these leeches of the Christians, because if we do not exterminate these locusts we will disappear—so peasants to the stick, flail, and scythe, in order to exterminate the locusts. From the social committee of Kalwaria. We will see each other soon.

Source: Central State Historical Archives of Ukraine in Lviv (Tsentral'nyi Derzhavnyi Istorychnyi Arkhiv Ukrainy; TSDIAL) 146/4/3126, p. 46. Translated from the Polish by Daniel Unowsky.

Flyer 2

Hurrah! Hurrah! at the Jews.
   Since it is happening all over Galicia, we should be ashamed if we do not also brush away their stinking kaftans, and therefore drive them away, let them take up the flails, scythe, and skeins and let them work as we do. And still the Jews have not taken enough. You have shed the blood of our Savior, you have shed our blood, you have dishonored our country, you rob our people, you enrich yourselves from our

---

* The Polish word in the flyer for "ink stain" was *żyd* (Jew). In this half-literate community, ads for a new remedy to remove ink stains transformed into tickets of permission to beat Jews.

labor, you are everywhere. Go to Palestine already; there your Messiah is looking for you—So away with you scabs, away you infection, we despise you, as God despised you—we will not stop beating and burning you until we can no longer see you. We will blow you up with dynamite and you will fall down from the clouds like frogs. Hurrah brothers, Hurrah at the Jews, Hurrah!! The Holy Father has granted a complete indulgence to those who drive the Jews from among the Catholics. Rally together, and you know when. Do not forget about the fair. Hurrah! Hurrah! Hurrah!

Source: TSDIAL 146/4/3124, p. 87. Translated from the Polish by Daniel Unowsky.

Document 2.6. The Lutcza Indictment

The first trials took place at the beginning of July, the last in January 1899. Some included a handful of defendants; others featured dozens or even hundreds of accused. The Lutcza indictment stemmed from an attack by some eight hundred people on an isolated group of Jewish houses and businesses. The case resulted in many convictions and was repeatedly cited in the anti-Jewish press as confirmation by the authorities themselves that the Jews were ultimately to blame for the violence.

Riot in Lutcza

Rzeszów, August 22. Tomorrow a hearing about an antisemitic riot will open before the local court of judgment. Sitting on the bench of the accused will be eighty-six peasants. One hundred six witnesses will be called, and aside from that the testimony of fifty witnesses will be read. The indictment presents the matter in the following manner:

In the spring months of this year 1898 riots with antisemitic character took place almost without pause in localities in western Galicia, and although their instigators have not been discovered, it appears the incitement was done for some hidden purpose by the same personalities, because the nature of these riots and the way in which they revealed themselves was almost everywhere one and the same. The population succumbed to antisemitic attacks, preserving the persons and the lives of Jews, taking almost nothing, destroying taverns, breaking the windows [of taverns], breaking furniture, pouring out liquor. It appears to have been the intention of the attackers to protect the life and entire physical person of the Jews, to destroy their economic dominance, which, especially in the spring months becomes difficult and unpleasant for those hard laborers and workers lacking employment. News about the outbreak of rioting, whether spread by rumor or by journalists, quickly gave rise in other communities to antisemitic movements, the fever of which spread swiftly to almost all districts of western Galicia, spreading especially among the populations of the political counties of Kraków, Wadowice, Nowy Sącz, Jasło, and Strzyżów. Especially in these last three the rioting took on truly alarming dimensions, and the scenes that played out during the attacks in the communities of these last two counties will remain for a long time a dark card in the history of the cultural development of their populations.

The people of the village of Lutcza in the Strzyzów court district were among the first to internalize the general current and to act on their disgust and hatred of their semitic neighbors. It is true that in this village the local population felt the advantage of the Jewish element more than in others, because the manor and the estate lands passed into Israelite hands (Chaskel Wallach), which remained unpleasant for the neighboring poor rural population. [. . .]

Moreover, a few dozen Jewish families lived in Lutcza, and at the head of them stands Hersch Felber, who earns his living with usurious loans on account of which he has had to answer to the court.

In these conditions, rumors about attacks on the property of Jews and the destruction of their belongings found fertile ground and willing listeners. Unreasonable rumors were spread in part by some agitators hoping to kill two birds with one stone and in part by the inhabitants of Lutcza and its region simply out of stupidity and lack of education. Tidings about supposed permission from the emperor, from the government, or from political authorities to destroy the property of Jews for thirty days while preserving their lives, spread with the speed of lightning among the population that lent an eager ear to these terrible and improbable tales [. . .] it is enough to point out [. . .] the story (spread by Jedrzej Szurlej from Lutcza) that "some Jews bribed the emperor's barber so that when he shaved the emperor [the barber] would rip his throat, but the barber felt sorry for the emperor and informed him about what the Jews had persuaded him [the barber] to do to the emperor's throat. The emperor was then so angry at the Jews that he sent an order to take vengeance on the Jews for thirty days. Immediately the empress begged the emperor to reduce the order to permit attacks on the Jews for fourteen and not the initially determined thirty days."

[. . .]

This rumor was received as genuine, and in Lutcza, Godowa, Żarnowa, and other villages in the Strzyzów district on the days of the sixteenth and seventeenth, and above all on the night of the nineteenth, dangerous antisemitic riots broke out in connection with attacks on taverns, homes, and Jewish buildings and with thefts of Jewish belongings.

Who first cast out into Lutcza, whose fate is the subject of this indictment, the fantastical rumor about permission to destroy the property of Jews, and just who were the first to mark June 18 of this year as the moment for the assault on Jewish fellow citizens in Lutcza, this investigation has not and it appears will not be able to identify.

Source: *Kurjer Lwowski*, August 23, 1898, 1. Translated from the Polish by Daniel Unowsky.

Documents 2.7 and 2.8. Three Trial Excerpts

Wieliczka Trial

In mid-March, a group of salt miners rioted against the local Jewish population. The miners worshipped in the local parish church, whose priest, Andrzej Szponder, was a leading member of the Christian People's Party. Szponder had already promoted the pamphlet Jewish Secrets *to his flock. The miners acted on the rumor that the Jews planned to waylay their pastor because of his exposure of the alleged truth of the Jewish threat. During these events, the first serious anti-Jewish attacks of 1898, a group of rock throwers attacked booths run by Jews in the market square of nearby Krasno, including that of the butcher Mendel Kraus and his father Izrael. Due to Mendel Kraus's aggressive self-defense, he was put on trial, along with the Christians who attacked him and other Jews. This is one of the few trials in which Jews faced criminal charges. Kraus was sentenced to two months in prison, longer than Andrzej Konopka, identified by Kraus and other witnesses as one of the ringleaders of the violence.*

Judge: For what reason did you come out with the rock? After all you are accused of throwing the rock into the crowd.

The accused [Mendel Kraus] insisted that he did not throw a rock into the crowd; he threw the rock about five or six steps away from himself, and he saw that the crowd stood about eighty steps away.

Mr. Counselor Pogorzelski: So you only threw that one rock, and no other stones?

Accused: No. I only threw into the yard that one [rock] that had whizzed by my ear.

The accused Mendel Kraus, who flew out at Konopka with a knife, insists that when he was working in the butcher's stall, rocks hit the windows of the store, shattered the windows, and hit the accused in the chest, after which many rocks fell into the store. Terrified, he ran out of the store and met Konopka, who was coming toward him; the accused was so frightened that he does not remember if he grabbed Konopka or not. The accused guesses that he threatened Konopka with his knife because he was very frightened by the flying rocks. The accused does not know whether Konopka threw rocks.

Mr. Counselor Pogorzelski: For what reason did you run at Konopka with a knife, since you did not know that he threw the rocks?

Accused: Because Konopka was walking at the head of the crowd and I was terrified.

Mr. Counselor Pogorzelski: A person hides out of fear, but does not run with a knife at another person.

Accused: So I should let myself be killed by rocks? I do not remember whether I had a knife. The accused denies that he threatened Konopka that he would stab him with the knife.

The confronted Konopka denies that he was at the head of the crowd or broke windows; he walked alone peacefully until suddenly Kraus came at him with a knife. The accused Kraus insists again that Konopka is not speaking the truth.

Source: *Czas*, July 22 and 23, 1898. Translated from the Polish by Daniel Unowsky.

Strzyżów Trial

Here, on June 17, one day after the gendarmes shot down twelve Christians in nearby Frysztak, a group of cavalry officers were directed by local officials to graze their horses in the old Jewish cemetery. Jakób Hagel, described in the Jewish press as the caretaker of the cemetery, called on the officers to graze in the Catholic church cemetery instead. He was arrested and tried for insulting a "legally recognized church or religious community" and for supposedly provoking Catholics who overheard him to do violence. Hagel received a one year prison sentence, which was reduced to two months by the High Court of Appeals in Vienna, still longer than many of those who physically attacked Jews. This trial attracted great attention and was cited as evidence that Jewish arrogance and provocations had led to the violence. Jewish journalists denounced the novel theory of the prosecution that Hagel incited others to violence by expressing his outrage at the insult to Jews and Judaism.

The hall of the proceedings began to fill with intelligent listeners—a sight rare among us—Jews were not lacking among the public, weighted down with gabardines, and their own special stench made staying in the hall almost impossible. [. . .] The accused himself had the usual look of the Galician type of Jew—long *peyos*, and an even longer black beard decorating his pale face. His beady eyes cast glances in all directions.

The state prosecutor accused him of the following criminal act:

On June 18 in the morning, two platoons of hussars marched to Strzyżów to assist in calming the antisemitic riots. The troops set up on the market square, exposed to the tropical heat. The mayor of Strzyżów delegated Władysław Wyżkowski to find suitable quarters for the soldiers. The officer in charge requested a shady place where the horses could be placed at least temporarily.

Behind the synagogue in Strzyżów is an old cemetery surrounded on three sides by a rampart, behind which grow wide oak trees. Under these oak trees the officer wished to find shade for the military horses. As far back as anyone can remember, no one has been buried there—this has been the case, witnesses have confirmed, since the year 1869. At present the grass is cut and cattle graze all year round there.

The delegate of the mayor, Władysław Wyżkowski, quite correctly sought to accommodate the wish of the officer, which angered the accused, who has an interest in renting out the grass; he began shouting loudly and then yelled at Wyżkowski: "So you are an official and you have to lead the horses to our Jewish cemetery? Take your horses to your own cemetery or your church."

The officer heard the yelling and, not understanding Polish, ordered the accused to leave. The accused walked away some dozens of steps and then went to Roman Wyżkowski, who stood together with some local Catholic inhabitants, mostly educated people, and began to say again: "What is this, your brother wants to put horses in our cemetery, you should lead them to your church, there they will be fine." When, however, Roman Wyżkowski drew attention to the accused that he should not express himself in this way about the church, he replied: "Take your horses to your own cemetery."

Source: *Głos Narodu*, July 8, 1898. Translated from the Polish by Daniel Unowsky.

Frysztak Trial

Most defense attorneys conceded that their clients were inebriated; however, they cited this fact as proof of the corrupting influence of the Jewish alcohol purveyors and as a major reason for their clients' violent behavior. Dr. Baranowski, a defense attorney involved in the Frysztak trial concerning the events leading up to the deadly confrontation between rioters and gendarmes on June 16, 1898, offers this defense in the following excerpt. One of the most inventive arguments was put forward by Tadeusz Dwernicki, another defense attorney in the Frysztak trial. Dwernicki denied that any individual can be responsible for specific acts when participating in a violent crowd.

In an excellent argument, Counselor Dr. Baranowski first refuted the prosecutor's claim that the accused should be referred to as robbers. Then he splendidly portrayed the material and moral misery of the simple folk and pointed to the fact that society is responsible for this, that more than fifty years of constitutional life has not been able to remove this ignorance, and he asked the court for understanding and indulgence for these victims of ignorance. The alcohol monopoly [*propinacja*] is protected and other misfortunes spread in our province. Then he demonstrated with a very apt legal argument the innocence of his clients.

In his speech, the next defense attorney, Dr. Dwernicki, relied on a broader scientific basis to consider the criminal liability of the offender. This question is very difficult when it concerns an individual; it is much more difficult when it concerns a large group of perpetrators acting villainously together—so many diverse factors must be taken into account by those sitting in judgment—these difficulties become even more acute when dealing with a collective person—with a crowd.

Science has not yet determined to what extent the individual is responsible for the action of the crowd, whether one's responsibility is full, or whether the individual's crime in the crowd should be measured with the same measure—as when one acts spontaneously.

Science is in agreement, however, that the crowd is something entirely different from the individual, the spirit and the mood of the crowd is something different. The individual in the crowd loses his capacity for judgment—he is impressionable, he becomes subject to suggestion—the individual will loses the ability to resist—a slogan thrown into the crowd intensifies, flies farther, its echo grows stronger the more hearts and minds it penetrates. The intoxicated crowd moves forward blindly, carrying everything and everyone with it. The individual is then in a state of irresponsibility due to a lack of strength to resist.

The greater the predisposition to do bad, the less the resistance. This predisposition lies in the nature of humanity, in which evil instincts are greater than those to do good, and with the weakening of the will as a result of collective mental pressure, instinct will take over all the easier the more factors that push the crowd in a certain direction. [...]

When the stubborn rumor that the Jews can be beaten circulates for a long time among the people and is not countered by political and civil authorities, it is no wonder that the crowd would believe it and be so easily seduced into carrying out reprehensible excesses.

However, can the individual be responsible for crowd action? After all, the individual in the crowd is like a drop of water in an overflowing mountain stream that breaks and destroys everything in its path. Can it possibly be asserted that this drop of water—this specific one—causes havoc?

Postcard of Frysztak around 1900. On June 16, 1898, the main street depicted here was filled with Jewish merchants selling goods to Polish-speaking peasants and townspeople on market day. During the ensuing riot, gendarmes shot and killed twelve Christian rioters and bystanders.

The individual in the crowd disappears, dies, and is reborn as a new organism whose name is crowd. One may be a hero—or a greedy beast. In this case the crowd paid bloodily for its action—paid with its heart and its blood, and the memory of the Frysztak Vespers [when twelve people were killed by the gendarmes to restore order] will not fade soon and will be remembered by the people as a painful wound and a serious wrong.

The individual, therefore, should not be made to answer for the crowd.

Source: *Kurjer Lwowski*, August 19, 1898, 2. Translated from the Polish by Daniel Unowsky.

Document 2.9. Second Stary Sącz Proceeding

More than two thousand people took part in the June 25 riot in Stary Sącz, the largest single violent event in Galicia in 1898. In December, 249 peasants and townspeople, including members of the town council, were tried in four proceedings.

The second in the series of those accused of being involved in the riot against the Jews in Stary Sącz came before the local court today, [the accused] numbered seventy, men and women, mostly peasants from nearby villages. [. . .]

They are responsible for the destruction and plundering on June 25 of this year of more than thirty Jewish stores and for inflicting damages of around 80,000 gulden.

Ninety-one witnesses were called to the trial.

After the storm went through Nowy Sącz and the tavern in Kamienica like a hurricane, it came next, on June 25, to Stary Sącz. Whispered rumors about plunder having been allowed in other places circulated from cottage to cottage through the entire district, electrifying the people; all of the peasants knew about it, they knew about it in Stary Sącz too, and there was a slogan on everyone's lips: "Saturday, the twenty-fifth." On the hot afternoon of June 24, fire engines and firefighting equipment were deployed in the Stary Sącz market square. At night, the military arrived. Soldiers stood guard in homes, and one armed unit was positioned in the middle of the square. The Sabbath day arrived. Stores were shuttered, and a stifling atmosphere dominated the town. In the morning, peasants from the surrounding villages began to gather: individually, in twos, and in larger groups. The peasants arrived with sticks and poles in their hands, followed by women with baskets and sheets. The market square filled up, as it did on market day, only the physiognomy of these people was different than usual: now and then from the middle of the crowd came the whispered murmur "today the Jews will be beaten," a louder din came from among the women who sat in a row under the walls, and somewhat louder were the words spoken by townspeople, who walked with purpose around the market square. Otherwise, all was quiet and still, as before a storm.

Around noon a drum beat on the square. A crowd, waiting for some announcement, gathered around the figure of the local policeman. A snare drum sounded a short beat and the curious raised their ears with interest. It was announced that everyone had to leave the town by 8 or be forcibly expelled. And again silence and waiting. No one listened to the mayor's announcement. In the afternoon around 4:00 p.m. a great commotion started in the town offices, a moment later a trumpet sounded, the cavalry swiftly mounted, the hooves clattered, and the detachment disappeared from the town. A telegram had come from Rytro [a village just a few miles south of Stary Sącz] calling for military assistance because of the threatening mood of the population. Again, there was silence on the Stary Sącz market square, the sun went down in the west, dusk set in. In that moment the monastery tower bell struck heralding 8:00 p.m. Townsmen joined with the peasantry. Someone in the crowd raised up a stick and yelled out a few abrupt words. Finally one shout boomed out like thunder, it grew and grew, and finally enveloped the whole town: "Hurrah at the Jews!" It drowned out the German voice commanding soldiers to raise their weapons to attack. Every living soul threw himself into plunder, smashing the bolts of Jewish stores, doors and windows fell, large quantities of goods were thrown outside and quickly snatched up. In first one, then a second, then a third window, lights shone on what proved to be holy images, as signs that these were Christian houses and that they should not be plundered. These lights illuminated the market square, and the peasants, reddened by the glow, ran like the damned in a crazy hellish dance. A mix of bonnets, homespun coats, a shiny bayonet here, a blue cap with a brass button there, the four-cornered hat of a policeman, arcs of water gushing from the fire engines because of the danger of fire, the buzz and din of exhortations, and above all one terrible shout of "hurrah" and another terrible cry of despair and fear. A really tragic day!

Around midnight the steady step of military reinforcements could be heard. The infantry from Nowy Sącz stood in the square followed by the cavalry returned from Rytro. The crowd began to dissipate, the yelling ceased, and stolen goods were only taken away in back alleys.

Sunday June 26 dawned. The bright sun revealed a terrible picture of desolation. Warehouses and stores completely devastated, piles of broken glass all over the square, store shelves and equipment broken, doors and windows shattered.

At the same time, for several miles around, a day of punishment and judgment dawned over the misled people, who were only the blind tools of some criminal and cursed hand. The hunt for the "guilty" commenced. Day after day the prison gates closed behind crowds of unfortunate peasants who were torn away from urgent work in the field, almost mad from sorrow. So began the lengthy, lengthy and difficult, investigation that led to today's hearing. Based on the indictment, you can get a picture of the riots in Stary Sącz, for which today seventy peasants stand before the court accused of the crime of public violence, theft, and violations of the public peace.

Source: *Kurjer Lwowski*, December 13, 1898, 2–3. Translated from the Polish by Daniel Unowsky.

The historic market square of Stary Sącz, site of the single largest anti-Jewish attack in Galicia in 1898.
Photograph by Daniel Unowsky

Document 2.10. Parliamentary Debates on the Anti-Jewish Riots

Politicians maneuvered to take advantage of the riots to promote themselves to their potential constituents. On November 22 and 24, 1898, politicians, some elected from the newly instituted fifth universal manhood suffrage curia, debated the riots on the floor of the Vienna parliament. Ignacy Daszyński, the Galician socialist leader, opened the debate by charging that the institution of a state of emergency was unnecessary, harmful, and unlawful. A series of speakers followed, supporting or opposing Daszyński's charge.

Ignacy Daszyński *denounced antisemitism and criticized the government but conceded that corrupt Jews working with exploitative nobles bore a large share of the blame for the violence.*

Ignacy Daszyński: Gentlemen! Those are the facts that cannot be changed. I can relate to you litanies of names of people who are involved in this process. Each of us knows it, it is not secret, that entire districts of Galicia are leased out to the powerful Szlachta [Polish nobility], and that these powerful Szlachta simply steal thousands and thousands in pure profit from the public purse and shift the entire hatred, the entire contempt of the ignorant people onto the only accomplices, namely, onto the village Jews. It is the task of a reasonable politician, it is the holiest duty in politics to bring this truth finally here into the open, to say finally here, that all of the blame for these shameful deeds, which took place in Galicia under the influence of schnapps—and they are not a few crimes—that all the guilt for the decline of the entire people in Galicia, as far as it stems from schnapps, must be ascribed by history and politics to the Szlachta as much or to a greater degree than to the village usurers, the villages taverns, the village Jews (*So right! from party colleagues*).

There is a close connection between the village lords and the village Jews. The village lord, the landowner, owns the tavern building. An inn cannot however be founded on any old location; no, it must stand near a church—yes, that is the custom in Galicia—on a public road. Exactly this location is occupied by the building of the landowner, and the landlord has at every moment the village Jew in his hand. But he needs him. He himself is economically wasteful, he cannot think economically, he does not know what is to his advantage and what is to his disadvantage, and for this he has his village Jew, his factor, his ever-ready agent. And because of this he protects him [the Jew] from his crimes and swindles. From whom? From the district captain above all.

I know an instance where an official, an imperial-royal official, found fraudulent weights. He took the Jew briefly into custody, told him a few truths, and threatened him of course with an investigation. The Jew said to a neighbor: "Nothing will happen to me," ran to the landowner, who ran to the district captain, and the district captain took care of everything. He reprimanded the official and the village Jew, and the village Jew returned to his community safe and sound and possibly continued to do business with fraudulent weights.

The system of concessions, of protection, of corruption, of bribery, of connection, of nepotism, feeds on our body in Galicia; that all brings about the situation where even the village usurer feels so powerful compared to society. Everyone complains about this, the officials receive petition after petition to deal with them [the Jews] firmly according to the law—but they gloat about all of these persecutions. Why? Because in the Szlachta, in this powerful agent of the land, they have a patron, the natural historic protector.

And it is very tragic, that also in Galicia the Jew has a mission, a social mission. He has to negotiate between the manor house [of the noble] and the cottage of the peasant.

Austrian Minister President and Minister of the Interior Franz Anton von Thun und Hohenstein responded to Daszyński by defending the state of emergency, the employment of deadly force, and the rule of law. He proclaimed that Jews, like all citizens, are equal before the law and that the state had the duty to protect them and to preserve public order.

Franz Anton von Thun und Hohenstein: I do not doubt that you gentlemen have all had the opportunity through the press to closely follow the events that have played out in Galicia. I will allow myself therefore to very briefly recapitulate these events. The movement began on March 11 and 13 in Wieliczka and the surrounding region, it continued and increased in intensity and spread to more and more localities. Although in the beginning it consisted of nothing more than the breaking in of window panes and, if I can be permitted to say so, insignificant damage of property, such as the destruction of taproom equipment, the developments by the end of June took on an ever more threatening and serious character such that 5 acts of arson, around 150 cases of looting, and an uncountable series of thefts, property damage, and robbery took place.

All efforts to curb this movement of misled people *(heckling from the left)*—I beg the two gentlemen who posed questions to answer the various questions themselves *(cheers from the right)*—despite all warnings, despite the enhanced readiness of the gendarmerie, despite the military preparations, despite the military assistance, despite the strengthened assembly of the gendarmerie, did not succeed in putting a stop to this movement. The gendarmes were wounded by slashing scythes and thrown rocks, the military and the gendarmes, unfortunately—and by each of us fully and completely deeply regretted—had to make use of their weapons and a series of victims is ascribed to this use of weapons *(heckling from the left)*.

This means only that this movement was not such an innocent one and that exactly, if all is just as the gentleman representative Daszyński claimed, that we are dealing here with a deluded and inadequately educated population, these happenings are to be taken even more seriously, because it is very difficult to come to terms with this very class of people in order to stop such a movement. But the question here is not where it stops; what has happened is already enough. [This movement] was directed against a religious community, against the Jews, and the Jews are completely equal citizens of this state *(Bravo!)*, and whether one is a Jew or a Christian, whether he belongs to this or that nationality, it is the duty and task of the state to protect that person to the fullest measure and to ensure the maintenance of law and order *(lively agreement from the right; heckling from the left)*.

*Representative **Emil Byk** denounced Daszyński's complete lack of empathy for the Jewish victims of the riots. This longtime leader of Lemberg's Jewish community defended the government's resort to violence and blamed the antisemitic agitation of populist political parties for the attacks.*

Emil Byk: I understand that police laws and police measures are seldom very popular and can be the least popular among those directly affected. I also recognize that for a populist representative it is more appreciated and reasonable to speak against the suppression of the people's freedom and for the lifting of the state of emergency.

I concede that I myself would wish rather to speak against the state of emergency than, as my duty and conscience dictate, to speak for it. [. . .]

No matter how one has spoken here against the taverns—I would be the last to want to defend them, if they prove themselves corrupting of the population—in fact the relationship between the Jewish and the peasant population has been a tolerable one, often a friendly one. In the spring of this year in the western districts of Galicia there began slowly some isolated, I concede, [at first] marginal and insignificant riots against the Jews. These attacks became more potent and they multiplied, and when we were here [in Vienna] at the beginning of June—and I have preserved the complete correspondence—a whole pile of telegrams and letters came to us Jewish representatives from the affected districts. *(Representative Stojałowski: From Jews! Shout: Certainly! They would not come to you!)* What do you mean by this? The affected were in fact Jews. Of course, you did not point that out, to you it was important to hide these things. These telegrams brought the complaint that the movement had arrived and that it was beginning to seethe. From one side a person wrote: Everything was completely calm here until the publications were disseminated. And again in other districts it was completely calm, until the arrival of the brochure by the priest Jeż; true, it was later confiscated, but hundreds of copies had already been disseminated in the communities and unrest set in. According to other reports, meetings where the gentleman cleric Stojałowski played a conspicuous directorial role gave rise to the turmoil. [. . .] However, since the beginning of the month of June things took on a completely different character. On June 11—to identify this with calendar-like precision—the typical Fear and Shame of the whole movement came to light. What happened? Hundreds gradually growing into thousands of peasants left their homes and farms, provided themselves with baskets *(Representative Stojałowski: Not true!)* and in Jasło, at the first sign of trouble the burgher, without distinction of religion—a few Jews, mostly educated Christians—armed themselves with flints in order to protect the citizens of Jasło from a horde of peasants. *(Representative Stojałowski: That is not true!)* I can prove this with documentation. *(Representative Stojałowski: Not true!)*. [. . .]

The typical movement began in Jasło, hundreds and later thousands of peasants came with baskets in order simply to plunder and to get their hands on the belongings of the Jews, not in order to carry out random bodily assaults and riots. Admittedly, some went beyond this program, and in Jasło even went as far as arson that destroyed a refinery. The movement can be graphically described as it moved south from Jasło and seized other communities and then sprang to other districts. It positively haunted all of these districts and the culmination point came on the days of June 24 and 25 in Nowy Sącz and Stary Sącz, where nearly six thousand peasants came to lay siege and plunder the town and caused damages of more than 100,000 gulden, in the face of these excesses all measures of repression, even the military, stood by helpless. That is how things were, gentlemen, the fear grew among the population and I can assure you—I am here prepared for every interruption, and so it

THE 1898 ANTI-JEWISH VIOLENCE IN HABSBURG GALICIA   67

is—hundreds of pale figures came with their worldly possessions to Lemberg to store them because they felt uncertain. The trains were filled with refugees, in all the newspapers—not in the Jewish liberal press, as you are so used to saying, but even in those you would define as entirely classic Polish local papers, frightening reports could be read every day. The fear in the commercial and industrial circles of western Austria grew, such that in Vienna's chamber of commerce the question concerning how things stood with the credit situation and what a catastrophe could arise from these events. In the face of all of this, should one stand with crossed arms and do nothing? . . .

Should Austria, which still claims to be a *Rechstsstaat*, despair of restoring order in its own house? Should there be open season on the life and property of citizens because it is about Jews? There was no other way out, something had to happen. [. . .]

Allow me a word about antisemitism. The antisemitism is in my humble view a brutality, it is the brutal term for a very simple sentence: We antisemites are the majority, you are the minority, and therefore your value is less and you are therefore trouble, and therefore you are due no rights. And if that is not the simplest theory: Might makes right, I know no other definition.

And what do you tell the rural population? You say that the Jews are usurers. If you use that argument with all minorities, you would say that is complete madness. How? Should the entirety be made responsible for what one individual does? This only applies to the Jews. You say, the Jews are usurers. Count just one time the wealthy Jews in your hometowns that have anything to do with the credit business. Compare that with all those who pursue commerce, crafts, trade, bureaucrats, lawyers, and doctors, and finally the overwhelming number of Jewish beggars among them, who not only lend no money, but are more likely to need to borrow it. [. . .]

A few years ago, when I spoke about this question, I could point out with satisfaction that the rude form of Viennese antisemitism was foreign in our province, was unknown in our province *(agreement from the right)*.

Unfortunately, honorable gentlemen, things have changed. This form [of antisemitism] has now come into our province, and when one asks who are the main carriers of this movement, so I must say that it is the so-called Polish Christian-Social Party, whose leader is the cleric Mr. Stojałowski.

Stanisław Stojałowski denied that he and his Christian People's Party instigated or supported the violence, but made clear his anti-Jewish sentiments and those of his political movement. He labeled himself and his party antisemitic.

Stanisław Stojałowski: Honorable House! In today's debate much has been brought forward that I really must correct. However, since I am next according to the daily order to come to speak about the state of emergency in Galicia, I will not tire the high house, but will instead correct today only that which is most important.

At the start I must express my admiration that so little has been spoken of those who provoked and caused the state of emergency, the Jews. *(Laughter)* I believe that this above all requires a real correction, because here just those that caused the state of emergency remain so very spared by the speakers.

So I must correct what the honorable representative Karatnicki cited here [in an earlier speech], that the excesses began on June 9 in Jasło, and I have to recall it to his memory that already earlier in Kalwaria two peasants had been shot down *(Hear! from his party colleagues)*, and that the Minister President himself countered Mr. Karatnicki by asserting that already in March excesses had taken place. The honorable representative Winkowski also asserted the same, and even the honorable Dr. Byk, who tried to link the excesses in Jasło to a people's meeting of our party. Accordingly, I hereby note that our election gathering in Jasło took place on May 17 and that after this election meeting, calm reigned for the following three weeks and it broke out into rioting only on June 9. [...]

Now I must correct what the honorable spokesperson for the Polish Club, Dr. Byk, brought forth in the first place and I must repeat what the honorable Dr. Pattai already stated, that I stand decidedly opposed to being lectured by Dr. Byk as to what is Christian and what is Polish. He gave here a historical overview of antisemitism and so presented this matter as if our party was the one that, as he had the audacity to put it *(laughter from the left)*, brought rude antisemitism to Galicia.

Against this I declare that thank God our party has been active for more than twenty years and through this time has certainly always fought against the Jews and has always been antisemitic but has never struck the Jews. If it then came to rioting, it was not our party that encouraged or incited the people, but it was rather the national and confessional brothers of the honorable Dr. Byk themselves, which I will prove to him. [...]

Furthermore, he made the accusation against us that our party abused the press and assembly freedoms not in order to enlighten the people, but to flatter the instincts of the people. That sprang entirely from the honorable Dr. Byk's brain. After all, since he was never in one of our meetings, he does not know what happens there. I must state that we never appeal to the base instincts of the people, but one thing we must say to the people resolutely: Do not let yourselves be exploited by the Jews! ...

We have to awaken the realization so that the people recognize that they are exploited and treated unfairly. That is no appeal to base instincts, that is the duty of any man of the people and of any representative. [...]

In our meetings there are no assaults *(lively laughter and calls: But outside!)*. If outside of our meetings *(again lively laughter)* there is violence, then it happened for the most part in the taprooms, where Jews sit and brandy addles the minds, or during other situations, I don't know. I am not responsible for what the Jews do in their taverns. [...]

I still have to correct one thing that the Minister President said in the debate and what follows from it. He said: On March 13 the excesses began, and the government instituted the state of emergency only on June 28. So every person should consider, from March through June there was ongoing unrest in Galicia, and the poor government did not know how to remedy the situation, other than through the police measures of the state of emergency and by the law, which the Minister President called a just one and which I call a shameful one, martial law.

Source: Stenographische Protokolle über die Sitzungen des Hauses der Abgeordneten des österreichischen Reichsrathes in den Jahren 1898 und 1899. XV. Session. II. Band. 19 bis 37 Sitzung. Vienna, 1899, 1361–62 (Daszyński); 1377 (Thun); 1438–44 (Byk); 1480–81 (Stojałowski). Translated from the German by Daniel Unowsky.

3

Kishinev Pogrom

Steven J. Zipperstein

For Kishinev's Jews, little set apart the unpleasantness of midday April 2, 1903, Easter Sunday, from previous years.[1] There was jostling with drunks, rocks tossed mostly—at least, at first—by children at the windows of Jewish-owned businesses. This erupted in a market square adjacent to a small church with a capacity of no more than one hundred or so, with all these familiar annoyances occurring year after year in the Easter season. Jews gravitated here, too, on this the final day of Passover, eager to rub shoulders with the holiday crowds on the last day of the lengthy Jewish Passover festival.

In the months before, a rumor had circulated in the Kishinev region regarding the murder of a fifteen-year-old for Jewish ritual purposes in a nearby town. The charge was soon disproven by a series of coroner reports—demonstrating that no blood had been drained, which was believed to be a trademark of Jewish ritual killings—with further proof that the murder was the work of a relative intent on robbing the boy of an inheritance. Still, the charge persisted.

How influential these anti-Jewish charges were in the region remains unclear. Few Jews seem to have altered their pre-Passover behavior because of them: reports of Jews trapped in Kishinev during the pogrom describe many out-of-town guests. Jews from the rural regions of Bessarabia—a mostly landlocked slice of the Russian Empire at its southwestern edge—continued, as in years past, to flock to the homes of relatives for the Passover festival.

Still, Jewish shop owners reported that they took home for safekeeping bank records, receipts, and similar financial documents. Fear of attacks on Jews prompted synagogue announcements on the last day of Passover warning that they stay indoors. Reports of Jews roughed up near the church surfaced around midday. Police intervened and the attacks soon took on a more sinister character. Liquor stores—the city had some eight hundred mostly very small ones, nearly all owned by Jews—then clothing shops, followed by other Jewish-owned businesses, were now ransacked by adults and many were emptied of stock. Liquor, discarded clothing, and shoes filled

---

[1] This essay draws on Steven J. Zipperstein, *Pogrom: Kishinev and the Tilt of History* (New York: Liverlight, 2018).

Steven J. Zipperstein, *Kishinev Pogrom* In: *Pogroms*. Edited by: Eugene M. Avrutin and Elissa Bemporad, Oxford University Press.

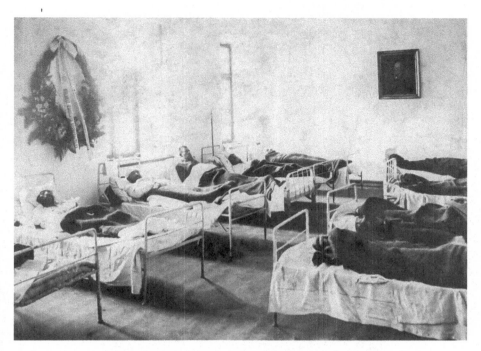

Kishinev victims. Forty-five Jews were murdered in the immediate wake of the Kishinev pogrom, rumored at first to have left hundreds dead, and four died from wounds incurred afterward. The photograph was taken in Kishinev's Jewish hospital.
Courtesy of Iurie Şveţ

a cluster of Kishinev's streets. By early afternoon, homes of Jews were attacked, and building after building was swarmed by rioters in the area near the city square where the riot first erupted. Already by four that afternoon, police admitted they were outnumbered—some two hundred rioters participated that day—as attackers moved across a small, densely Jewish slice of the city, wreaking havoc well into the night.

Likely leading the riot at the outset were far-right students enrolled at the local seminary, together with a small clutch of antisemitic ideologues—numbering no more than five or six—linked to the region's only daily newspaper, *Bessarabets*, owned by one of the empire's most enterprising, committed antisemites, Pavel Krushevan (1860–1909). *Bessarabets* daily trumpeted the ritual murder charge long after the authorities had disproved it, insisting in issue after issue that Jews were responsible for a plethora of other vile deeds as well. These included plans to produce wine without grapes, which would devastate Bessarabia's crucial wine market amid a steep fall in agricultural prices over the course of the past year or so.

A club launched by the newspaper with the goal of resisting a Jewish immigrant onslaught circulated word of a secret meeting in Kishinev's largest synagogue, where a plot to unleash horrible deeds was revealed. And Krushevan and the circle close to him were at the same time almost certainly at work on an anti-Jewish document, the first version of what would become known as *The Protocols of the Elders*

Pavel Krushevan. Krushevan, a novelist, essayist, and newspaper publisher in Kishinev and later in St. Petersburg, was among the most influential antisemites of his age. He died of cancer in 1909 at age forty-nine. Much of his life was shrouded in secrecy, despite a public role in journalism and, eventually, as a member of the Second Duma. He wrote the first, sustained guidebook of Bessarabia, a detailed—fiercely antisemitic—portrait of Russia at the turn of the twentieth century, and published, as well as likely authored or coauthored, the first version of *The Protocols of the Elders of Zion*.
Public Domain, Wikimedia Commons

of Zion. The text would appear soon after the pogrom's end under a slightly different title in a St. Petersburg newspaper owned by Krushevan.

From Krushevan's vantage point, Kishinev had become little less than a powder keg, a place fed up with the exploitation of Jews and ready to explode. In contrast, as seen by the city's long-standing mayor, Karl Schmidt—by 1903, he had been in office twenty-five years—Jews were a singularly positive presence in local commerce and trade. The Bessarabia governor-general R. S. von Raaben harbored no particular antagonism toward Jews—his sole passions being card-playing and women. Kishinev, like much of the rest of the empire, was underpoliced and, as was often the case, the army garrison stationed nearby was resistant to the quieting of civil disorder. Only on the second day of the riot in mid-afternoon would Raaben order that the army put down the disturbance, which they rapidly did.

By Sunday's end, no more than two or three of the city's main thoroughfares had been engulfed. Violence continued into the night with apartments broken into and women and girls raped. How many were attacked remains unclear; a local rabbi would later report that he knew of forty, but the number was likely greater. Sixty rioters were arrested that day; nine hundred would be in prison by late afternoon the next day. On Monday morning Raaben provided a guarantee to a Jewish delegation of local leaders that order would soon be re-established. Rain had continued through the night, promising a respite by early morning.

Late in the morning on Monday, rioting, looting, and murders were now widespread throughout the city in nearly every quarter. Rioters would later claim in trials starting in the summer and lasting well into December that their deeds constituted little more than acts of self-defense. These actions, they insisted, were a response to the aggression of Jews who had broken into a church and murdered its priest. None of this was true, but on that same morning a large group of Jews, numbering as many as two hundred, attacked rioters of Jews armed with knives and guns. Some were arrested together with pogromists, who were now jailed alongside them.

Jewish memory of the pogrom would mostly recall Jewish timidity, particularly the shameful cowardice of Jewish males. All Jews murdered in the pogrom—at first hundreds were reported in the press abroad with, in fact, forty-nine dead—were killed between late morning and mid-afternoon on the second day of the riot. The worst of the atrocities occurred in the poorest neighborhoods at the city's edge in Lower or Old Kishinev. There gentile neighbors attacked Jewish acquaintances, while others saved Jews by hiding them in their homes until the violence ended with the military's intervention late that afternoon.

By mid-May, this violence would surface as the best-known of all events in Russian Jewish life, sidelining the Dreyfus affair on the pages of Jewish newspapers. News of Kishinev would prompt President Theodore Roosevelt to declare, "I have never in my experience known of a more immediate or deeper expression of sympathy."[2] The pogrom's unprecedented notoriety is traceable to several factors: it occurred at the start of the new century as well as at a moment of authority with regard to Jewry's political movements; Theodore Herzl, still at Zionism's helm, would die the following year; and the Jewish Socialist Labor Bund was then at the height of its popularity. The eminent Anglo-Jewish writer Israel Zangwill would build Kishinev's horrors into the core of his 1909 Broadway play *The Melting Pot*, which offered one of the most resilient depictions of American exceptionalism—message far more than mere specialness.

A populous, keenly political Lower East Side New York Jewish community would embrace Kishinev as its major concern, thus propelling the *Yiddish Daily Forward* into sudden, long-lasting prominence. The Hearst press also took up the cause in a significant way—William Randolph Hearst was then courting Jewish support for a run for New York governor or, perhaps, on the Democratic ticket for

---

[2] Cyrus Adler, ed., *The Voice of America on Kishineff* (Philadelphia: The Jewish Publication Society of America, 1904), xvii.

Jacob Bernstein-Kogan. A Zionist activist and founding head of the Zionist movement's correspondence bureau based in Kishinev, Kogan was largely responsible for the spreading of news about the Kishinev pogrom immediately after its end, and would likely be the model for the Jewish Elder at the centerpiece of the first version of *The Protocols of the Elders of Zion*, published in a somewhat revised version under a different title in a newspaper owned by Pavel Krushevan.
Miriam Bernshtain and Yitshak Koren, eds., *Sefer Bernshtain-Kogan*. Tel Aviv, 1961

president. He dispatched to Kishinev the well-known Irish nationalist Michael Davitt, whose reportage and soon best-selling book *Within the Pale: The True Story of Anti-Semitic Persecutions in Russia* galvanized readers. This was the first widely read work on Russian Jewish life in a Western language. By fall, Kishinev's tragedy would be widely integrated into the High Holidays synagogue ritual throughout the United States. Photographs of shrouded Kishinev dead would appear in dozens of newspapers in the United States, Europe, and elsewhere: "Even Hell is preferable," declared Kishinev's Jewish communal leader Jacob Bernstein-Kogan (1859–1929) at the Sixth Zionist Congress in the summer of 1903.[3]

More than the pogrom itself, prompting by far the greatest worldwide outrage—indeed, for the first time Leo Tolstoy would be moved to denounce anti-Jewish

[3] Yitshak Maor, *Ha-tenuah ha-Tsiyonit be-rusyah* (Jerusalem: The World Zionist Organization, 1973), 244.

outrage—was a document that surfaced three weeks after the pogrom's end, signed by Minister of Interior V. K. Plehve. It gave a green light to progromists to attack Jews without reprisal. Now recognized as a forgery, its accuracy was emphatically believed both at the time and for many years after. Hence, now the term "pogrom," which before Kishinev was one of a medley of descriptions used in Russia for violence, would come to refer primarily to Jews, at least, in regard to a government-sponsored or -condoned attack on Jews.

The publication later that year, in November/December, of the Hebrew poet Hayim Nahman Bialik's (1873–1934) searing Hebrew-language poem "In the City of Killing"—which is widely regarded as the finest poem written in a Jewish tongue since the Middle Ages—offered an unforgiving portrait of the weight of age-old oppression now fully revealed on Kishinev's streets. Bialik saw the riot as having caused irreparable harm not only to the bodies but, no less crucially, to the souls of the city's Jews, especially its cowardly men. The poet arrived in Kishinev soon after the pogrom ended, to record the recollections of victims and bystanders for the writing of a document about the massacre. The extensive notes he took during his stay were then sequestered—for reasons still unexplained—for more than seventy years. His poem exerted a major influence on the attitudes of Jews, Zionists as well as non-Zionists, and his notes perhaps represent the most detailed, authoritative account of the massacre.

"In the City of Killing" was soon translated into Russian by Vladimir Jabotinsky and would become for Jews of all political affiliations a clarion call for resistance to the regime during the 1905 revolution and later. Eventually it would also enter the curriculum of Jewish Palestine, later Israel, as among the most influential of all portraits of exilic Jewish misery.

With pogroms having emerged into the American lexicon as synonymous with race riots, it was hoped that Russia's horrors—as now claimed by many independent African American newspapers—would sensitize the American public to the need for an urgent reaction to their own country's indignities, especially lynching. The belief that such travesties were born of causes similar to those of pogroms, including the connivance of authorities and the rightlessness of victims, helped expose the lynching of Blacks with a prominence not previously seen. The convergence of the call for protection of Blacks from lynching and Jews from pogroms would soon serve as the backdrop to the establishment, in 1909, of the National Association for the Advancement of Colored People (NAACP).

A vastly different by-product was the belief, still resilient in Russian conservative and far-right circles, that the overwhelming distrust created by the Kishinev pogrom—particularly the Plehve letter—rendered the Russian regime incapable of weathering an eventual onslaught of opposition within the empire and beyond. In his 2001 book, *Dvesti let vmeste (1795–1995)* (Two Hundred Years Together [1795–1995]), Alexander Solzhenitsyn (1918–2008) draws a straight, tragic trajectory, starting with Kishinev's weakening of Russian resolve, all the way to the horrors of the Bolshevik revolution.

Anna Strunsky. A well-known radical in northern California circles at the turn of the twentieth century, Strunsky collaborated closely with Jack London—with whom she cowrote a book—and later with her husband William English Walling, who in 1909 was named co-chair of the National Association for the Advancement of Colored People (NAACP). The idea for an organization designed to protect Blacks from persecution, especially from lynching, was first formulated by Strunsky, inspired by her having witnessed pogroms in Russia in the wake of the 1905 revolution.
Courtesy of Christopher English Walling

Marketplace Jews. This photograph in Pavel Krushevan's *Bessarabia*, published in 1903, was accompanied by a text that described the insidious effect of Jews on the local economy. They were accused by Krushevan, the region's most influential antisemitic ideologue, of many economic sins, including accosting peasants outside the city limits of Kishinev and urging them to sell their grain for cheaper prices than they would otherwise earn. The photograph is meant to portray Jews as dark and conspiratorial.

Document 3.1. On Hayim Nahman Bialik's "City of Killing"

Pesakh Averbakh was a teacher of Hebrew and a correspondent for the St. Petersburg daily Ha-Zeman. *His witness accounts of the pogrom published in the Hebrew daily* Ha-Zeman *were the first newspaper reports of the riot. Averbakh assisted Bialik during his stay in Kishinev, and also helped Michael Davitt as a translator. He acknowledges in this brief reminiscence, which appeared in 1935 shortly after Bialik's death, that he never understood why the extensive transcripts recorded by Bialik during his five-week Kishinev stay—many of which were translated by Averbakh from their original Yiddish to Hebrew—still remained unpublished and were released only years later in 1991.*

Bialik came to the "city of slaughter." The same day he came I was asked to join him and to aid him in the fulfillment of his important mission. He brought some kind of working plan, and we followed it in our work for five weeks. In great pains we succeeded in collecting numerous and very interesting materials. The main part of our work involved visiting places where the pogroms occurred and obtaining evidence from the injured parties and the eyewitnesses. We wrote down most of this evidence almost verbatim and translated it into Hebrew literally without changing form and content.

   Bialik revealed a marvelous gift for getting mute souls to talk . . . and prompting them to tell their stories. Jewish types of all classes went before us, including many simple Jewish men and women. The wretched and the tortured could tell openheartedly in simple trustworthy language about hidden matters and unseen secrets buried in the depths of their souls. The source of Bialik's influence . . . was undoubtedly his attitude toward them, an attitude full of warmth and simplicity, humility and affability, and wisdom.

Source: The item appeared originally in *Ha-Aretz*, reprinted as "H. N. Byalik ve-'ir ha-hareigah," in H. Shorer, ed., *Ha-pogrom be-Kishinev bi-melot 60 shanah* (Tel Aviv, 1963). Translated from the Hebrew by Asia Lev.

Document 3.2. Hayim Nahman Bialik, "City of Killing"

Hayim Nahman Bialik's poem, written in the summer of 1903 after he had spent five weeks interviewing victims and witnesses of the Kishinev pogrom, is by far the best-known account of the pogrom. Viewed by many as the most definitive description of the event—and the most cogent summation of the horrors of Jewish exile—the poem has also been criticized as a viciously skewed depiction of Jewish behavior amid urban savagery. The many rapes Bialik recorded in the transcripts of his interviews in

Kishinev are sidelined in the poem, which give prominence to a lacerating account of the cowardice of the city's Jewish males.

> And you will go down from there and come to the dark cellars
> where the pure daughters of your race were defiled among the pots and pans
> woman by woman under seven after seven uncircumcised,
> daughter in front of mother and mother in front of daughter,
> before killing, during killing, and after killing . . .
> under this bench and behind that barrel
> lay husbands, fiancés, brothers, peeping out of holes
> at the flutter of holy bodies under the flesh of donkeys
> choking in their corruption and gagging on their own throats' blood
> as like slices of meat a loathsome gentile spread their flesh—
> they lay in their shame and saw—and didn't budge,
> and they didn't pluck out their eyes or go out of their heads—
> and perhaps each to his soul and then prayed to his heart:
> master of the universe, make a miracle—and let me now be harmed.
> [. . .]
> And now go and I'll bring you to the places where they hid:
> The outhouse, the pigpen and the other places smeared with shit,
> and you'll see with your own eyes where they were concealed—your brothers,
>   your people,
> the descendants of the Maccabees, the great grandchildren of lions
> from "Merciful Father" and the seed of the great "martyrs"
> were twenty souls in one hole and thirty upon thirty
> and they have made great my place in the world and sanctified my name to the
>   multitudes . . .
> They fled the flight of mice and hid like tics
> And died like dogs there where they were found.

Source: *Songs from Bialik: Selected Poems of Hayim Nahman Bialik*, trans. Atar Hadari (Syracuse, NY: Syracuse University Press, 2000), 2–3.

Document 3.3. Testimony of Israel Rossman

The shop owner and businessman Israel Rossman, interviewed by Bialik with the assistance of Averbakh, provided a keenly detailed account of the pogrom's escalation on the morning of its second day. His report offers vivid detail with regard to how overwhelmed Jews were by its sudden, unexpected violence and the inability of police to intervene successfully. He was witness to some of the first killings.

On Sunday after lunch I sat with my household members at home, imprisoned in my residence because of the announcement in the synagogue not to walk outside. My wife was sitting on the threshold of the window facing the street. Suddenly she saw the gang of gentiles shower stones into the windows of [the] houses. A stone of approximately five pounds flew above my wife's head into the bedroom. My wife shut the window blinds and immediately the sound of a blast was heard in the other room. Stones smashed the good oil lamp hanging from the ceiling and the rest of the good housewares—the decoration of the house for the good day. "They smash the windows already," my wife said quietly and carefully in order not to scare me out of my nap (I was in the middle of my afternoon nap). I stood up and opened the blind that was shut in order to see the gang by myself. It was there. Some big ruffians leading and about fifty smaller men and women armed with stones walking behind them. Policemen and horsemen walked silently after the gang. I jumped into the yard—as I was, without a shirt— and found there about one hundred men, women, and children who came to visit their [Jewish] relatives. In the meantime, the noise and the tumult spread down the street. We hastened to close the gate of the yard. And one saw a yeshiva student running and screaming: "The ruffians took the leg and the thigh from the butcher shop!" Many ruffians were armed with axes and knives. The day turned into night. With great effort we persuaded our wives to get in and to sleep at least in the corridor and promised to guard them the whole night. For them this night was full of wrath and wanderings. Every time a baby woke up and cried, they woke up in a big fury and anxiety and said: Here, the murderers come! The cold and the darkness arose, and we the men sat or stood under the open clouded sky, pressed together and talking about what was happening. Maybe this rain will become the "good emissary" that came to save us from the cruelty. However, unfortunately, the rain did not become stronger. It ceased and the dawn arose. The great silence is around. We begin to hear the sound of human steps. We open the narrow gate and see the Jews, men and women, each of them goes to his store in the market to see its condition after the day of wrath. On the street corners the policemen stand on guard. We came close to one of them and asked: "What will be today?" "I don't know," he answered, "but you better sit in your homes." The passing Jews told us that the goyim boast that today they are going to slaughter all the Jews. In the meantime, we heard the galloping of horses patrolling the street. In less than two hours the tumult in our street grew stronger and the bad animal-like roaring reached our ears. We ran to the gate and came back in great fear: outside, near the gate stands the healthy rioter with a big axe in his hand and calls and heralds: "Zhidy, seichas!" (Jews, now!).

Source: Yaakov Goren, ed., *'Eduyot nifga'ei Kishinev, 1903: kefi sh-nigbu 'al yede H. N. Byalik ve-haverav* (Tel Aviv: Hakibutz Hameuhad, 1991). Translated from the Hebrew by Asia Lev.

Document 3.4. The Kishinev Pogroms, Jacob Bernstein-Kogan

Jacob Bernstein-Kogan's role in transmitting information about the Kishinev to for-eign newspapers and influential figures abroad was critical in the quick spread word of the riot. This he managed to do because of contacts forged as the founding head of the Zionist movement's Kishinev-based correspondence bureau. In his memoirs, written originally in Russian then translated after Bernstein's death into Hebrew by his daughter, he devotes a lengthy chapter to his activities during and immediately after the tragedy. It is likely that it was Bernstein-Kogan—a mild, gentle man—who would come to be seen by Krushevan as a result of these activities (the two were, as it happens, former schoolmates) as the prototype for the dreaded Jewish Elder as portrayed in the original version of The Protocols of the Elders of Zion.

The Jewish self-defense groups were surrounded by the police and the army that unarmed them pushing them into big yards. There the defense people were arrested and sent to the police station "in order to guard them from the arbitrariness and rage of the wild mob," as the police and the government would apologize later. The dusk came slowly; I went home, closed myself up in my apartment like all the Jews in the city, blocked the window and the doors with barricades of furniture. I did not move from the telephone. All the night we stood on guard and did not know that in our nearest neighborhood the acts of horror and terror were committed. At night all the windowpanes in our wing were smashed, they started to damage the frames of the windows, but we were lucky to be saved by our nanny, one of the Old Believers. Early in the morning we were told that thirty-three Jews were murdered during the night. Part of them were drowned in latrines, another part was hanged on roof rafters, and part of them were killed by batons. Many women and girls were raped and robberies and vandalism were too many to count. The rumor was spread in the city that they are looking for some Jewish doctor who killed our servant in order to squeeze her blood for baking matzo....

On Tuesday evening, in the darkness, when the streets had not yet dried from the saints` blood, and when the army shifts were marching on the streets to make order...we started to make the rounds at 10:00 p.m. entering every house in which it was possible to get help for rescuing our miserable brothers. We announced briefly the purpose of our night visit and right away we set up the sum that was imposed on the visited. There were also argumentative men who did not want to give what was asked and gave excuses, and who offered bills instead of cash, and so on. And we then threatened them with another pogrom that will be managed this time by the Jews themselves. And almost everyone—some with animosity and unwillingness—provided the demanded sums. The next morning, I sent telegrams to Europe (to almost all the capital cities), to America and to Africa that informed about the pogrom and about the sum immediately demanded to help people.

Source: Miriam Bernshtain and Yitzhak Koren, eds., *Sefer Bernshtain-Kogan* (Tel Aviv: Hugyotsei Besarabia, 1946), 127–28. Translated from the Hebrew by Asia Lev.

Document 3.5. Solzhenitsyn on the Kishinev Pogrom

Alexander I. Solzhenitsyn's two-volume work, available in French and German translations but still largely untranslated into English, Dvesti let vmeste (1795–1995) (Two Hundred Years Together [1795–1995]), *contains a compendium of late imperial conservative and right-wing charges against Jews as inimical to the Romanov regime because of their large numbers and economic as well as political activities. Solzhenitsyn absolves Jews of primary responsibility for the 1917 revolution, but he insists that the canard that the government had planned the Kishinev pogrom and other attacks on Jews so weakened its standing inside Russia and beyond that it was ripe for the Bolshevik takeover. Much of his description in the following regarding Jewish economic rapacity in Kishinev is influenced by early twentieth-century antisemitic accounts. Still, his insistence that no evidence exists to implicate the pogrom as the work of the central authorities is almost certainly accurate.*

We can confidently say that it was a forgery, for many reasons. Not just because A. A. Lopukhin, a harsh Plehve critic, refuted the fact that it was [accurate]. Not just because Prince Urusov, who was favorably disposed toward the Jews, immediately replaced [R. S. von] Raaben and controlled the governor's archive, never found any "letter from Plehve" there. Not just because the deposed Raaben, whose life had been ruined, never once complained, in his tearful attempts to restore it, that he had been following orders from on high—even though that would have instantly fixed his civil service career and, as an added bonus, made him a hero of liberal society. It was above all because Russia's state archives were not the Soviet doctored ones, where any document could be created if needed, or, inversely, secretly burned; there, everything was stored eternally, untouched. And immediately after the February Revolution, the Provisional Government's Extraordinary Investigative Commission, and, even more zealously, the special Commission for Studying the History of the Pogroms, involving such esteemed researchers as Simon Dubnov and Grigorii Krasnyi-Admoni, not only did not find the document itself in St. Petersburg or Kishinev, but found not even a record of it in incoming or outgoing messages; all they found was a *translation* from the English text by the Ministry of Internal Affairs (and also papers containing "references to strict punishments and suspension . . . for any unlawful action by executive agents in regard to the Jews"). Besides, after 1917, what was there to fear? And yet there was not a single witness or memoir author who explained how that immortal telegram ended up in Braham's possession, or who boasted of their own involvement. Not a word from Braham himself—not then, not later.

And even after all that, on March 19, 1917, the Kadet paper *Rech* (Speech) still wrote confidently, "The Kishinev bloodbath—the counterrevolutionary pogroms of 1905—were organized, as has been thoroughly established, by the Department of Police." And in August 1917, at the Moscow Government Meeting, the chairman of the Extraordinary Investigative Commission publicly claimed that he would "soon present documents from the Department of Police on organizing the Jewish pogroms," but not a single such document has been presented, neither soon nor not soon, neither by his commission nor later by the Bolsheviks. The lie was so ingrained—and remains so even now. (In my novel *November 1916*, one of the characters mentions the Kishinev pogrom, and in 1986 the German publisher added its own footnote for German readers: "A carefully orchestrated two-day Jewish pogrom. Internal Affairs Minister Plehve instructed the governor of Bessarabia, in the event of a pogrom, not to try to use force to contain it.") The modern (1996) *Jewish Encyclopedia* states confidently, "In April 1903, the new Minister of Internal Affairs, V. Plehve, organized a pogrom in Kishinev with the help of his agents." (Paradoxically, one volume earlier the same encyclopedia tells us that "the text of Plehve's telegram published in the London *Times* . . . is believed by most researchers to be a fake.")

And so the false history of the Kishinev pogrom has become more prominent than its true sorrowful story. And will another hundred years be enough to make sense of it?

Source: A. I. Solzhenitsyn, *Dvesti let vmeste (1795–1995)*, vol. 1 (Moscow: Issledovaniia noveishei russkoi istorii, 2001), 334–35. Translated from the Russian by Eugenia Tietz-Sokolskaya.

Document 3.6. Pavel Krushevan's Description of Sordid Jewish Economic Activity

Pavel Krushevan's book on Bessarabia, published soon before the pogrom in 1903, was on the whole a detailed, loving portrait of the province. The bulk of the work focused on the area's rural life with glimpses, by no means uniformly inaccurate, of its urban life as well. Its treatment of Jews was brief, rather cursory and condemnatory. The fiercest treatment of Jews in the volume—filled with photographs of the region's quiet, undramatic, lush countryside—was its description of the chicanery of Jews in the city's marketplaces. The following passage was accompanied in the volume by a photograph of raven-like images of Jews—dark, alien, eerily thin, their faces obscure, their designs on unsuspecting locals anything but clear.

When livestock is sold at market, the Jews arrange among themselves to go on strike, and the prices are set for the livestock according to their wishes, where they pay next to nothing for it, but in lean years, when everyone needs to sell their ox, cow, or horse, then there's no limit to the Jewish exploitation; the peasant weeps and sells the animals for what the Jews give him, and yet the meat sold by those same Jews is never cheap. In short, Bessarabia's peasants are entirely under the Jews' thumbs, even three-quarters of the landlords are controlled by the Jews, and they obediently execute the Jews' wishes.

Then, in the past three to four years, proclamations clearly of a Jewish provenance began appearing in Kishinev "to the intelligentsia, the people, the workers," those sorts of underground publications; workers were called on to go on strike, to disobey the authorities, and the strikers were promised cash rewards. More and more proclamations and appeals were being thrown around, and they were read, and even the illiterate talked about them. There were a few strikes.

In general, the workers have recently changed for the worse under the influence of Jewish agitators. But clearly the common people have not lost faith in their renowned tsar, whom they love, and all it took was for an appeal to circulate around Easter that the Jews were planning ill deeds against the tsar and for that the tsar had ordered the Jews punished, and the people took it upon themselves to deal with the Yids, unleashing a long-simmering hatred. On April 6, after the Jews beat a woman, this punishment first manifested itself as breaking windows in Jewish homes, but sufficient measures were not taken to put a stop to it, and on April 7 a full-on pogrom of Jewish homes and stores erupted. Troublemakers dispersed across the city in small groups of five to ten people and conducted pogroms here and there. Where the Jews took to beating Christians, the crowd would bear down on them, and this would frequently result in one or two Jewish deaths, while the thugs moved on. In particular, the killings became more frequent after Jews fired a shot from inside the gates of Stopudis's store, killing a teenager, who was later identified as Grigory Ostapov.

It was notable that the thugs themselves didn't take any property; people who happened to be watching and did not take part would pick it up from the street, and no one held it against them. All the crowd's actions and exclamations gave the impression that it was convinced it could act with impunity.

Source: Pavel Krushevan, *Bessarabia* (Moscow, 1903). Translated from the Russian by Eugenia Tietz-Sokolskaya.

Document 3.7. Pogroms and Lynching

The Broad Ax *was a fiercely independent newspaper launched in 1895 by Julius F. Taylor. Published during much of its existence in Chicago, it was one of several newspapers of the time critical of the politically moderate leadership of Booker T. Washington—arguably, it was the most critical of them all—but one of several raising questions repeatedly in the immediate wake of the Kishinev pogrom as to why the lynching of African Americans received so little attention while the Kishinev pogrom garnered so much, even from Black leaders like Washington.*

Booker T. Washington has written a letter to the Kishineff Relief League of this city, expressing his sympathy for the Hebrew sufferers across the sea in which he says, "the reports that have come of the horrors of Kishineff are shocking to the last degree, and civilization justly revolts against the cruelties that have been visited on the heads of the people so law-abiding and peace-loving as the Jews." This is all very well on the part of Booker Washington, but why is he mum or silent as to the existence of slavery in Alabama? Is he not cognizant of the fact that right now, Negro men and women, girls and boys, are alike shackled and handcuffed, beaten to death with buggy traces and gin stains, bought and sold and hunted down by ferocious bloodhounds by the slave drivers of his locality? Has he no sympathy for those unfortunate, innocent victims who are subjected to such hellish treatment simply because their skin is black? If he has not, then his hypocrisy is more than enough to shame the very devil himself and all the imps of hell!

Source: *The Broad Ax*, June 20, 1903, 1.

4

1905

Russia's Encounter with Revolution and Pogroms

Robert Weinberg

In mid-October 1905 the non-Jewish residents of Odessa went on a four-day rampage against their Jewish neighbors.[1] The anti-Jewish violence resulted from social and political turmoil and the instability that characterized late imperial Russia in the early years of the twentieth century. Violence against Jews in 1905 stemmed in part from long-standing prejudices toward Jews, but it took a confluence of particular social, political, and economic factors to spark physical attacks on Jews. The pogrom was the culmination of trends that had been unfolding in Odessa since the beginning of the year, making the city a tinderbox ready to explode. The erosion of autocratic authority and widespread labor unrest in the city transformed antisemitism into violent behavior. And once antisemitism turned violent, local authorities had trouble restoring law and order.

Throughout the year workers, students, professionals, national minorities, and revolutionaries and liberals in all parts of the country organized to demand political reform. Matters reached crisis proportions by mid-October, culminating in a general strike that paralyzed the country and prompted the tsar to grant civil and political rights and promise the formation of a popularly elected legislative assembly. The announcement of the October Manifesto on October 17 set the stage for the pogroms that broke out as the forces for reform, revolution, and reaction took to the streets to celebrate or decry the erosion of autocratic power. The pogroms were the expression of the crisis besetting the Romanov dynasty as the tsarist government tried to stem the tide of revolution, and its supporters mobilized to defend the autocracy.

The ethnic composition of Odessa helps to explain why the crisis gripping the country turned violent and pitted Russians against Jews. By the turn of the twentieth century, Jews composed some 35 percent of the nearly half million inhabitants

---

[1] Material for this chapter is based on Robert Weinberg, "Workers, Pogroms, and the 1905 Revolution in Odessa," *Russian Review* 46, no. 1 (1987): 53–75 and Weinberg, *The Revolution of 1905 in Odessa: Blood on the Steps* (Bloomington: Indiana University Press, 1993). I provide sources only for direct quotations.

Robert Weinberg, *1905* In: *Pogroms.* Edited by: Eugene M. Avrutin and Elissa Bemporad, Oxford University Press. © Oxford University Press 2021. DOI: 10.1093/oso/9780190060084.003.0005

Postcard from 1905 depicting a medal honoring members of the Black Hundreds
who participated in attacks on "high school students, Kikes, and intellectuals." The
drawing of a double-headed eagle, symbol of the Romanov dynasty, underscores the
Black Hundreds' unconditional support of the autocracy. The banner under the skull
and crossbones states "Down with Freedom." The words in the margin read, "To the
Suppression of the Rebellion of Educated Persons."
Courtesy of the Blavatnik Archive

of Odessa. Russians formed just about half of the city's population and Ukrainians
made up approximately 10 percent. Odessa was an economic juggernaut as it became the country's most important port and was home to banks, brokerage
houses, food-processing plants such as sugar refineries, and other manufacturing
enterprises. The city also boasted a vibrant intellectual and cultural scene that re-
flected the influence and effect of trends found in other cosmopolitan centers of
Europe.

The large number of Jews living in the city and their visible presence in the commercial and industrial life of the city contributed to resentment against Odessa's
Jewish community. For example, in the 1880s, firms owned by Jews controlled
70 percent of the export trade in grain, which grew to over 90 percent by 1910. In
addition, Jews and Russians competed for work at the docks as stevedores and day
laborers. Already predisposed to dislike Jews due to well-entrenched antisemitism
in late imperial Russian society, gentiles in Odessa seized upon the economic role
of Jews in the city and accused them of exploiting non-Jews. But this popular belief
that Jewish capitalists exploited Russians had less basis in reality than was commonly supposed. The bulk of the wealth in Odessa, not to mention political influence and power, remained in the hands of non-Jews, who controlled half of all large

commercial enterprises and brokerage firms and the majority of factories. Despite this disparity between popular perception and the reality of Jewish wealth and power, Jews found it difficult to dispel this attitude. The truth of the matter was that the vast majority of Jews eked out meager livings as shopkeepers, secondhand dealers, salesclerks, petty traders, domestic servants, day laborers, and workshop employees. In 1905, nearly eighty thousand Jews requested financial assistance from the Jewish community in order to buy matzoh during Passover, a telling sign that well over half of the Jews in Odessa experienced difficulties making ends meet.

In Odessa the populace and city authorities tended to associate civil unrest and political opposition with Jews, a word synonymous with revolutionaries. While many reports of Jewish revolutionary activity were exaggerations or even fabrications, Jews were behind some of the social and political ferment enveloping Odessa. The police arrested a group of Jewish revolutionaries for making and stockpiling bombs during the summer and urging Jews to arm themselves, struggle for civil and political freedom, and overthrow the autocracy. They organized rallies at the university and directed student strikes and public demonstrations. Jewish youths, students, and workers filled the ranks of the crowds that attended rallies at the university in September and October. In short, Jews actively participated in the work stoppages, demonstrations, and street disorders that overwhelmed Odessa by the time the general strike in mid-October brought the country to a standstill. Moreover, Jewish youths joined forces with the revolutionary parties to organize self-defense units designed to protect the Jewish community. These groups procured weapons and formed armed brigades that were ready to act at a moment's notice. Such preparation saved Jewish lives and protected Jewish property, but it also reinforced the perception of Jews as revolutionaries and the instigators of trouble.

Politics in Odessa polarized during 1905 as anti- and pro-government forces coalesced and mobilized. Militant monarchist organizations were taking shape that appealed to conservative Odessans. In addition to the revolutionary parties that had been active for several years in Odessa, radical student groups also emerged as a significant political force. The stage was set for a confrontation between the forces of revolution and reaction, and the pogrom occurred in the context of this unrest that converted antisemitism, normally dormant and passive, into a paroxysm of bloodletting.

Soldiers killed several students supporting striking workers on October 16, sparking confrontations between government forces and radical students, revolutionaries, and workers who had walked off the job in protest. The storm broke on October 18 as thousands of people thronged the streets to celebrate the October Manifesto. As one university student exclaimed, "A joyous crowd appeared in the streets—people greeted each other as if it were a holiday."[2] Many non-Jews joined Jews in enthusiastically celebrating the granting of civil rights and political liberties.

---

[2] *Materialy k istorii russkoi kontr-revoliutsii. Volume 1: Pogromy po offitsial'nym dokumentam* (St. Petersburg: Tipografiia Obshchestvennaia pol'za, 1908), 97.

"Feast after the Pogrom." Postcard depicting pogromists celebrating the murder and mutilation of Jews with shots of vodka. It was commonly believed that alcohol fueled the unrestrained violence that characterized the killing of defenseless men, women, and children. Note the simian features of the pogromists; the heavyset man in the middle is wearing what may be a policeman's hat.
Courtesy of the Blavatnik Archive

Soon after the demonstrations began, several individuals began to unfurl red flags and banners with antigovernment slogans. Others shouted slogans like "Down with the Autocracy" and "Long Live Freedom." Apartment dwellers hung pieces of red cloth from their balconies and windows, while groups of demonstrators forced passersby to doff their caps or bow before the flags. In the city council building, demonstrators ripped down the portrait of the tsar, substituted a red flag for the imperial colors, and collected money for weapons. The city governor Dmitrii Neidgart also reported that one group of demonstrators tied portraits of the tsar to the tails of dogs and then released them to roam the city. The mood of the demonstrators grew confrontational as the day wore on. Groups of demonstrators—primarily Jewish youths, according to official accounts—viciously attacked and disarmed policemen. By mid-afternoon Neidgart had received reports that two policemen had been killed or wounded and twenty-two disarmed, and that many others had abandoned their posts order to avoid possible injury. He ordered the police back to their stations and permitted only patrols in groups.

The clashes were not limited to attacks on policemen by angry demonstrators. Toward the end of the day tensions between those Odessans who heralded the manifesto and those who disapproved of the concessions granted by the tsar had reached a breaking point. Outraged by the sight of desecrated portraits of the tsar, supporters of the monarchy gave vent to their anger and frustration not by attacking

Russians celebrating in the streets, but by turning on the entire Jewish community, which they viewed as the source of problems besetting the country. Clashes occurred as groups of armed demonstrators, chiefly Jewish students and workers, fought with bands of gentile vigilantes. These instances of violence underscored the deep-seated ethnic animosities in Odessa.

Armed confrontations broke out in the afternoon and early evening of October 18. The clashes apparently started when a group of Jews carrying red flags in celebration of the October Manifesto demanded that a group of Russian workers doff their caps to the flags. Harsh words were exchanged, scuffles ensued, and both groups scattered, only to reassemble in nearby streets and resume their fighting. The clashes soon turned into a full-fledged pogrom, as Russians indiscriminately attacked Jews and began to vandalize and loot Jewish homes, apartments, and stores.

In mid-morning on October 19, hundreds of patriotic Russian children, women, and men gathered in various parts of the city and readied themselves for marches to display their loyalty to the tsar. Day laborers, especially those employed at the port, made up a major element of the crowd that assembled at the harbor. Factory and construction workers, shopkeepers, salesclerks, workshop employees, and vagrants soon joined the rallies, where organizers distributed flags, icons, and portraits of the tsar. The marchers also passed around bottles of vodka. Some plainclothes policemen reportedly handed out not only vodka but also money and guns. Onlookers and passersby joined the processions as the demonstrators from all parts of Odessa made their way to the center of the city. Singing the national anthem and religious hymns, they stopped at the city council building and substituted the imperial colors for the red flag that students had raised the previous day. They then headed toward the city's main Orthodox cathedral, stopping en route at the residences of Baron Aleksandr Kaul'bars, commander of the Odessa Military District, and Neidgart. Kaul'bars, fearing confrontation between the patriotic marchers and revolutionaries, asked them to disperse. Some heeded his request, but most members of the procession continued their march. Neidgart, on the other hand, greeted the patriots enthusiastically and urged them to hold a prayer service at the cathedral.

After the service, the procession continued to march through the streets of central Odessa. Suddenly, shots rang out, and a young boy carrying an icon lay dead. Most accounts of the incident assert that the shots came from surrounding buildings. No one knows for certain who was responsible for the shots, but evidence indicates that revolutionaries or members of Jewish and student self-defense brigades initiated the shooting and reportedly threw homemade bombs. The crowd panicked and ran through the streets as more shots were fired from rooftops, balconies, and apartment windows. The shootings triggered a chain reaction. Convinced that the Jews were responsible for the shootings, members of the patriotic demonstration began shouting "Beat the Kikes" and "Death to the Kikes," and went on a rampage, attacking Jews with wild abandon and destroying

"Home at Last." Postcard reproduction of M. L. Maimon's 1906 painting of an invalid
Jewish soldier who, having returned home from the Russo-Japanese War, finds
the bodies of his family who had died at the hands of pogromists. An elderly Jew,
presumably the father of the soldier or of his wife, mourns their deaths through prayer.
Courtesy of the Blavatnik Archive.

Jewish apartments, homes, and stores. The course of events was similar in other
parts of the city; members of student and Jewish self-defense brigades fired on
Russians who were holding smaller patriotic processions and provoked similar
pogromist responses. By mid-afternoon a full-fledged pogrom had developed,
and it raged until October 22.

The pogrom was the most violent incident of anti-Jewish violence in terms of destruction of property and number of people wounded and killed to date in Russia.
The pogrom wave of 1881–1882 was far less deadly, and no other Jewish community experienced the carnage endured by Odessa's Jews. Police in Odessa claimed
that at least 400 Jews and 100 gentiles were killed and approximately 300, mostly
Jews, suffered injuries; some 1,632 houses, apartments, and stores belonging to
Jews incurred damage. But these figures are estimates at best, particularly in terms
of the number wounded, which was higher than the police reported. The list of
atrocities perpetrated against the Jews is too long to recount here and beggars the
imagination. But suffice it to say that pogromists brutally and indiscriminately beat,
mutilated, and murdered defenseless Jewish men, women, and children who were
not involved in the attacks on defenders of the autocracy. They hurled Jews out of
windows, raped women of all ages, and slaughtered infants in front of their parents.

The pogrom assumed the characteristics of a secular ritual whereby some
pogromists hoped to celebrate and reinforce their identity as Orthodox Christians
devoted to tsar and motherland. From their perspective the challenges confronting

the autocracy threatened to unravel the bonds that tied them to the tsar. The destruction of portraits of Nicholas II (1868–1918) elicited feelings of resentment and anger and helped mobilize the forces of reaction eager to stand up to the provocative behavior of those rejecting the values that undergirded the autocracy. The pogrom can be viewed as an effort to strengthen the foundation of tsarist rule by physically attacking the regime's existential enemy, the Jew, in the hope of destroying all perceived threats to autocratic institutions and values. Like the pogrom wave that targeted Jews as responsible for the regicide in 1881, pogromist unrest and violence in 1905 viewed Jews as threats to the body politic and fabric of late imperial Russian society.

The October 1905 pogrom in Odessa illustrates how antisemitism could become a potent force in politics. The pogrom served the cause of political reaction by revealing how a potentially revolutionary situation could quickly became defused when the target of the people's wrath was no longer the autocracy but the Jews, a convenient scapegoat viewed as responsible for personal difficulties and political uncertainty. But the wave of pogroms that broke out in mid-October would not have occurred without the polarized political atmosphere that had developed over the course of 1905. The issuance of the October Manifesto and the mobilization of anti-tsarist and monarchist forces in such an emotionally charged setting triggered the outbreak of bloodletting at a time of political anxiety.

"Seal of Approval." Postcard commemorates the gratitude of "a grateful Russia" to the Black Hundreds for their actions on October 19, 1905. Note the skulls and images of a *nagaika* (whip) on the monument and the seal of approval from the press of the Black Hundreds.
Courtesy of the Blavatnik Archive

Document 4.1. Government Inquiry Links Pogrom to Civil Unrest

In the aftermath of the pogrom, the government appointed Senator Aleksandr Kuzminskii to investigate the causes of the unrest. Kuzminskii offered a detailed account of the events in mid-October that underscored how Odessa was a powder keg ready to explode even before Tsar Nicholas II announced the October Manifesto: labor unrest and the formation of armed militias of university students, Jewish self-defense groups, and revolutionary parties set the stage for open confrontation between the forces of reform and reaction. Kuzminskii also noted that the events of October were more than the result of ethnic and economic tensions; they were a consequence of the political crisis besetting the regime since January. Kuzminskii's report was published in 1908 as Materials on the History of the Russian Counter-Revolution. *The following excerpt describes the events of October 14.*

From October 18 through October 22, 1905, the city of Odessa was the site of an extraordinarily lengthy pogrom accompanied by the beating of Jews, the destruction and looting of their property, and numerous victims, casualties, and injuries, not just Jews but also Christians. In its force and demonstrated cruelty it surpassed all those that had preceded it, which had typically been akin to fights sparked primarily by ethnic and economic concerns, while this last one must be considered as a phenomenon of a different type, in which the causes seen previously were overshadowed by other ones arising from the current state of the country.

The investigation showed that the tragic events of the October days are a phenomenon of Odessa political life that is linked by cause and effect to the entire progression of the local revolutionary movement, for which reason, in order to correctly determine their causes, it would be necessary to present a brief summary of this movement in the preceding time period.

[. . .]

The political strike that began in the first days of October in many cities across the empire manifested itself in Odessa first by a gradual cessation, over the course of time between the twelfth and the fourteenth, of work and train movement on Odessa's railroads and of classes at secondary educational institutions. The first to stop classes, on October 12 and 13, were the students of the Emperor Nicholas II and Faig Commercial Colleges, which were the most susceptible to revolutionary propaganda because a majority of the students were Jewish. The following day, October 14, the students at the striking commercial schools appeared at the university, where at a meeting in which the students participated it was decided that classes would be stopped at all the other secondary educational institutions in Odessa. In order to implement this decision, the commercial students, led by the university students, headed toward the Sokolovskii Electrotechnical School located near the university and tried to have the students there walk out of classes, after which the crowd of youths, having split into groups, began going to other educational institutions and stopping classes there by force. The majority of the students who walked out joined the strikers, and in this way the crowd gradually grew. Around two in the afternoon, the crowd, which had grown to just over two thousand people, approached the Berezina Women's Gymnasium ... several university and commercial students from the crowd entered the women's school and upon emerging announced that they had stopped classes and the students should be coming out soon. At that time a detachment of twenty policemen ... appeared suddenly. ... Upon approaching the crowd, the policemen began dispersing it and in doing so caused various injuries to persons in the crowd with their unsheathed swords. ...

Source: *Materialy k istorii russkoi kontr-revoliutsii*. Volume 1: *Pogromy po offitsial'nym dokumentam* (St. Petersburg: Tipografiia Obshchestvennaia pol'za, 1908), cv–cvi, cxix–cxx. Translated from the Russian by Eugenia Tietz-Sokolskaya.

Document 4.2. Students, Workers, and Revolutionaries Clash with Soldiers

On October 15, high school and university students took to the streets and appealed to workers to join the general strike that was paralyzing the country. Headquartered at the university, they joined forces with revolutionary parties to solicit funds to arm civilian militias. The following excerpts, taken from Kuzminskii's report, describe the violence that erupted the following day as students, workers, and revolutionaries clashed with police and soldiers, resulting in the deaths of five students.

On October 16 an armed crowd set out from the university to the barricades, when, under orders from St. Petersburg, soldiers and police cut off access to the rally at the university; nursing units and medical help were sent out from the same place to previously defined posts. . . . Of that day's casualties, five bodies were brought to the university, embalmed, and placed in coffins, and then held there ... waiting for favorable conditions for a formal burial, which could not take place on its initially scheduled day, October 19, due to patriotic demonstrations in the city. Thus, for over two months the constant threat of new riots and associated violence hung over the peaceful population, and it was only when martial law was reinstated on December 15, at the governor-general's request, that these bodies were buried without formalities.

The armed clash with soldiers on the barricades on the sixteenth, and the preceding forced walkout at Berezina Gymnasium on the fourteenth, which caused the police to get involved, gave the university a pretext for protests in which the Academic Council placed responsibility for the events of the sixteenth on the city governor for not allowing a rally open to the public, and thereby, in the council's view, infringing on the university's autonomy. In another protest, the pretext was that the police had beaten children, despite the investigation's clear finding that none of the children had been harmed and the students had not even come out of the school into the street. Both protests were due to significant misinterpretations, both of the facts and of the definition of autonomy that led to resolutions overflowing with indignation and claiming it was impossible to continue classes at the university, even though they were not, in fact, in session.... The same level of exaggeration and excess that had been so salient at rally speeches was also present in the discussion of current events by faculty of the university, even though one could have expected them to have a more sober outlook.

Source: *Materialy k istorii russkoi kontr-revoliutsii.* Volume 1: *Pogromy po offitsial'nym dokumentam* (St. Petersburg: Tipografiia Obshchestvennaia pol'za, 1908), cciv–ccv. Translated from the Russian by Eugenia Tietz-Sokolskaya.

Document 4.3. Calm before the Storm

October 17 passed without any public disturbances or confrontations, but life did not return to normal. Soldiers patrolled the city, while schools and many stores remained closed. Even though not all workers responded to the appeal for a general strike, thousands of workers—many of whom were Jewish—walked off their jobs. Groups of workers congregated outside stores that opened for business, singing songs and drinking vodka. At the university, professors and students, along with representatives of revolutionary parties, continued raising money for guns and ammunition. City Governor Neidgart took the opportunity to condemn the university's administration for allowing it to become the epicenter of resistance to the regime. He issued a printed notice circulated widely in the city. In it he cautioned the people of Odessa to resist the urge to support the forces of revolution headquartered at the university.

City Governor Neidgart noted: "At the university, which has been granted self-government, but not the right of assembly for outside persons, the meetings being held were accompanied by prohibited and appalling collections to arm fighters. I pointed out . . . that such collections, which would inevitably lead to a bloody outcome, were not permissible, but neither the president nor the council took any measures to prevent the collection of money for weapons. On October 13 there was a strike among the students of commercial colleges, and no one touched them until they became violent themselves, by initiating violence on October 14 . . . After that, tales started circulating through the city that almost all the children at all educational institutions had been chopped to pieces by savage policemen. Well-meaning people, please be more careful with rumors; there are now great multitudes of them, one worse than the next. Yesterday morning the drugstores were closed at the strikers' demand, and first-aid stations were set up at certain specified places next to the future sites of barricades. Who organized all this, who predicted and prepared for it? Yesterday barricades were being built in eleven places . . . Troops fired several times, and reports from hospitals speak of up to eighty wounded and killed . . . The rioting and strikes have terribly increased prices on all basic necessities. Decide for yourselves, well-meaning people, who is to blame for it all.

Source: *Materialy k istorii russkoi kontr-revoliutsii*. Volume 1: *Pogromy po offitsial'nym dokumentam* (St. Petersburg: Tipografiia Obshchestvennaia pol'za, 1908), cxxx–cxxxi. Translated from the Russian by Eugenia Tietz-Sokolskaya.

Document 4.4. The Pogrom Begins

Senator Kuzminskii's report provided a detailed description of how the confrontation between demonstrators celebrating and protesting the October Manifesto during the course of October 18 developed into the pogrom. Testimony collected by Kuzminskii makes it clear that blame for the escalation of violence fell on both opponents and defenders of the autocracy. He presented evidence that policemen and soldiers were active participants in the violence against the Jews, an understandable response, from his perspective, because Jewish revolutionaries were responsible for the civil and political unrest in 1905. Moreover, Jewish revolutionaries had organized armed, self-defense units that stood up to pogromists and even shot at those policemen and soldiers who were seen as egging on the mobs and failing to stem the bloodshed.

Meanwhile, already in the evening of the eighteenth rumors began spreading through the city that on the outskirts, on Prokhorov Street in the Mikhailov district, some kind of armed confrontation had taken place. It turned out that a crowd of demonstrators with red flags, consisting mostly of Jews, had tried to get workers at a . . . factory to walk out, demanding that they join the demonstration. But the workers did not satisfy their demand; later, when the same crowd met Russian workers on Golovkov Street, the crowd demanded that they take off their hats before the red flags. When the workers refused, shots were heard from among the crowd; the workers, despite being unarmed, were able to disperse the crowd and follow it to Prokhorov Street, where the crowd was joined by another crowd of up to a thousand armed Jews, who began shooting at the workers. According to the report of the Mikhailov district police chief, who arrived at the confrontation with fifty Cossacks, four workers were killed. The Cossacks and police were met with shots, not just from the crowd but also from the rooftops, balconies, and windows; in various places fights and armed clashes broke out between Russians and Jews; Russian workers and persons without clearly defined occupations—so-called hooligans[3]— began catching and beating Jews, then transitioned to breaking into and destroying Jewish houses, apartments, and stores. The riots grew to such proportions that the

---

[3] In Russian the word for "hooligan" has the same connotation as "thug" or "hoodlum" in English.

police chief deemed it necessary to summon the soldiers on-call from the station, who prevented further clashes and restored order by eight in the evening. During the armed clashes in that area, people were killed and wounded, but members of the crowd would immediately carry them away, so the number of casualties remains unknown.

[...]

The mood in the crowd of protesters was quite peaceful and calm, although one witness . . . claims that when he came across that crowd between eight and nine in the morning on Kanat Street, heading toward the sea, there were yells of "long live the Tsar, long live freedom, down with the Yids, they should be beaten," while the staff at the Merchant Marine Academy . . . said that the crowd was on its way to "raise the Moscow guild to go beat the Yids together."

Due to the appearance of this crowd, the funeral service for those killed on the barricades on October 16 was abruptly canceled by its own organizers, out of fear of a clash between the two opposing groups. From then on, the corpses, embalmed and lying in sealed zinc coffins, remained at the university clinic, until an opportunity to bury them presented itself. Thus, the indefinite storage of these corpses at the university continually threatened to give rise to a new demonstration and rioting, the extent of which was difficult to predict. However, this wait for a good opportunity was cut off in the last third of December by the city governor, who demanded immediate burial.

[...]

But even in those cases when police patrols would show up at the scene of the action with detachments of soldiers, according to almost all witnesses questioned during the investigation, they would typically take no measures to stop the rioting or havoc being wreaked because all the police officers, believing as they did that the Jews were responsible for all sorts of political disturbances and strikes and judging them to be revolutionaries, were quite in favor of the pogrom under way against the Jewish population. They did not even think it necessary to hide that fact, and therefore naturally did not have stopping the pogrom as their goal, and because in many cases it was the police officers themselves directing groups of hooligans to destroy and plunder Jewish houses, apartments, and shops, supplying them with clubs from felled trees, personally taking part in the devastation, plunder, and murder alongside the hooligans, and directing the mob's actions.

[...]

The soldiers were similarly quite indifferent about who was responsible for the pogrom because, on the one hand, they were not familiar with the substance of their duties and, in the absence of any directives from police officers, when they arrived at the scene of the action and saw the pogroms taking place and the armed self-defense groups, they would not know against whom or in what order they were supposed to employ military force. On the other hand, on seeing how the police officers condoned the destruction of Jewish property, the soldiers could assume that the pogrom had begun with the authorities' knowledge and approval. As a result, according to witnesses, soldiers and policemen typically beat only students and shot only at Jewish self-defense groups and student militias; sometimes policemen would say to those they were beating, "Here's your freedom and your 'down with autocracy.'" In one case, according to Dr. Radetsky, an officer witnessing hooligans brutally beating Jews watched indifferently and commented only: "You didn't want government, so now there is no government." The soldiers did nothing to stop the rioters, even though it was often in the presence of the police and military that they would break into Jewish shops and apartments, destroying and stealing Jewish property . . . In general, the mobs of hooligans were entirely unchecked, thoroughly convinced that neither the police nor the soldiers would do anything to stop them or detain them at the scene of the crime, while many students, Jews, and others engaged in self-defense were detained by the dozen merely for being found carrying a weapon. They were held at police stations in the toughest of conditions, often subject to beatings by police officers, soldiers, and Cossacks. As a result of this attitude, the culprits were not identified in a timely fashion, and it would be extremely difficult to establish their guilt at this time.

Source: *Materialy k istorii russkoi kontr-revoliutsii*. Volume 1: *Pogromy po offitsial'nym dokumentam* (St. Petersburg: Tipografiia Obshchestvennaia pol'za, 1908), cxlvii, cxlix, cliii, cliv–clv. Translated from the Russian by Eugenia Tietz-Sokolskaya.

Document 4.5. Military Commander Describes the Outbreak of Violence

General Kaul'bars recounted his experiences during the pogrom when Kuzminskii was conducting his investigation. In this excerpt, Kaul'bars describes the events that transpired during the course of October 19, including his brief encounter with a group of pro-tsarist demonstrators that had congregated outside his house in the hope of receiving his blessing.

October 19

In response to the demonstrations that took place on October 18, when the overwhelming majority of participants were Jews carrying red flags, starting on the morning of the nineteenth, patriotic demonstrators began appearing in the streets with portraits of the tsar. . . . These demonstrations were composed exclusively of Russian workers: huge crowds of them marched in the streets, singing the national anthem and the hymn "God Save Thy People." Crowds of these demonstrators were marching on the boulevard around ten in the morning, and at 10:30 a huge crowd carrying portraits of the tsar had gathered across from my apartment, demonstrating in an entirely peaceful manner.

I came out to the crowd and asked the people to disperse, to not go into the city center, since the funeral for the victims of October 16 was planned for that day.

After that, part of the crowd, heeding my advice, dispersed, but part remained. Then this crowd headed past the City Duma building toward the cathedral; in many places it was met with revolver shots from a crowd of hostile Jews, and a bomb was thrown at the demonstrators from the same Jewish crowd. In response to this reception, shouts of "beat the Yids!" were heard from the crowd of demonstrators. Their peaceful attitude changed abruptly. Reports of rioting started coming in from all quarters.

At 9:20 a.m., a statement arrived from a gun shop that . . . the student militia had demanded that it hand over all of the store's revolvers. Under threat of destruction, the store acceded to the demand and gave over sixteen revolvers. Meanwhile, the students said they would get ammunition from the stores of Rauchwerger and Sterenberg.[4]

The patriotic demonstrators, who had marched along the city streets in complete order and without any violence, faced gunfire along their route from windows, roofs, and balconies. For example, the crowd of demonstrators marching on Ekaterina Street was met with shots from the upper stories of houses on Zhukov Street, and in the same place a bomb was thrown into the crowd from a basement.

The platoon of Cossacks that was then accompanying the city governor, who was returning from the cathedral after the conclusion of a church service in honor of the October 17 Manifesto, was ordered by the city governor to escort the demonstrators from the rear. When the crowd faced gunfire from houses, the platoon dismounted and opened fire at the windows from which shots were heard and into the basement from which the bomb had been thrown.

Another crowd of demonstrators, on Gavan Street, faced the same sort of gunfire. After receiving the signal to open fire, the company of the 59th reserve battalion that was marching behind the crowd fired a round into the windows from which the shots were being fired.

News of all these attacks against patriotic demonstrators spread through the populace incredibly quickly, causing extreme anger and hostility against the Jews, who were believed—not without reason—to be behind all these attacks and whose behavior the previous day had outraged and angered the lower classes of the Russian populace.

Source: *Materialy k istorii russkoi kontr-revoliutsii*. Volume 1: *Pogromy po offitsial'nym dokumentam* (St. Petersburg: Tipografiia Obshchestvennaia pol'za, 1908), 188–89. Translated from the Russian by Eugenia Tietz-Sokolskaya.

---

[4] By police order, ammunition had been removed from stores beforehand.

Document 4.6. The Western Press Describes the Pogrom

News about the pogrom appeared in the English-language press in England and the United States and did not spare its readers the details. In this account the number of casualties is grossly exaggerated, as is the number of pogromists apprehended, a mistake due in large measure to the inability to collect accurate information while the pogrom raged and a predisposition to view Russia's treatment of Jews in a negative light. Like the account in Document 4.10, this report suggests that the police helped to mobilize the pogromists and direct their actions.

"Odessa Drenched in Blood. Five Thousand People Reported Killed or Wounded There."

The *Standard*'s correspondent says: "Within three hours of the declaration of martial law, which came to the unspeakable relief of peaceable citizens, no fewer than 5,000 ruffianly Loyalists had been disarmed by the students and the military. . . .

The rigorous curfew law is welcomed as a deliverance from the terrors of the last two days. Anyone in the streets after nightfall is liable to arrest: anyone appearing at open windows or on balconies risks being shot without warning."

A dispatch to the *Evening Standard* from Odessa, timed 2:30 p.m. today, says:

The city rings with the reports of rifles and revolvers, and occasionally a volley is fired. Every house and tenement is [*sic*] bolted and barred. The infantry patrols are doing their duty perfunctorily, declining to fire on the mobs unless they themselves are attacked. The Cossacks are said to have lost over a hundred men by bombs and shots from windows. Cossack patrols carry carbines and have their fingers on the triggers. The streets are absolutely unsafe for civilians.

The casualties yesterday are believed to have amounted to 5,000 killed and wounded. In the Jewish quarters bodies still strew the streets and sidewalks. Jewish women and children were strangled and hacked to pieces in the streets where the mobs gained the upper hand. A Red Cross doctor tells me that the Kishinev horrors were repeated a hundredfold. The students alone saved the city from wholesale sack and massacre. The military are now placing a hundred machine guns at various points. Twenty-six carts full of wounded have just passed my door.

Odessa. November 2—The massacre of Jews continues. They are being hunted down in the streets and killed and beaten, while their shops are given over to pillage. The streets are in possession of a wild, disorderly mob. Several bombs have been thrown.

Killing and plundering by bands formed of hundreds of Loyalists continued this morning. The night was made hideous, bodies of Loyalists, with whom the police are fraternizing, marching through the principal streets, bearing national flags, portraits of the Emperor and ikons, singling the national anthem, smashing everything in their way and looting shops and houses. Hospital wagons passed through the streets incessantly, carrying off the killed, wounded and mutilated. The population is panic-stricken.

The troops wreaked terrible vengeance on the residents of three houses from balconies from which shots were fired by unknown persons on the soldiers. The troops immediately stormed the houses and massacred all the inhabitants with unheard of barbarity. It is persistently asserted that the unknown persons who fired on the troops were disguised policemen, who purposely provoked the troops.

The city is a dismal sight. The streets are filled with Cossack patrols and flying detachments of the Red Cross, which follow the bands of murderous rioters. The firing has been uninterrupted all day and still continues as this dispatch is filed at 5 p.m. Many hundreds have been killed or wounded.

The Cossacks eagerly attack the student militia, which is courageously trying to check the bands who are massacring and pillaging, principally in the Jewish quarter. The looters openly divide the goods, the Cossacks in many cases participating in the proceeds of the robberies.

Source: *New York Tribune*, November 3, 1905, 1.

Document 4.7.   Eyewitness Accounts of the Odessa Pogrom

The following two passages appeared in a book compiled by a Jewish revolutionary organization, Poale-Zion. Titled The Odessa Pogrom and Self-Defense, *the book is primarily a compilation of eyewitness accounts to the pogrom. The first selection is an overview of the events written by someone on a fact-finding mission by Poale-Zion. The second is an account offered by several milkmen. These passages reveal that the unrest affected all districts of the city, regardless of wealth, and were not limited to neighborhoods with large concentrations of Jews. They reveal the passions unleashed by publication of the October Manifesto. These accounts also underscore the extent of the bloodletting and they hint at police involvement in the organization of the violence. The testimony indicates that Jewish self-defense limited the destructive and deadly force of the mobs.*

By nine in the morning there was a young man riding in a tram down Pushkin Street, waving a red flag and yelling "freedom!" Soon the manifesto became known to the entire city, and the city was transformed. All the central streets were packed with people celebrating; there were processions, red flags waving, songs sung, speeches given at the city council and university. At the same time, crowds of demonstrators headed to the outlying streets—Malorossia, Dal'nits, and others—to bring the good news to residents in the outskirts.

It was the beating of one such crowd of demonstrators on Dal'nits Street that started the pogrom. The beatings began at two in the afternoon and continued for two whole hours; at four, a crowd of thugs, organized by one of the policemen, emerged from Gutmants's tavern and trashed Roizman and Tsipinyuk's tobacco shop. It was the first shop destroyed. That was how the pogrom began.

It continued for four days. It took over all of Odessa. Then again, the streets in wealthy neighborhoods, like Deribasov and even Richelieu, were only lightly touched by the pogrom, but several streets that housed the Jewish poor were completely destroyed. The pogrom was not like an avalanche, destroying everything in its path, then moving on and not returning to the same place twice. No, the pogrom was everywhere almost simultaneously, and on many streets it continued all four days. That shows the sheer number of its participants. The pogrom was not like a flowing river, but more like a lake, boiling and churning while remaining in place. And the general pattern of the pogrom, so to speak, was also the same almost everywhere. On Tuesday night they smashed windows and trashed shops; on Wednesday they were already getting into apartments; that was also the day of patriotic demonstrations and isolated murders. On Thursday and Friday there were murders in attics and cellars. Apparently, the crowd needed a day and a half of rioting and drinking to finally rise to mass murder. In some places the first crowd of thugs came from outside, as it did in Peresyp, then spread to the locals.[5] Some streets and blocks, on the other hand, were, so to speak, independent in terms of the pogrom. For example, in Slobodka-Romanovka,[6] the pogrom was strictly autonomous: it was organized by the local police, executed using local manpower, and it was local Jews who bore the brunt of the beatings; neither thugs nor anyone to help with self-defense went there from the city, and even now little is known in the city about the Slobodka pogrom.

[. . .]

The three previous days they had been in hiding. By Friday afternoon the pogrom was wrapping up. Friday night their neighbors, who were Russian, assured them that they could go home. They went and sat down for tea. And those same neighbors, it would seem, quietly let the killers in, since they never heard them knocking in the hallway. Suddenly, there was a knock on the door and strangers' footsteps. The tea drinkers all hid: the servant by himself, the father by himself, the mother and daughter together. The killers found the mother and daughter first. They hit the mother in the head with an axe and cut the daughter's arm. Their screams brought the father running, and he was taken down on the spot. The wounded mother was later taken to the hospital, while the daughter got off lightly. Why? Unclear, as much is unclear and mysterious in all these murders. Maybe she was saved because they thought her dead, or because she fainted. The girl did not tell me everything about the murder, and of course I did not question her further. She did not tell me that they had cut off her mother's nose and widened her mouth by a *vershok* on each side,[7] and maybe that was not all . . . Hideousness always brings about shame. These

---

[5] Peresyp, a factory district on the outskirts of the city, was home to Russian workers.
[6] Slobodka-Romanovka was a neighborhood outside the city center where mostly Russians lived.
[7] A unit of measure equal to 1.75 inches.

people, these innocents, not their killers, will always be ashamed of the hideous thing done to them. This mother will always diligently hide her "defect" behind a handkerchief, while her daughter, who can clearly and sonorously relate how cruelly, but not hideously, her father was killed, cannot utter a word about it. The horror, the shame!

"Who were the killers?"

"This time it was pickpockets. And also neighbors—they'd lived nearby for a few years."

"Will you tell the investigator about them?"

"What's it to me? I'll tell everyone."

Death defeats fear. I found this to be true on numerous occasions while roaming Odessa. Those whose loved ones have been killed are not afraid to name the killers, if they know them.

Source: *Odesskii pogrom i samooborona* (Paris: Impremerie Ch. Noblet, 1906), 17–18, 31–32. Translated from the Russian by Eugenia Tietz-Sokolskaya.

Document 4.8. Government Inquiry Accuses Jews of Inciting the Violence

From the government's perspective, the pogrom was a spontaneous display of outrage against the Jews for fomenting revolution and instigating the violence. In its eyes the pogrom was an understandable response by patriotic Russians who felt offended by the celebrants of the October Manifesto: they acted in self-defense and sought to punish the Jews for desecrating portraits of the tsar and forcing bystanders to pay tribute to revolutionary flags. In the following excerpt from his report, Kuzminskii outlined his thinking about the causes of the pogrom.

At the end of last year, Odessa, despite its outward signs of culturedness, was a depressing sight due to the heavy burden on all of the external manifestations of its life. Anxiety among the population was constantly maintained by bombs being discovered or thrown in the city and by individual shots fired; on strike days, the streets were dark, trade and movement ceased, the port was deathly quiet; there were unlawful and violent acts, such as the seizing and shredding of bundles of the newly launched patriotic newspaper *Russkaia rech'* [Russian Speech],[8] demands for money for revolutionary purposes under threats that were then carried out, crowds of truant students from secondary education institutions, and so on. All this had an inevitable effect and eroded confidence in the future. The population was clearly oppressed by the revolutionary movement, which was led by youths, primarily Jews, who paid no heed to the rights of individuals and demonstrated extreme

[8] *Russkaia rech'* was a monarchist newspaper that opposed political reform.

intolerance toward the views of opposing camps. The frightened state of the population was taken advantage of by its lowest classes, such as Odessa's large numbers of hooligans, who used these circumstances to pursue their own self-enriching, criminal objectives. Martial law instituted a relative, albeit forced, calm, but the three and a half months that have passed since the terrors of the Potemkin days and during which it was in place have shown that a mere few days are sufficient for revolution to flare up when it is removed.

The aggregation of all the circumstances described, elucidated by my investigation, give me, in connection with the considerations noted above, grounds to conclude that the October unrest and rioting arose due to undoubtedly revolutionary causes and concluded with a pogrom against Jews solely as a result of members of that particular ethnicity playing a predominant role in the revolutionary movement, and their provocative actions enraging the Russian segment of the city population. As for the horrific scale of the destruction, in terms of both its duration and the resulting significant amount of human death and material damage, it should be primarily attributed to: (1) the unlawful nonfeasance in office of the former Odessa city governor ... Neidgart, against whom I petitioned the State Senate to initiate criminal prosecution, and (2) the criminal actions of several middle and lower ranks of the Odessa city police, whom I have held accountable in court.

In conclusion, it is my duty to most humbly inform Your Imperial Majesty of the excellent work and outstanding effort put forward by the staff placed under my direction by the Ministry of Justice.

Source: *Materialy k istorii russkoi kontr-revoliutsii*. Volume 1: *Pogromy po offitsial'nym dokumentam* (St. Petersburg: Tipografiia Obshchestvennaia pol'za, 1908), ccxiv–ccxv. Translated from the Russian by Eugenia Tietz-Sokolskaya.

Document 4.9. Government Inquiry Accuses City Governor of Malfeasance

Senator Kuzminskii castigated Neidgart for his decision to withdraw all police from their posts on the afternoon of October 18. The reasons for Neidgart's action are unclear, since his reports were contradictory and conflicted with accounts of other police officials and civilian leaders. The city governor claimed that he was seeking to protect the lives of policemen, for they were subject to attack by celebrants of the October Manifesto. Kuzminskii found that Neidgart violated protocol that was supposed to ensure that he would enlist the assistance of the military during times of civil unrest. The government concluded that Neidgart had left Odessa defenseless, thereby giving free reign to those Odessans intent on toppling the autocracy. Kuzminksii felt he had no choice but to recommend the dismissal of Neidgart and the bringing of criminal charges against him.

The information laid out clearly points to the fact that on October 18 City Governor Neidgart did not, whether personally or through his subordinate police force or using the troops, take any measures to disperse the revolutionarily inclined crowds that had assembled in the city streets, clearly expressing a lack of respect for the Supreme power and a sympathy toward the rebellion whose aim was the coercive destruction of the existing order in the country, but instead, without any worthy reasons and contrary to the provisions of the law, ordered the removal of policemen from their posts and thereby stripped the population of protection and himself of the agents of authority through which he could have suppressed the revolt and restored order. At the same time, the student militia, which turned out to consist of members of the extremist revolutionary parties, was allowed into the city; it did not restrict its actions to repelling attacks on Jews and their property, but rather fired on troops passing by in the streets; and nevertheless the City Duma resolved during its meeting on October 18 "to express sincere and deep gratitude to the students of the Novorossiiskii University for their energetic, reasonable and selfless actions to protect the peace in the city on October 18." For his part, Police Chief Golovin reported to City Governor Neidgart that same day on the need to remove the militia and re-institute the police posts, pointing out that it was impossible to restore order while the militia was allowed in the city, and since his report was not given due weight, he submitted his resignation and was replaced by another person.

[...]

Neidgart ... exhibited complete inaction when it came to taking efficacious measures to quell the riots. His inaction also affected the police force: after he recalled the policemen from their posts on the eighteenth, even though he ordered that they be sent to patrol around the city, there was no organization imposed on this kind of service, the patrols acted without any oversight, and their appearance did nothing at all to stop or at least lessen the destruction. The city governor himself rode through the city only once, under the protection of a strong escort, and that was not until the fourth day of the riots, when the pogrom began to quiet down; the rest of the time he stayed at home, requiring the police chiefs to be constantly present at the stations. Fearing for their lives, they and their deputies very rarely appeared in the streets, and would not appear at all where the major skirmishes were happening. Other than the occasional assignment to a patrol ... policemen either sat in the stations with nothing to do or, as the investigation discovered, appeared in the midst of the action, often having changed clothes, as participants in the pogrom and looting.

In addition, City Governor Neidhart's inaction also manifested itself in his refusals to assist persons and institutions who sent him requests for protection from attacks and destruction, saying that he was unable to do anything and sending the petitioners to the university: "Go to the university," he told Brakhman, the director of a mutual loan society, "the protection of the city is gathered there now." In response to numerous requests from residents of Odessa to reinstate posted police protection, he published a print announcement dated October 20, in which he informed the population that "this is possible only if ten citizens will stand next to each policeman, to whom he can entrust his life." . . . Thus, the protection of the city . . . was left to the initiative of the residents themselves. . . .

Neidgart is subject to the accusation that, in his position as city governor of Odessa, having the ability to prevent and suppress the armed conflict between Odessa's Russian and Jewish populations, he permitted Jewish revolutionary mobs to hold demonstrations throughout the city and to affront insolently the Imperial Government and Russian patriotic feelings, and did not use the means at his disposal to disperse these mobs. . . . The next day he allowed a Russian patriotic demonstration, without giving warning of the threat of a confrontation with Jews who had once again gathered in the streets, and not only did not take any measures at all to prevent such a confrontation, but instead, at the very start of the marches on the eighteenth, having no right under law and no legitimate grounds to do so, ordered without permission that the police be recalled from their outside posts, and, having thus left the city with no police protection, did nothing himself to restore order and at the same time did not transfer to the military commander the authority to independently use force to quell the riots that had arisen . . . thereby engaging in malfeasance of office, which to a large extent contributed to the fact that the conflict that began on October 18 between two hostile factions of the population did not end until October 22 and was accompanied by a great many people killed and wounded, as well as by the destruction and looting of property worth a significant amount—in short, in a criminal act as described by Article 341, Part 2 of the Penal Code.

Source: *Materialy k istorii russkoi kontr-revoliutsii*. Volume 1: *Pogromy po offitsial'nym dokumentam* (St. Petersburg: Tipografiia Obshchestvennaia pol'za, 1908), clxxvi–clxxvii, 11–13. Translated from the Russian by Eugenia Tietz-Sokolskaya.

Document 4.10. Testimony Given by Witness Teplitskii to Senator Kuzminskii on November 25, 1905

Many contemporaries blamed civilian and military authorities, particularly Neidgart, for not only encouraging but even sponsoring the pogromists. Some testimony collected by the government inquiry hints at lower-level police involvement in the planning and organization of the patriotic counterdemonstration and pogrom. The violence and destruction were in large measure made possible by the failure of the authorities to adopt any countermeasures. In fact, policemen reportedly compiled lists of Jewish-owned stores and Jews' apartments to facilitate attacks. Other evidence indicated that policemen were instructed not to interfere with pogromists. An army captain stated that a policeman had told him that his superiors had given their permission for three days of beating because Jews had destroyed the tsar's portrait in the municipal duma. Low-ranking policemen and soldiers did not interfere with the pogromists, and in several instances some participated in the looting and killing. At times, policemen, seeking to avenge the attacks of October 16 and 18 on their colleagues and on themselves by self-defense brigades once the pogrom broke out, went so far as to provide protection for pogromists by firing on members of the Jewish self-defense units. Some policemen discharged their weapons into the air and told the rioters that the shots had come from apartments inhabited by Jews, leaving the latter vulnerable to vicious beatings and murder. Eyewitnesses reported seeing policemen directing pogromists to Jewish-owned stores or Jews' apartments, while preventing the rioters from damaging the property of non-Jews. In addition, policemen and pogromist agitators went door to door and spread rumors that Jews were slaughtering Russian families, urging Russian residents to repel the Jews with force. For their part, soldiers, concluding from the actions of the police that higher authorities sanctioned the pogrom, stood idly by while pogromists looted stores and murdered unarmed Jews. The following excerpt is the testimony of Lev Teplitskii, a reserve soldier who told Kuzminskii that he believed soldiers and police were planning to use force against Jews as punishment for their perceived role in instigating the current wave of strikes and disorder in Odessa.

Before being drafted from the reserves, I served as deputy auditor in the Odessa city administration, where I still work. To provide military protection for the city in case of rioting, the entire city was divided into sectors, each of which was entrusted to a specific military unit for protection. The troop in which I serve was responsible for the Aleksandrov sector; from the fifteenth to the sixteenth of October, I had to be with my unit . . . and I gathered from the conversations of police officials that they all believe Jews to be behind the . . . displays of various forms of unrest and for that reason are dead set against them. One could conclude from their words that there was some action being planned against the Jews, like a pogrom; police officer Ratsishevskii himself, not at all inhibited by my presence and apparently not considering the possibility that I may disagree with him on this matter, stated openly: "They wanted freedom—now we'll take down two–three thousand of them, then they'll know what freedom is." From what lower-ranking officers told me, I knew that similar conversations were also taking place among the policemen, who were talking favorably about beating the Jews. These same lower-ranking officers communicated that, according to the policemen, Neidgart had recently come to the station and trained the lower-ranking officers in how to slash and use their weapons, conducting experiments with using sabers to cut ribbons and inspecting the sabers to ensure they had been sharpened. The soldiers themselves saw the policemen practicing with their sabers on dummies labeled "striker" and "student."

    I spent the twenty-four hours between the seventeenth and eighteenth protecting the city's water supply; early in the morning on the eighteenth, a group of poor workers, looking like tramps and somewhat drunk, stopped near me . . . and addressed me, saying: "We're coming from the police station, Your Honor, got 'structions' (probably 'instructions') from there, we'll make a killing this evening." I did not enter into a conversation with the half-drunken group and did not clarify the meaning of these words; but, in conjunction with the prior conversations in the station, including the statement cited, I began to suspect that a Jewish pogrom was in the works, one that would erupt in the near future.

On October 18, when we received news of the manifesto, I spent all morning walking around various streets; everywhere there were large groups of people, composed of respectable, middle-class intelligentsia; everyone was in a joyous mood, there was general gaiety everywhere, but in every place it was orderly and completely calm. Around four in the afternoon, crowds of a different nature began appearing: large groups of some sort of tramps, workers, and young people walking around the streets with icons, portraits of the tsar, and national flags. These groups comprised exclusively Christians, whereas the other groups had both Christians and Jews, as well as red flags without any revolutionary slogans. Only on Kherson Street, not far from the university, there were two black flags in the crowd with the inscription "Rest in peace, fighters for freedom." I think there was a third such flag. I did not hear anything to the effect that Jews had destroyed the "God save the tsar" inscription in the Duma building; on the contrary, I was told that this inscription had been accidentally destroyed by lower-ranking officers who had been instructed to take down a red flag from the Duma building. By evening, rumors began coming in that on Dal'nits Street on the outskirts there had been a confrontation with Jews. This news surprised me greatly, as it completely contradicted what I had seen myself in the central part of the city. . . . I had not seen any entirely Jewish groups in the city that day. I headed toward Dal'nits Street, but was unable to reach the actual scene of the action, as a rifle barrage sounded—troops were already there and the area was cordoned off. Students and both the student and Jewish self-defense groups wanted to get through, but the troops did not let them, shooting not at the mob that had started the riots, but off to the side, as if shooting back at those who wanted to get closer to the mob.

Signed, *Teplitskii*

Source: *Materialy k istorii russkoi kontr-revoliutsii.* Volume 1: *Pogromy po offitsial'nym dokumentam* (St. Petersburg: Tipografiia Obshchestvennaia pol'za, 1908), 100–3. Translated from the Russian by Eugenia Tietz-Sokolskaya.

5

Pogroms in World War I Russia

Polly Zavadivker

The Jewish population in the Russian Empire experienced mass violence during World War I. Widespread atrocities against Jewish civilians typically involved extensive destruction and theft of property, as well as physical brutality and the rape of women. The majority of wartime pogroms against Jews were carried out in 1914–1915 by the Russian military in war zones. Isolated pogroms also occurred in home-front cities, driven not by the army but by local residents; in these pogroms, the victims included Jews along with others associated with the German enemy, namely, Germans, Poles, and Mennonites.

The role of the Russian army constituted a fundamental feature of wartime anti-Jewish violence. The military's participation also distinguished war pogroms from earlier "pogrom waves" in Russian imperial history (1881–1882, 1903–1906). These wartime attacks on Jews, which one historian has called "military pogroms," should be understood as part of a sweeping campaign waged by the Russian government against "enemy aliens," or subject populations that the state and military identified as unreliable and disloyal groups, and thus as national security threats.[1] However, it is important to register distinctions between the kind of violence that the Russian army visited upon Jews and other "enemy alien" groups such as Germans, Poles, and other foreign subjects. The sheer numbers of documented anti-Jewish pogroms (in the dozens), as well as the dehumanizing nature of the violence—the rape of Jewish women most notably—occurred on an unparalleled scale.

This campaign against "enemy aliens" and its ideology led to the Russian army's decision to order deportations of hundreds of thousands of Jews, Germans, Poles, Latvians, and other populations from front zones in 1914–1915. It is in the framework of these military expulsions that extensive violence against Jewish communities repeatedly unfolded at local levels. Moreover, some army commanders tolerated the participation of not only soldiers but also local civilian populations in these pogroms. In this way, the Russian army's wartime policies and practices legitimized acts of popular violence against Jews, sending the message to soldiers and civilians alike that their actions against "enemy aliens" could be perceived as reprisals and thus go unpunished.

---

[1] Eric Lohr, *Nationalizing the Russian Empire: The Campaign against Enemy Aliens during World War I* (Cambridge, MA: Harvard University Press, 2003), 145.

Polly Zavadivker, *Pogroms in World War I Russia* In: *Pogroms.* Edited by: Eugene M. Avrutin and Elissa Bemporad, Oxford University Press. © Oxford University Press 2021. DOI: 10.1093/oso/9780190060084.003.0006

К. Говоаровъ. 1914.

Л Объявили мобилизацію
И казакъ сталъ какъ гроза
Хватитъ съ нѣмцами лизаться
Намозолили намъ глаза.

Postcard celebrating the heroism of Cossack soldiers in the Russian army, 1914. The soldier is drawn in an iconic folk style. He sits astride a horse with his saber drawn. Drawing by K. Govoiarov. The poem reads: "Mobilization was announced / And the Cossack rose like thunder. / Stop cuddling up to the Germans, / They are a thorn in our side."

Courtesy of the Blavatnik Archive

Military pogroms of 1914–1915 played out as part of the wartime encounter between Jewish civilians and the Russian army. The tsar's war statute of July 16, 1914, granted almost unlimited control to the army and commander in chief over civilian populations under military rule. The front line between Russian and German forces, and between Russian and Austro-Hungarian forces, traversed large parts of the Pale of Jewish Settlement.

Postcard of Russian cavalry with weapons drawn, speeding on horseback through a town in flames. Observers described pogroms being started by advance cavalry units. The image conveys the power and force that armed combatants possessed and could wield against defenseless civilians. Unknown artist.
Courtesy of the Blavatnik Archive

The Russian military carried out anti-Jewish violence in two distinct areas under its control, first in the Habsburg provinces of Galicia and Bukovina, which the Russian army occupied early in the war, from the fall of 1914 to the spring of 1915. In September 1914, Russian troops in passing military units carried out unsanctioned atrocities against Jews in the Galician cities of Brody and Lwów (Lemberg), burning Jewish neighborhoods and killing dozens of people (an estimated seventeen Jews and two Christians in Lwów, and eighteen Jews and one Christian in Brody).[2] Eyewitnesses in Brody claimed that some officers alleged that a "Jewish girl" provoked the attacks by shooting at Russian troops. Anti-Jewish violence in Galicia assumed increasingly brutal forms over the following months and spread to surrounding towns. The well-known Russian Jewish writer S. An-sky witnessed the aftermath of an attack in Sokal in the spring of 1915, where stunned residents recounted the perpetrators' savagery. The Russian Jewish soldier Aba Lev's harrowing account of a pogrom in the city of Buczacz revealed that the army inflicted equally if not more vicious atrocities after occupying Galicia a second time in the summer of 1916.

The Russian army unleashed a second spate of pogroms along its northwestern front during the Great Retreat of April to September 1915. Over nearly five months, Austro-Hungarian and German armies forced the Russians hundreds of kilometers

---

[2] Semion Gol'din, *Russkaia armiia i evrei 1914–1917* (Moscow: Gesharim, 2018), 286.

Русская пѣхота на улицахъ Львова.

Photograph of Russian infantry forces marching down a main street in occupied Lemberg, Habsburg Galicia (now L'viv, Ukraine), 1914. Civilian onlookers watch the triumphant procession from the sidewalks. Shortly after occupying Lemberg in September 1914, Russian troops carried out a pogrom in the city's Jewish neighborhood.
Courtesy of the Blavatnik Archive

to the east, managing to occupy large sections of Poland, Lithuania, and Belarus. The Russian army's scorched earth practices during the retreat enabled the pogroms. Soldiers received orders to burn crops, destroy property, and remove "unreliable" populations to keep them from enemy hands. These orders provided commanders with a framework to sanction violence against civilians whom the army had a priori declared to be "enemy aliens."

Thus, while prior to April 1915 there were a few documented cases of pogroms, between May and October 1915 the army carried out dozens of them. One observer, G. M. Erlikh, described these pogroms in an essay of January 1916. Erlikh argued that Cossack units had played a dominant role as perpetrators of the army's 1915 pogroms in Kovno, Vilna, Minsk, and Volhynia provinces. This fact may seem overdetermined, given the iconic status that Jewish collective memory has assigned to Cossacks as proverbial pogrom-mongers. Yet only during World War I did Cossacks first play a widespread role in waging pogroms. An investigation into fifty-four pogroms from April to October 1915 found that soldiers initiated fifty-one of them; in forty-one of those (about 80 percent), violence had commenced only after Cossack units arrived.[3] This is partly because Cossacks made up 70 percent

---

[3] Eric Lohr, "The Russian Army and the Jews: Mass Deportation, Hostages, and Violence during World War I," *Russian Review* 60, no. 3 (2001): 416.

of wartime cavalries—units that led advances and often first appeared in towns in which the residents were targeted for deportation. Army commanders thus effectively positioned Cossack soldiers, men known as merciless warriors, in locations where they could carry out pogroms. Furthermore, while Cossacks carried out the violence against Jews, they also found willing helpers among the local peasants. A pattern emerged whereby the appearance of Cossacks drew peasants to a town, equipped with carts, prepared to retrieve loot. While both the Cossacks and peasants acted with agency, they received their cues from a pervasive culture of anti-Jewish violence.

We have little evidence of Jewish responses to pogroms other than flight and hiding. There are few records of Jewish self-defense. In one case, forty Jewish soldiers defended people during the pogrom of September 1915 in Smorgon; elsewhere, Jews appealed to local officers to disperse the rioters, which led to at least one successful intervention. Otherwise, it appears that troops brutalized Jews with untrammeled impunity and sometimes a nudge from their officers, as the Russian nurse Sofia Fedorchenko's account reveals.

As noted earlier, Jews were the primary, but not exclusive, targets of wartime pogroms in Russia. Popular violence was also directed at German subjects. One of the most widely documented incidents occurred in Moscow on May 26–29, 1915, when local mobs wounded and killed Germans and destroyed vast numbers of homes and businesses, resulting in estimated damages of 72 million rubles. In comparing wartime violence against Germans and Jews it is important to underline a basic feature of the state's wartime campaign against enemy aliens, whose messages depicted the "problem" and "solution" in simple terms: an incitement to action against Jews and Germans as foreign dominators of the Russian economy whose presence should be reduced, if not eliminated.

Why did the state and military label Jews as "enemy aliens"? The stereotype of Jews as spies, traitors, and profiteering speculators had its roots in nineteenth-century Russian military discourse and literary culture. For decades before the war, Russian military academies instructed officers that whereas loyalty and patriotism were supposedly inherent qualities of ethnic Russians, Jews constituted an "unreliable" population with proclivities to commit treason.[4]

These negative stereotypes—familiar antisemitic canards presented in the guise of "military science"—influenced the Russian High Command's policies regarding Jews. Conspiracy theories voiced by the commander in chief, Grand Duke Nikolai Nikolaevich, and Chief of Staff Nikolai Ianushkevich, alleged that Jewish spies lurked within and beyond the army. Army commanders also treated Jewish civilians as potential saboteurs. Wartime espionage tales seemed to borrow from medieval examples: in one town in Volhynia province, a local priest alleged that

---

[4] Peter Holquist, "To Count, to Extract, To Exterminate: Population Statistics and Population Politics in Late Imperial and Soviet Russia," in *A State of Nations: Empire and Nation-Making in the Age of Lenin and Stalin*, ed. Ronald Grigor Suny and Terry Martin (Oxford: Oxford University Press, 2001), 115.

Jews hid a telephone in a cow's stomach to communicate with the enemy. In a self-fulfilling feedback loop, each Russian military defeat spurred further allegations of Jewish espionage. In the town of Kuzhi, it was alleged in April 1915 that Jews sheltered German soldiers in their homes. A government investigation proved the allegations baseless—most likely the invention of officers who "slept through" an enemy attack. The contents of Russian counterintelligence files suggest that hundreds of similar charges appeared, leading to the arrest and execution of the alleged spies.[5] Rumors of Jewish espionage also supplied a basis for military orders to expel Jewish communities. Did these claims have any truth to them? While Jewish enemy agents undoubtedly existed in wartime Russia, the accusations of widespread espionage were wildly exaggerated, and hundreds of thousands of Jews were punished for the actions of a dozen or at most a few hundred people.

As the war continued into its second and third years, new varieties of rumors emerged. A reshuffling of government ministers and the High Command in August 1915 augured the chance that the state and army might cease to blame Jews for their own failures. This did not happen. If before then the main charge against Jews was espionage, by late 1915 it morphed into their alleged responsibility for most of the state, economy, and society's basic problems. As food shortages and the high cost of basic necessities grew, the message that Jews and Germans dominated the declining economy fueled popular anger of a kind that periodically exploded into riots.

Two government circulars in 1915 and 1916 played a notorious role in cementing views of Jews as "unreliable" and "unpatriotic" subjects. These circulars spread claims that Jews plotted to subvert the Russian war effort using economic means, including hoarding, speculation, and revolutionary incitement. The first circular of July 23, 1915, from the Ministry of Finance to its departments throughout the country, stated that Jews were collaborating with Germans to burn crops in Russia. A second circular dated January 9, 1916, from the acting director of the Department of Police, K. D. Kafafov, stated that Jews were hoarding currency and food. The latter document reveals the extent to which some Russian military and bureaucratic elites believed in some secret conspiracy among Jews to destroy Russia through military defeat or socialist revolution. When the historian S. M. Dubnov referred to the Kafafov circular as a "pogrom circular," he keenly intuited its creators' sensibilities.[6] Such rumors did often precede the eruption of pogroms. Similarly, the pogrom in the Siberian city of Krasnoiarsk on May 7, 1916, which began as a protest over food shortages and inflation, was directed almost entirely at Jews.

The pogroms in Russia's Great War remain a little-known chapter in the history of anti-Jewish violence. In retrospect, they might be viewed as a prologue to pogroms of the Russian Civil War from 1918 to 1921. Many Jewish activists who chronicled atrocities in those years looked back to 1914–1915 as a reference point,

[5] Gol'din, *Russkaia armiia*, 209–22.
[6] Diary of February 8, 1916, in S. M. Dubnov, *Kniga zhizni: Vospominaniia i razmyshleniia: Materialy dlia istorii moego vremeni*, ed. Viktor Kel'ner (St. Petersburg: Peterburgskoe vostokovedenie, 1998), 360.

knowing that anti-Jewish massacres in 1919 capped nearly five years of uninterrupted warfare. The years from 1914 to 1921 can be characterized as a period of continuous excesses, beginning with the anti-Jewish violence of 1914 and culminating in the Russian Civil War pogroms. Continuities among the pogrom perpetrators are telling: a majority of Volunteer (or White) Army officers in 1919 had served in World War I with the imperial army, as had a large number of soldiers; and during both the world war and the civil war, military violence toward the Jewish population was ordered from above and was reinforced by libelous propaganda. Yet, in contrast to the Russian army pogroms of 1914–1915, *all* belligerents in the civil war practiced anti-Jewish violence in 1918–1921: Ukrainian troops, the Volunteer Army, and, to a lesser extent, the Red Army. The Russian imperial army's violence during World War I provided them with a model for how to channel popular aggression toward Jews, along with vocabulary and imagery to justify it: the treasonous or "enemy agent" Jews, whose very existence threatened their cause. The exact nature of the threat that Jews allegedly posed remained remarkably malleable—they could be as easily depicted as Bolsheviks as they could "enemies of the revolution." At various times during the civil war, the Reds, Whites, and others imagined themselves to have been lethally betrayed by Jews. The idea endured in the Russian popular imagination and as an effective incitement to violence in the years ahead.

Document 5.1. A Jewish Military Doctor's Account from Galicia

Eyewitnesses who traveled with the Russian army described pogroms that took place in September 1914, soon after the Russian army occupied Austro-Hungarian Galicia. These pogroms were among the first carried out by the Russian army during the war. The author is a self-described Jewish military doctor and activist from Petrograd. The account draws from the author's experiences while traveling throughout Galicia as part of an army division.

I stopped at Brody to make inquiries. All over the town are obvious notes of riot and fire. The main street of the town and all Jewish quarters bear evidence of shooting and destruction. The ancient synagogue was not spared. Happily no one was in it during the cannonade, and no fight took place there. Some officers and officials explained to me that the shooting and the rioting were provoked by a Jewish girl, who killed a Russian officer when the Cossacks entered the town.

Nine Jews were killed and by an accident one Christian woman was shot. A glance at Brody and its population suffices to show that all crimes of military character ascribed to the Jews are complete nonsense. If a Russian officer were really killed, it is more reasonable to believe that a disguised soldier shot him. The reprisals were taken only on the Jews. In the windows of the Christian flats and houses were and are still to be seen crosses and holy pictures. Everything reminds you of the Jewish pogroms in Russia.

Although seven weeks have passed, the Jewish population has not yet recovered from the horrors they suffered. But the situation of the Jews of the Galician towns and villages, where the Russian troops passed, is still worse. Robbery and murder, arson and complete demolition of Jewish property, violation of women and physical insult of everybody else were common occurrences. I have heard it from the victims of these exploits, I have heard it from the soldiers themselves, who naively reported what they had done, being sure that no wrong was committed by them, since it was permitted by the *nachal'stvo* (authorities). [...]

The ruin of the Jewish population of Galicia is almost complete—the houses are leveled to the ground and the property destroyed. The methods were everywhere the same: after some provocative shot of a never disclosed person came robbery, fire, and massacre. The estates of the Jewish landowners have been ruined. Troops arriving at an estate asked only if the owner was a Jew. Jewish estates were at once wildly devastated. Many of the Jewish estates have been confiscated.

That the army officers are antisemites is a commonly known fact. Everybody who has had a chance of being in their company affirms it. I (the author of this letter, a military doctor, a Jew, and a well-known and very active social worker in Petrograd) once spent a night with a great number of officers of different ranks and regiments, and I am compelled, although with deep sorrow, to acknowledge that I have heard and seen things which surpassed all my fears. The "Jew" was the chief topic of conversation, anecdotes, menaces, and songs. One young officer, whose only exploits had consisted in demolishing Jewish houses, gained the sincerest applause of the company by his very picturesque tales of his deeds of destruction in the numerous Jewish towns of Galicia which had been visited by him and his troops.

Source: Institute for Jewish Research Archives (YIVO), Lucien Wolf and David Mowshowitch Papers, Record group 348, folder 58, microfilm #4760–63.

Document 5.2. S. An-sky Describes the Radivilov Pogrom

The Russian Jewish folklorist and writer S. An-sky (1863–1920) traveled throughout the front zones in 1914–1915. He worked on behalf of the Petrograd-based Jewish Committee to Aid War Victims. During his travels he recorded stories of his encounters with Jewish civilians. In the diary entry that follows, he describes accounts of a pogrom in Radivilov that Cossacks in the Russian army perpetrated in August 1914.

January 16, 1915

Radivilov. A large border town. At first glance it appears to be full of life. There is a crowd of soldiers in the market, brisk bargaining. However, complete ruin is concealed behind this exterior. Apart from the destruction of the town's custom-house, the town itself, which made its living from the border, was also destroyed. The Austrians entered the town one week after war was declared, but stayed for only a few hours and then left. Cossacks entered the town right after they left, and bacchanalia immediately ensued. They destroyed the best stores and warehouses; whatever they couldn't take was smashed to bits, and peasants from surrounding villages took what was left. Precious few trading stalls survived the destruction, which continued for several days. What is curious is that these Cossacks had been stationed in Radivilov for the past twelve years and were familiar with everyone. Several hundred people hid in the synagogue. The Cossacks wanted to break in there, but apparently one Christian who was guarding them came out, shielded the door with his body, and started to rebuke the Cossacks for attacking poor defenseless people.

Source: S. An-sky, *The 1915 Diary of S. An-sky: A Russian-Jewish Writer at the Eastern Front*, trans. Polly Zavadivker (Bloomington: Indiana University Press, 2016), 48.

Document 5.3. S. An-sky Witnesses the Aftermath of the Sokal Pogrom and Flight of Jews from Gorokhov, June 1915

In spring and summer 1915 An-sky traveled alongside the Russian army as its forces retreated from Galicia. He later recounted episodes from this time in a six-hundred-page Yiddish memoir known as The Destruction of Galicia *(Khurbn Galitsye). In the first passage, he describes the aftermath of a Russian army pogrom in Sokal, a large town in Galicia northeast of Lwow. In the second passage he portrays Jewish refugees passing through the small town of Vatyn, in Volhynia province of the Russian Empire.*

Sokal is a city center. It used to be known as a rich and beautiful town. I arrived there on the Sabbath, and at first glance I couldn't figure out the reason for the deathly silence and closed shops—was it because of the Sabbath, or because of the pogrom that the town had just endured? When I looked more closely, however, I saw broken and nailed-up doors, shattered windows, and twisted iron gates that had been ripped from the storefronts. When I peered beyond the battered doors inside the stores, I saw pogrom destruction: everything had been broken, ripped, shot up. There wasn't a single Jew walking along the main streets.

I turned off into the side streets. I wandered along them, one after another. I didn't see a single soldier here. Just small Jewish houses. Then a bit farther, an enormous, gigantic old stone synagogue from the seventeenth century, among the most beautiful of all synagogues. Old people, women, and children sat on the porches of the little houses nearby, all with their heads hanging low, depressed, as if reciting lamentations on the ninth of Av. [. . .]

I went into a hotel, rented a room, started talking with the owner (an old Jewish woman), and asked her what happened in the city. "They ruined the town. They spent the whole week stealing, breaking, beating people. They didn't spare a single home or shop. How many Jews were killed or badly wounded? Maybe a few hundred. A clockmaker was murdered, leaving behind a wife with eight children. [. . .] That's what we do know, but there's a lot we don't. People have found children without mothers wandering in the woods, and no one has any idea to where their mothers have disappeared. [. . .] A Cossack chopped off my daughter's hand with his sword." She spoke in a monotone, quietly and with tears streaming from her eyes.

[. . .]

Vatyn is a large town, about thirty versts from the old Russian border, between Vladimir-Volynsk and Lutsk. [. . .] Apparently Vatyn was a transit point for refugees from locations that were near the front. From morning to night, wagons with homeless Jews, mostly from the shtetl of Gorokhov [Horokhiv], rumbled past the house that our division had occupied. Long wagons were packed with all kinds of household items. Children sat in the middle of them, with old people and women surrounding them, like birds in a nest. Men followed behind each wagon on foot. It had the appearance of a funeral procession.

It seemed that they had fled from their shtetl out of fear of a pogrom, and more so that they would be suddenly expelled. [. . .] They didn't want to travel very far from their homes; maybe they would be allowed to return shortly. [. . .] Since I crossed the old Russian border a few weeks ago, I had realized that this vast area, which contained several dozens of Russia's Jewish cities and small towns, had been struck by an awful dark cloud of terror and despair. [. . .] The mood here was the same it had been among the Galician Jews. Everywhere, from hour to hour, they await two plagues: a pogrom and a sudden mass expulsion. This had completely para-lyzed normal life in the shtetls, causing widespread panic and flight without order, without destination—only to save themselves and fast.

Source: Sh. An-ski, *Der Yudisher Khurbn fun poylen galitsye un bukovina, fun tog-bukh 1914–1917*, in *Gezamelte shriftn in fuftsen bender*, vols. 4–6 (Vilna, Poland: Farlag An-ski, 1921–28), 5:97–98, 116–18. Translated from the Yiddish by Polly Zavadivker.

Document 5.4. Causes of the Anti-German Pogrom in Moscow, May 26–29, 1915

Like Jews, the Russian Empire's German subjects were labeled as an "enemy alien" group during World War I and became the targets of the state's nationalizing economic policies, as well as widespread popular anger. The latter reached a fever pitch in a wave of anti-German pogroms that swept Moscow on May 26–29, 1915. Over four days, local mobs robbed, set fire to homes and businesses, and murdered several Germans, causing nearly 72 million rubles in estimated damage. An independent government investigation into the causes of the riots, led by Senator I. S. Krasheninnikov, chairman of the Petrograd Chamber of Justice, released its findings in September 1915. In a 1916 article published in the journal Vestnik Evropy, *the Russian liberal politician and legal scholar V. D. Kuzmin-Karavaev (1859–1928) cited from the Krasheninnikov report, singling out the role of the Moscow chief of police A. A. Adrianov, who had allegedly witnessed the pogrom but took no measures to disperse the crowds until after they had already inflicted significant damage.*

In an entire series of orders concerning the Moscow police issued in preparation for potential unrest, General Adrianov declared the use of weapons completely imper-missible and suggested that words of exhortation be used to influence the crowd. [. . .] General Adrianov, in trying to influence the pogrom-mongers, even walked with them at one point along Myasnitskaya Street. When the crowd ahead of them stopped at one company's store and a hooligan who had split off from the crowd went into the store to "check their papers," General Adrianov addressed the crowd with these words: "Gentlemen, this is a Russian company, let us move farther on." The crowd heeded him, did not ransack this store, moved on, and ransacked stores that were "farther on." [. . .]

This phrase, uttered by General Adrianov to a crowd of pogrom-mongers on the second day of unrest, after nearly half of Moscow had been ransacked, at least on the outskirts, and after brutal murders had taken place, this phrase "Gentlemen, this is a Russian company, let us move farther on," essentially covers all the other information that Senator Krasheninnikov collected. Indeed, could the crowd have interpreted a phrase like this in any way other than as, if not explicit permission, then as tacit consent by the police to ransacking non-Russian companies? Could the crowd not believe that it was engaging in a patriotic act when it saw the highest executive of police authority walking with it, his head bare?

In response to a plea from N. I. Prokhorov, the owner of one of Moscow's largest factories, to stop the crowd's movement, General Adrianov said: "When a crowd walks with a portrait of His Majesty, sings 'God Save the Tsar' and 'God Save Your People,' then I am willing to line up at its head and will not disperse it." This was at the very beginning of the unrest. But even when the rioting was in full swing, General Adrianov did not change his understanding of how to approach a crowd that was singing prayers and the national anthem and walking with His Majesty's portrait, no matter what such a crowd did. [...]

If a crowd is dominated by one political movement, shots are fired into it the moment it is formed, even if it is a peaceful demonstration showing no signs of a threat; if, on the other hand, different movements dominate, repressive measures are applied only when it is too late. This is what the vast experience of the tragic memories of Jewish pogroms tells us. This is how the May rioting in Moscow became such a horrific scene.

[...] Horrific riots have taken place, accompanied by 50 million rubles worth of damage, looting, arson, and the murder of several persons. The rioting took place in the context of an irrefutably established lack of countermeasures by the police. It has been equally irrefutably established that orders from above came from both the minister of internal affairs and the governor-general. And both public officials are defending themselves by shunting responsibility from one to the other. Neither one says simply and succinctly: "I'm at fault." Both, therefore, consider themselves guilt-free before their own consciences. What is this responsibility of which so much has been said, which is used to justify the granting of emergency powers to top administrators, and which, as soon as there is a concrete question about it, dissipates like a wisp of smoke? Who, then, is at fault in what happened? The minister says, "Not I." The governor-general says, "Not I." So who? Is it really going to be the proverbial fall guy time and time again? [...]

On May 27, after listening to a report that the crowd is "currently" beating one Karlsen, General Adrianov said nothing, got into his car, and left. Afterward, Karlsen was killed. A different report, concerning the murder of two women, similarly elicited no order from Adrianov. He again said nothing and ordered the chauffeur to drive. On May 28, while the Einem store was being ransacked, Adrianov was standing about twenty paces away from where the crime was being committed, but issued no orders. In the evening on the same day, during one of the governor-general's outings, a subordinate police officer reported that the Koss and Dur office near the Red Gate was under attack, in view of the police patrol posted at Prince

Yusupov's residence. Without exiting his car, Gen. Adrianov watched the attack, did not summon the patrol, and left. The office was ransacked, still in view of the police patrol posted nearby. This last incident is the most typical illustration of the legal nature of what Gen. Adrianov is guilty of. He condoned looting and should be tried together with the pogrom-mongers.

Source: V. D. Kuzmin-Karavaev, "Raport senatora Krashenininkov o maiskikh bezporiadkakh v Moskve," *Vestnik Evropy* 51, no. 2 (February 1916), 363–64, 367–68. Translated from the Russian by Eugenia Tietz-Sokolskaya.

Document 5.5. Russian Military Pogroms in Kovno, Vilna, and Minsk Provinces

G. M. Erlikh was a well-known Bundist leader in Petrograd. Together with a team of Jewish activists in 1914–1915, he took part in compiling a wartime narrative history and document volume titled From the "Black Book" of Imperial Russian Jewry. *Nearly one-third of the volume is devoted to the subject of anti-Jewish pogroms carried out by the Russian army from July to October 1915. The following accounts describe a series of military pogroms in Kovno, Vilna, and Minsk provinces.*

Our army's retreat, which began on April 18, 1915, with the German breakthrough at Gorlice (in Galicia) and ended far to the northwest along the line from the Kovno fortress to Brest-Litovsk, was accompanied by two phenomena: scorched earth in the abandoned territories and mass expulsions of the male populations from seventeen to forty-five years old, on the one hand; and an endless string of violence against the civilian population on the other. [. . .] The second of these, pogroms, was the exclusive privilege of the Jewish population. [. . .] The time and place [of the pogroms] were both determined in part by a series of military actions, and namely the movement of retreating forces from west to east. [. . .]

However, the Jewish pogroms that took place in summer and fall 1915 are internally and logically linked to all of the central governmental and military authorities' policies regarding Jews, which appeared earlier, at the start of the war. These conscious and systematic policies found their complete expression in the mass expulsions of May, which placed Russian Jewry beyond the boundaries of civil society and outside the law, and in this manner, created a foundation for the pogroms. [. . .]

Pogroms in Kovno Province, July 1915

During the first half of July, the Germans, who had begun an advance on their left flank toward the Baltic territories, turned toward the southwest and southeast, transferring the operation to the borders of Kovno and Vilna provinces. At the end of July, after Warsaw was taken, the enemy strengthened its activities in the Vilna and Kovno regions. An evacuation of Vilna began on August 5, although the city remained in Russian hands until early September. Kovno fell on August 7 and Grodno was cleansed on August 20. [. . .]

The retreat of our [Russian] forces was accompanied on every front by anti-Jewish pogroms, and often by mass expulsions of the Jewish population, usually carried out under orders from the commanding officer, and sometimes even at the whim of soldiers without any higher orders. It was primarily Cossacks and dragoons who looted and wrecked property. The infantry took part only in rare instances. On the contrary, sometimes the arrival of infantry units helped to stop pogroms, as in Dokshitsy. With the exception of a few purely military pogroms, some parts of the local Christian populations wrought havoc alongside the Cossacks. [. . .]

According to the available information, fifteen towns [in Kovno province] suffered pogroms: Suboch, Onikshty, Vol'niki, Lotovo, Vizhuny, Trashkun, Dobeiki, Veshinty, Vobol'niki, Kovarsk, Rakiski, Abeli, Soloki, Shimonets, and Vidzy. These are all small shtetls where the majority of the populations are Jews and Lithuanians. Jews compose nearly half of the population in some of them, a majority in others. Before July 1915, relations [between Jews and Lithuanians] were completely civil. In July our retreating forces began passing through the province. They behaved properly by paying in shops, and even forewarned Jews about Cossacks in some places, advising them to evacuate (as in Abeli). The entry of Cossacks opened an era of robbery and violence. [. . .]

In Trashkun, Russian troops passed through starting on July 9. On July 12, a dragoon arrived and the townspeople became anxious. A pogrom began on the night of the twelfth. The soldiers broke down doors, smashed windows, broke into homes, looted, and beat people. From morning to night on the thirteenth one heard screams all around, the sound of shattering glass and dishes, and cracking furniture. Feathers were flying from ripped up pillows, flour was spilled from sacks. The rioters took valuable and worthless objects alike. [. . .]

In the shtetl Onikshty, troops appeared on July 10. Looting began on the thirteenth, and a pogrom that affected the entire Jewish population broke out on the fourteenth. Dragoons and Cossacks tore apart shops, and stole samovars, bristle brushes, flour, and women's clothing. They threw part of the wares onto peasant wagons, and wrecked and burned the rest. The peasants took energetic part in the pogrom. The commanders treated the Jews with obvious hostility. A dragoon officer arrested two Jews without any reason, sentenced one of them to death and ordered him to execute the other, a sixty-five-year-old man. When the younger man refused, the soldiers killed the old man. Many women were raped. [. . .] The Cossacks whipped one Jew until he fell unconscious because they noticed he had an umbrella hanging on the door of his house and took it as a sign that he was signaling to the enemy. As Jews ran away, all of the Jewish houses, shops, synagogues, and schools were burned. The pogrom was predominantly carried out here by infantry soldiers. [. . .]

Pogroms in Vilna Province, August–September 1915

Driven out by terror and the Cossack whip, the Jewish population of Kovno province fled to the east, to the cities and shtetls of Vilna province, and in so doing,
jumped from the frying pan into the fire. Russian forces steadily continued their retreat, the enemy close on their heels. In connection with this, the theater of pogrom
activities also shifted to the territory of Vilna province, and seized the victims of
yesterday's pogroms. If in Kovno province the pogroms usually accompanied the retreat of our forces, a "parting gift" of sorts from the army to the civilians it had been
called to defend, then in Vilna and Minsk provinces, the series of events tended to
follow an opposite course. In the shtetls, German units appeared in large numbers.
They would leave after a few days, retreating before Russian cavalry (Cossack) units.
As soon as the Cossacks appeared, violence against the Jewish population and destruction of Jewish property began. There were numerous shtetls that experienced
pogroms many times over, both before the Germans occupied the town and after
their departure. There were cases of "chronic" pogroms, when the Jewish population was subject to daily robberies, beatings, and rapes. [. . .]

The most brutal pogrom in Vilna province occurred in Smorgon, a large center
of the leather trade. This pogrom transformed a lively and rich industrial town into
a den of ruins. In early June, the residents of Smorgon had their first experience of
living in a war zone. Many soldiers appeared in the city, but they treated the Jewish
populations correctly. As the front line approached, relations between Jews and
Christians worsened. Fights broke out. [. . .]

On September 2, the Germans entered Smorgon. They carried out numerous
arrests and searches, taking leather, money, and valuable objects from many of the
residents. Suspecting Jews of espionage, the commandant took several hostages
from among them. The retreat of the Germans therefore made the residents very
happy, and when our troops entered the town, the Jewish population greeted
them as victors and regaled the soldiers. This joy lasted a short time, however.
The Christian residents denounced the Jews, saying they had allegedly supported
the Germans, and these denunciations caused a stir among the soldiers. Lootings
began on the night of September 7. Jews began to flee toward Minsk, leaving behind
all of their property. [. . .] The soldiers (who had been told to search for hidden
Germans), broke into houses, where they stole valuable items, beat the residents,
and raped women.

The authorities behaved in different ways toward the atrocities. Some officers
permitted and even aided the thefts; others chased away crowds and arrested the
looters. One officer even fired into a rioting crowd. But these distinct cases when
officers defended Jews could not save the population; the pogrom spread like fire.
At that time about forty Jewish soldiers, unable to watch the destruction with indifference, formed a small unit to defend the Jewish population. This unit fought
in front of the Old Synagogue with the Cossacks, where the brutes were raping
women. When the Jewish soldiers managed to get inside the synagogue, a horrific

picture appeared before their eyes: the Cossacks were smashing ritual objects, ripping Torah scrolls, and bickering over holy things. The corpses of tortured, raped women were lying on the floor. Near the body of one young girl lay the badly beaten body of her elderly father. An intense fight between the Jewish soldiers and Cossacks continued on the street. As a result two [Jews] were killed and many wounded; the Cossacks had significant losses as well. The commandant ordered the arrest of all participants in the clash and sent them off to frontline positions.

On September 11, horrors of expulsions were added to the horrors of the destruction. All of the Jews who hadn't managed to flee at the start of the pogrom were ordered to immediately leave the city. . . . In the home of the Sobols, a Cossack officer appeared and ordered everyone to leave. Leib Sobol answered that he could not leave his ailing, bedridden father behind. The officer shot the elder Sobol on the spot and informed the son that he was now free and could leave the town.

Fires were set during the expulsions. Groups of soldiers with an officer leading them went from house to house, setting them on fire. Some residents had attempted to remain by hiding in cellars. When the Jew Vilenchik came out of a cellar and was spotted by the officers, he barely escaped a hanging and bribed them for a mere 1,500 rubles. Those who didn't manage to escape from the cellars died in the flames. Kalman Rozovskii was wounded by soldiers and burned alive inside his house. Veinshtein, a paralyzed man, was carried to the Libavicheskii synagogue, by his request, and died in the fire there. There were many other cases of people killed in the fires. People who managed to get back to the town on September 15 saw many charred corpses that couldn't be identified. Among the soldiers who carried out the pogrom in Smorgon, Ussuri Cossacks and the ninety-ninth and one hundredth regiments of the twenty-fifth division distinguished themselves. [. . .] About seven thousand to eight thousand refugees from Smorgon arrived in Minsk.

Pogroms in Minsk Province, September 1915

At the end of August, large German cavalry units [. . .] approached the northern border of Minsk province. [. . .] On September 6, Russian forces cleansed Vilna, and retreated under protection of the rear guard toward the interior, until they managed to unite with other units, and close the front line.

The pogroms carried out during this extraordinary episode during the autumn 1915 campaign belong to the harshest excesses of the period under review. In this series of pogroms the first took place in Glubokoe, Vilna province, at the border of three provinces: Vilna, Minsk, and Vitebsk. On August 30–31, after the breakthrough at the Sventsiany front, masses of refugees and Russian troops started to arrive in Glubokoe. On the night of September 1, retreating Russian forces passed through the town. [. . .] The city's Jewish aid committee did everything in its power to feed the transient soldiers. Despite a severe flour shortage in the region, the

Jewish population managed in just a few hours to procure 70 poods [about 2,500 pounds] of bread for the Cossacks, in addition to other foods. Nonetheless, there were many cases of robberies and violence against the Jewish population that day and at night. But thanks to the energy of the Jewish Aid Committee and the intervention of an officer of one of the Cossack units, the riot was quelled. Robberies ceased on the night of September 2.

When the Cossack commander heard this on the morning of September 3, he said, "It is the duty of every Cossack to annihilate everything that comes across his path so it doesn't fall into the enemies' hands." The real pogrom began that same day, September 3, after the last of the Cossack hundreds had left. Separate groups broke away from their divisions and returned to the shtetl, and along with the local and surrounding Christian population, they robbed and destroyed Jewish property. This went on for two days. Over that time not a single Christian shop was attacked. [...]

One of the most brutal pogroms that took place in the region of Minsk province occurred in Dokshitsy. The city, in Borisovskii uezd [county], has a population of about five thousand, among that number four thousand Jews. On September 7 (September 5 according to other reports), Dokshitsy was occupied by the Germans. The German soldiers paid for their goods in the shops and behaved correctly toward the residents. After a week the Germans were pushed out from Dokshitsy and a Siberian Cossack hundred entered the town. After the first outrages they committed, the rabbi went to their officer, asking him to restrain the riot and promising to get the necessary food for the troops. The officer promised to restore order, and indeed, the problems stopped for a short time. The Jewish population gave each soldier one pound of meat and three pounds of bread, and distributed cigarettes and matches.

After the Siberians left, some Don Cossacks arrived, at first a small number, then a few thousand. The Jews were not in a position to satisfy these Cossacks. A pogrom began and continued almost entirely without pause for three days, on September 15, 16, and 17 (September 13, 14, 15 according to other reports). When news spread that Cossacks had come to Dokshitsy, many peasants came and together with the Cossacks they began to rob the Jewish population. Peasants broke into groups of thirty to forty people; Cossacks walked at the head of each one. Shops, stores, and private homes were subjected to destruction, along with cellars where residents (not only Jewish) hid their property. Cossacks took the more valuable and cumbersome items for themselves and threw all the rest onto the street, where peasants stood holding sacks and wagons they had prepared in advance. Lootings were accompanied by beatings, torture, and humiliation, and in some cases the rape of women. The civilian authorities (the bailiff) took no actions to quell the disturbances, claiming to be powerless. In the accounts of eyewitnesses there are only two instances mentioned when officers intervened to help pogrom victims. In general the military authorities not only made it difficult to stop the violence, but on the contrary, gave the rioters full support. [...] The pogrom was put to an end by

the appearance of infantry forces. [. . .] During the Dokshitsy pogrom 132 families suffered.
January 1916

Source: "Iz 'chernoi knigi' rossiiskago evreistva: Materialy dlia istorii voiny 1914–1915 g." *Evreiskaia starina*, no. 10 (1918): 195–296, here 267–68, 273–77, 285–88. Translated from the Russian by Polly Zavadivker.

Document 5.6. The Rape of Jewish Women during Russian Military Pogroms

Erlikh devoted a section of his essay on pogroms to the subject of rape of Jewish women. The following stories are based on police reports and personal accounts. Among the worst instances of rape are those described in the towns of Smorgon and Lemeshevich. The essay provides explanations and a descriptive chronicle of the violence.

What Jewish women underwent during the period we are studying deserves a special place in the military martyrology of Russian Jewry. There was almost no pogrom that was not accompanied by individual instances of women being raped; in several pogroms (Smorgon, Glubokoe, Vidzy, Lemeshevich, and others) rapes took place on a massive scale. We will note only these mass rapes, and of the individual instances only those that were marked by particular cruelty.

The appearance in a city of Cossack hosts, who spared neither girls nor old women, elicited a terrible panic in Jewish women. There were cases, as happened in Begomel in Minsk province, where the entire female Jewish population would leave the city upon hearing that Cossacks were approaching. By the time the Cossacks entered the city, finding safety became more difficult. Those with more means were sometimes able to ransom their wives and daughters from the rapists; even that option was not available to the poor. Driven to despair, women would frequently leap into the water (in Dunilovich and Lemeshevich), but they would be hauled out and raped. Defending women who were about to be raped or hiding them was dangerous. In Veshinty, Kovno province, a father trying to save his daughter from rape had his head split open with a saber. Five versts from Onikshty, dragoons killed a Jewish miller and his son for refusing to give up their wife and daughter. In Piskurno, Cossacks wounded a *shochet* (ritual slaughterer) who was defending his daughter, then raped her. . . .

The savage cruelty and indiscriminateness of the brutes who committed the rapes is astounding. [. . .] The rapes would, for the most part, take place in front of family members. Near Dunilovichi, Cossacks forced the wife of the Jew Gordon to go with them into the forest, supposedly to show them where Germans were hiding. Afraid to go alone, Gordon asked permission for her daughter and elderly father to accompany her. Along the way, the Cossacks tied up the old man and raped the woman in front of her daughter and father. In the shtetl of Bereznitsy, Volhynia province, three Cossacks climbed through the window into the room where a relative of landlord Perlmuter was sleeping and, one after the other, raped the girl in front of the master of the house and his son.

Sometimes the rapes were particularly brutal. In previously mentioned Bereznitsy, Volhynia province, Cossacks would frequently kill the women they raped. Hannah Goldman, a cobbler's daughter who had gone to ask a soldier for money, was found dead the next day, with signs of rape. Granted, Christian girls were subjected to the same fate here. [. . .]

The cruelest pogroms (in Vidzy, Smorgon, Glubokoe, and others) were accompanied by mass rapes. In Vidzy, the Jews who did not flee in time barricaded themselves in the synagogue; Cossacks broke in and separated the men from the women; the women were all raped; many old women were among them. [. . .] In Glubokoe the rapes also took on a mass scale. [. . .] Horrors also took place in Smorgon. Cossacks would burst into houses and cellars where Jews were hiding, strip women, ostensibly to search them, and try to rape them. Soldiers raped one woman, a wagon driver's wife, when they arrived, after striking the infant she was nursing from her arms. Many were raped in the cellar of the Pergament brewery, where three hundred to four hundred people were hiding. Soldiers burst in, separated out the young women, and led them away. One of the rape victims became mute; another, the joiner's daughter Chava Mitskevich, went mad, was taken to Minsk, and died there. [. . .]

The [pogrom] in Lemeshevich deserves special mention in this saga. After the men were arrested, the pogrom turned into one unbroken series of cruel rapes of women. The defenseless women, separated from their husbands and fathers, found themselves in the clutches of the enraged Cossack horde. Night brought with it the apprehension of horror. In the evening on September 6, a group of about forty Cossacks approached the barges where the women were sitting. The Cossacks lined up all the women and sorted them, separating out the adults, teenagers, and old women. There were two rape victims that night: the maiden Alta Livshits and the married woman Flaksman. They were raped by three batches of Cossacks, forty people in each. Many of the women hid, especially as morning dawned, in the mud and reeds. The child of one of the hiding women began crying from the cold; the mother, fearing that the crying would give away her presence, wanted to strangle and throw the child in the mud, but the other women did not let her. In the day-time, the Jewish women of Lemeshevich tried to find shelter with the peasants, but for the most part they refused to take the women in, saying that the Cossacks had ordered them all raped. The following night the Cossacks raped eighteen women, including four girls no older than fourteen. The infant of the rape victim Mirka Schmidt was ripped from her arms and thrown in the mud. The child was found in the morning, severely frostbitten. A few days later the infant died. The following night the Cossacks managed to catch the Livshits mother and daughters, whom they had been chasing from the very beginning, because the peasants had pointed out the daughters of the local rich man Livshits as beautiful girls. Maria Livshits tried to throw herself in the river, but the Cossacks dragged her out by the hair and, after a long and brutal fight, her strength exhausted, felled her to the ground.

One Cossack held an unsheathed dagger over her, another put the barrel of his rifle to her temple, while the third carried out the assault; after that they switched off. Livshits recalled three of them, then she lost consciousness, but it seemed to her that there were five of them. Maria Livshits's mother and twelve-year-old sister were also raped. Almost none of the Jewish women in Lemeshevich managed to escape the violence. The details of this dreadful case are laid out in a police report.

Source: "Iz 'chernoi knigi' rossiiskago evreistva: Materialy dlia istorii voiny 1914–1915 g." *Evreiskaia starina* 10 (1917–18): 195–296, here 292–96. Translated from the Russian by Eugenia Tietz-Sokolskaya.

Document 5.7. A Russian Jewish Politician Accuses the Russian Government of Complicity in the Incitement of Pogroms

Naftali M. Fridman (1863–1921) was a Jewish member of the liberal Kadet (Constitutional Democratic) Party and, during the war, one of three Jewish deputies in the Russian State Duma. A speech before the Duma on August 2, 1915, marked the first time that Fridman publicly denounced the Russian government during the war. He alleged that government officials played a role in spreading rumors of Jewish treason that, in turn, helped to provoke pogroms as well as legitimize the military's policies of expelling Jews en masse from front zones. The transcript of his speech appeared in the Russian liberal daily newspaper Rech *(Speech) on August 3, and in the* New York Times *on September 23, 1915.*

In a long war lucky events alternate with unlucky ones, and in any case it is naturally useful to have scapegoats in reserve. For this purpose there exists the old firm: the Jew. Scarcely has the enemy reached our frontiers when the rumor is spread that Jewish gold is flowing over to the Germans, and that, too, in aeroplanes, in coffins, and—in the entrails of geese!

Scarcely had the enemy pressed further, than there appeared again beyond dispute the eternal Jew "on the white horse," perhaps the same one who once rode on the white horse through the city in order to provoke a pogrom. The Jews have set up telephones, have destroyed the telegraph lines. The legend grew, and with the eager support of the powers of Government and the agitation in official circles, assumed ever greater proportions. A series of unprecedented, unheard of, cruel measures was adopted against Jews. These measures, which were carried out before the eyes of the entire population, suggested to the people and to the army the recognition of the fact that the Jews were treated as enemies by the Government, and that the Jewish population was outside the law. [...]

Yes, we are beyond the pale of the laws, we are oppressed, we have a hard life, but we know the source of that evil: it comes from those benches (pointing to the boxes of the Ministers).

Source: *New York Times*, September 23, 1915, 5.

Document 5.8.   A Russian Nurse's Notes from the Front

Sofia Zakharovna Fedorchenko (1888–1959) served as a Russian nurse with a division of the Zemstvo Union on the Russian army's southwestern front in 1915–1916. During her wartime service, she kept a diary in which she transcribed soldiers' conversations about their wartime experiences. In the following excerpt from her diary, she cites soldiers' descriptions of brutal violence they carried out against Jews. The account reveals soldiers' and commanding officers' sensibilities regarding Jewish civilians.

"And then the top brass put yids in with us," we read in another note from the front. "It was hilarious. [. . .] One, say, wails like a beluga, another lies down as soon as he gets there, like a dead man, all white, just his ears sticking out. [. . .] One time, me and Stepa Kovalyov went into a house and saw all sorts of good stuff. [. . .] We laid down a blanket and started laying things out, whose was whose we'd figure out later. [. . .] As we were piling things on the blanket, our little yid showed up."

"Guys," he says, "you can't do that." We say nothing. [. . .] He keeps mumbling, but we keep mum. [. . .] He got mad, started yelling, and the company commander came in. He thinks it's funny, but it's not allowed, he has to put a stop to it. He's roaring with laughter, but tells us to leave the stuff. [. . .] And the yid sure got it, both from us and the commander. [. . .] Ended up in the hospital." [. . .]

[Another soldier]: "I've seen so many messed up kids here. I just can't forget one little yid. In a single hour, the soldiers basically made a complete orphan of him. Beat his mother, hanged his father, tormented his sister to death, violated her. And this one, no more than eight years old, was left behind, and an infant brother with him. I tried to show him some kindness, gave him some bread, and kept reaching to pat him on the head. But he shrieked like some vampire, and took off yelling like that, stumbling over everything in his way. Even after he was out of sight, for a long time you could hear him screaming like an animal, in grief, as an orphan."

Source: S. Fedorchenko, *Narod na voine: frontovyia zapisi* (Kiev: Union of Towns and Zemstvos, 1917), 46, 66. Translated from the Russian by Eugenia Tietz-Sokolskaya.

Document 5.9.   The Kafafov Circular, January 9, 1916

K. D. Kafafov, acting director of the Department of Police in the Russian Ministry of Interior, sent the following circular to Russian provincial governors, mayors, and chiefs of police. It contains the claim that Jews are subverting Russia's war effort by means of economic warfare, primarily currency manipulation and hoarding. This document contained incendiary claims. Often these claims supplied the basis for rumors that preceded and triggered anti-Jewish pogroms.

According to information received from the Department of Police, Jews are currently using numerous underground organizations to conduct revolutionary propaganda with the aim to arouse general discontent throughout Russia. In addition to their criminal agitation among troops and in major industrial centers of the empire, including calls for labor strikes, they have also adopted two other methods: the artificial inflation of prices of necessities and the withholding of small denominations of money from circulation.

Knowing that neither military setbacks nor revolutionary agitation will have any serious effect on the masses, the revolutionaries, the Jews who inspire them, and their secret German supporters now intend to incite discontent and protests against the war by means of famine and the hyperinflation of basic goods. These malicious merchants are almost certainly hoarding goods and slowing deliveries and the off-loading of goods at railroad stations in whatever ways they possibly can.

Thanks to the lack of small coins in circulation, the Jews are attempting to instill a distrust of Russian currency among the general population in order to devalue it. They force depositors to remove their savings from state institutions and banks while hiding metal coins, the only money that has any intrinsic value. Following the release of equivalent [paper] banknotes, the Jews have actively participated in spreading the rumor among the populace that the Russian government has gone bankrupt, as it doesn't even have enough metal for coins.

Source: "Dokumenty o presledovanii evreev," *Arkhiv russkoi revoliutsii* 19 (Berlin, 1928), 267–68. Translated from the Russian by Polly Zavadivker.

Document 5.10. The First Jewish Pogrom in Siberia, May 7, 1916

The only anti-Jewish pogrom to take place in Siberia during the war occurred on May 7, 1916, in the city of Krasnoiarsk. One week later, the Russian Jewish lawyer and publicist I. A. Kleinman traveled there from Petrograd to investigate and report on the pogrom. He published his report in the journal Jewish Chronicle (Evreiskaia letopis'), *which he edited in 1924. On the basis of witness testimony, his report shows that the pogrom was planned and executed by local residents with the consent of the local police, and that the pogrom was incited by charges that Jews were hoarding currency and causing inflation—the same slander that appeared in the January 1916 Kafafov Circular (Document 5.9).*

A pogrom took place in Krasnoiarsk on May 7, 1916—the first Jewish pogrom in Siberia. This was a typical Jewish pogrom: its features, the composition of the victims, the slander and motives that caused it, and the attitudes of the governing authorities. . . . When I arrived in Krasnoiarsk, I met not only with Jews—pogrom victims, witnesses, and various representatives of the Jewish community—but also the Archbishop Nikon; the head of the military garrison, Martynov; the police chief, Ignatov; civil authorities, and others. . . . Despite their differences of opinion, all of them regarded the governor [Ia. G. Gololobov] to be a crucial figure [in the pogrom] and said that his politics were a form of pogrom incitement. Public opinion was also unanimous in this regard.

According to survivor accounts and a series of eyewitnesses, events in Krasnoiarsk unfolded on May 7 as follows: early that morning an unusually large crowd gathered in the market. A big group stood in front of Freida Sinets's meat shop. This was not by accident, but the result of premeditated incitement that preceded the events of the day. On May 7, Sinets had meat in her shop that she had gotten just a day or two earlier from the municipal food reserve, and since she didn't want to keep it around, she sold it at market rates. Nonetheless, the crowd started raving and wrangling with her. One woman ran up to her and yelled, "I'll kill you today, yid, and will beat up all the other yids!" Sinets tried to leave her shop and summon the police for help, but the crowd pounced on her with baskets and buckets. Sinets managed to break free and quickly walked to the nearest police station. Sinets asked the station chief to rescue her and her sister [. . .] but he told her, "They'll kill you anyway," and left. Then the crowd began to pelt her with rocks; then they tore down her stand and smashed it to pieces. [. . .]

The assembly of the crowd [in the market] had undoubtedly been planned in advance. The head of the local garrison, P. A. Martynov, confirmed that after arresting some looters he found that the women who had been in the market that morning brought baskets with them in which rocks and bricks had been packed on the bottom and covered with rags. [. . .]

[Governor] Gololobov's actions on that day were not unusual. The governor was not in the city while the pogrom was taking place. He arrived in Krasnoiarsk around noon, but took no actions to counter the pogrom, which went on the whole day until late that night. According to Archbishop Nikon, it would have been easy to disperse the crowds: "One word from the authorities, or a bucket of water, would have been enough to chase away the roiled crowds." [. . .]

The results of the pogrom of May 7 included the destruction of goods and property both in shops and homes belonging to nearly seventy families, who suffered significant damages. Sixty of those seventy families were Jewish. The pogrom had a clearly anti-Jewish character: Jews alone were robbed during the day in the city, but when the pogrom reached the outskirts that night (the so-called Nikolaev sloboda), a few Christian shops were robbed. Apart from material damages, there were also badly beaten and wounded victims. . . .

The Krasnoiarsk Duma responded to the pogrom that very day by holding a special meeting devoted specifically to the task of issuing a proclamation to the city's residents and devising measures to fight inflation. [. . .] On May 8, the proclamation appeared on the streets of Krasnoiarsk. The statement condemned the disturbances and pogroms and indicated that the city duma had adopted specific measures to fight inflation. It concluded by stating that the city duma "expresses profound regret that the character of yesterday's pogrom was predominantly Jewish. The duma, which insists that Jewish merchants have not acted in such a way as to deserve this treatment, is confident that yesterday's deplorable events will not be repeated—that the citizens of Krasnoiarsk will not lose their reason, and will find the inner strength to restrain themselves from any further riots."

Source: I. A. Kleinman, "Pervyi evreiskii pogrom v Sibiri," *Evreiskaia letopis'* 3 (1924): 124–34. Translated from the Russian by Polly Zavadivker.

Document 5.11. A Jewish Soldier Witnesses a Pogrom in Buczacz

Aba Lev was a Russian Jewish soldier stationed in Galicia during the first and second Russian occupations of the region. In a Yiddish diary that he kept during the war, he described the immediate aftermath of a pogrom in Buczacz following the Brusilov Offensive in the summer of 1916. His account describes his own responses and his attempts to aid the survivors and bury the dead. Excerpts of his diary were translated into Russian and published in 1924.

As I approached [Buczacz] I was gripped by the bitter smell of smoke and alcohol, and could barely breathe. The first thing that struck my eye was a wooden building, on which I noticed a sign in Yiddish that read, "This building is supported by charity." People scurried around the building, which was engulfed by flames, a few Jews among them, trying to put out the fire. Suddenly a drunk officer showed up, threw a bucket of water on the Jews, and began to beat them with the bucket. The burning building was a Jewish orphanage that the soldiers had set on fire while searching for vodka.

When I entered the synagogue courtyard, my vision grew dark from the terrifying picture of destruction, vandalism, and cruelty before me. A Jew with wild red hair ran up to me and shouted in a hoarse voice, "My name is Solomon. Tell me soldier, are you a Jew? Yes, I can tell that you're a Jew!" Another Jew with a terrified face and lifeless eyes approached me. I comforted them, asking them to tell me what had happened. They led me to a neighboring house, where there was a boy of ten, his hands broken; his mother lay next to him, her skull smashed and her legs cut off. This was the work of Cossack beasts. In the next house there was a dead woman, who had been raped and then beaten so badly that she died the same day in terrible agony. In the third and fourth buildings, there were raped Jewish women and girls, men with smashed heads and gouged eyes. In the almshouse I found five murdered people who had to be buried. [. . .] They showed me many other Jewish houses with dead people lying inside who had been strangled, burned; there were also wounded people who had been beaten and raped.

Devastated by everything I had seen and heard, I headed straight to my comrades to consider what to do. We decided it was necessary to bring a wagon of food to Buczacz that same night for starving people. The Buczacz Jews sensed that a ray of light had pierced their darkest night. They crawled out of their cellars to cry over their dead, who were soon taken to the cemetery.

When I came to the synagogue courtyard I found a rather different scene: it was filled with half-naked women with infants in their arms, children in bundles, and men with grim and lifeless eyes. We fed them and they recovered a bit, telling me that the Cossacks' rampage was now in its second week. The results of the Cossacks' exploits were felt everywhere. Torah scrolls stolen from twenty-three synagogues were strewn across the ground in the courtyard and near the synagogue.

At dawn the next morning, we gathered 250 destroyed Torah scrolls, cleaned them off, and brought them to the Great Synagogue, whose walls are as thick as those of a fortress. In spite of its metal doors and huge locks, everything in the synagogue that the wicked people couldn't steal had been smashed. Dozens of strong Cossack arms had tried to break down the metal doors the night before. [. . .]

Time passed unnoticeably in that nightmarish state. When the clock struck eight that morning on the city tower at the Uniate Church . . . I hastened to the headquarters to report to my unit's commander. . . . At ten o'clock, the captain (Kondratiev) received me very cordially. . . . I told him about what was happening in the city, where the defenseless Jews were at the disposal of the drunken Cossacks, and implored him to take strong measures to stop the outrages. [. . .] After thinking a bit, he sharply advised me [. . .] to avoid getting myself involved in this business [. . .] since only two days earlier a Jew had been caught making signals to the enemy from the high chimney of the brewery. [. . .]

During the last few days that I spent in Buczacz, I discovered several interesting details about the robberies and destruction committed there. Looters found twenty-seven cellars filled with wine, vodka, and liquor, on which most of the soldiers and officers got totally drunk. Since most of the city dwellers had fled and abandoned their houses and shops, the Seventh Army had issued an order to requisition all of the goods that were left behind.

Source: Aba Lev, "Razgrom galitsiiskikh evreev v krovavye gody mirovoi voiny: Otryvok iz dnevnika," *Evreiskaia letopis'* 3 (1924), 174–75. Translated from the Russian by Polly Zavadivker.

6

Anti-Jewish Violence in the Russian Civil War

Jeffrey Veidlinger

On Saturday, February 15, 1919, Ukrainian soldiers murdered over a thousand Jewish civilians in the town of Proskuriv (now Khmelnytsky) in what was at the time possibly the single deadliest episode of violence to befall the Jewish people in their long history of oppression.[1] The massacre in Proskuriv, though, was not an isolated event. Between 1917 and 1921, during the civil war that followed the Russian revolutions, over 1000 separate incidents were documented in about 500 different locales throughout the regions that had been the southwestern provinces of the Russian Empire and the eastern half of the Austrian province of Galicia, predominantly in areas that are now parts of Ukraine. The largest of the anti-Jewish massacres resulted in the deaths of 1,500–3,000 people apiece, but the vast majority left at most a few dozen dead in their wake. An estimated 30,000–40,000 Jews were killed during the pogroms, and another 60,000–70,000 subsequently perished from injuries sustained during the fighting, or from disease, starvation, and exposure as a direct result of them. In total, the violence resulted in over 100,000 Jewish deaths, forced approximately 600,000 refugees to flee across international borders, and displaced millions more internally. These casualties were part of a larger civil war that resulted in the deaths of about one million people in Ukraine.[2] It profoundly reshaped the demography of European Jewry and traumatized the affected communities for a generation.

Almost immediately after the first instances of mass violence began, the organized Jewish community sprang into action, both to raise funds to support the victims and to document the atrocities. Building upon the Jewish Committee to Aid Victims of the War, which had been established in August 1914 to coordinate aid and resettle Jewish war refugees, Jewish activists, led by Nokhem Gergel and Elias Heifetz, quickly redirected resources toward investigating instances of anti-Jewish violence that took place after the formal conclusion of the world war. The ensuing violence between various factions of Ukrainian independence fighters, Bolshevik Red Guard units, former tsarist soldiers fighting with the White Army of South

---

[1] This article draws material from Jeffrey Veidlinger, *In the Midst of Civilized Europe: The Pogroms of 1918–1921 and the Onset of the Holocaust* (New York: Metropolitan Books, 2021).

[2] Dietrich Beyrau, "Brutalization Revisited: The Case of Russia," *Journal of Contemporary History* 50, no. 1 (2015): 15–37.

Jeffrey Veidlinger, *Anti-Jewish Violence in the Russian Civil War* In: *Pogroms*. Edited by: Eugene M. Avrutin and Elissa Bemporad, Oxford University Press. © Oxford University Press 2021. DOI: 10.1093/oso/9780190060084.003.0007

An early nineteenth-century postcard depicting Aleksandrovskaya Street in Proskuriv, one of the main thoroughfares on which the February 1919 pogrom took place.
Wikimedia Commons

Russia, Polish legionnaires, and a number of insurgent bands quickly overwhelmed the aid agency's ability to provide relief. Its activities were further hindered by infighting among the organization's constituent political parties. But at least in areas that had not fallen under Bolshevik control, the Central Committee for Relief of Pogrom Victims was an effective investigatory body. The committee dispatched lawyers to the sites of pogroms to take testimonies, collect photographic evidence, and issue reports in the hopes of one day bringing the perpetrators to justice. The most prominent of these lawyer-investigators was Arnold Hillerson, whose report on the Proskuriv pogrom is included here.

During the tsarist period, Hillerson had established himself as a specialist on pogroms, famously representing victims of a 1906 pogrom in Białystok during an influential civil trial. On account of his courtroom speech at that trial, in which he condemned antisemitic groups tied to the government and exposed the tsarist military troops who provoked the violence, Hillerson was charged with inciting rebellion, treason, and the overthrow of the existing social order. The case against Hillerson became a cause célèbre in the late imperial period and a test case for the still relatively new Russian judicial system. For calling to justice the perpetrators of the pogrom, Hillerson was sentenced to one year in prison. Undeterred, he returned to the task of documenting anti-Jewish violence during the civil war period. The comprehensive reports he authored on the 1919 pogroms in Ovruch, Proskuriv, and Felshtin were widely distributed and subsequently published in multiple languages.[3]

---

[3] For a French translation, see Comité des Delegations Juives, *Les Pogromes en Ukraine sous les Gouvernements Ukrainiens (1917–1920)* (Paris, 1927), 43–52. An English version was published in Elias Heifetz, *The Slaughter of the Jews in the Ukraine in 1919* (New York: Thomas Seltzer, 1921), 203–34.

The Proskuriv pogrom began as an attempt by the newly formed Directory government of the short-lived Ukrainian People's Republic to put down a Bolshevik uprising that threatened their control of the province of Podilia. The Ukrainian People's Republic had been established by moderate socialist democrats, who were intent on creating a multiethnic socialist state in Ukraine tied to revolutionary Russia. The Directory had come to power in December 1918, following the departure of the German and Austrian armies, which had been occupying the country since April 1918 in collaboration with a conservative regime known as the Hetmanate. Throughout the summer of 1918, peasants and workers had risen up against the Hetmanate and the German occupation, bringing the government to its knees. When the German kaiser and Hapsburg emperor were overthrown in November, the soldiers occupying Ukraine eagerly abandoned their posts and returned home. The socialist Directory government then seized control in Kyiv (Kiev), while a Bolshevik government managed to take control of Kharkiv. Two rival states—a Ukrainian People's Republic and a Ukrainian Socialist Soviet Republic—laid claim to the same territory. In January 1919, Bolshevik forces advanced toward Kyiv, forcing the Directory to retreat.

Having abandoned their erstwhile capital, the socialist ministers who constituted the government of the Directory—mostly former writers, journalists, and intellectuals—set up governmental offices in a hotel in Vinnytsia, about 150 miles southwest of Kyiv, from where—with limited access to the railways or the telegraph—they tried to establish a functioning state. Their most immediate challenge was defending Ukrainian autonomy from the Bolsheviks, who attacked them on two fronts: Red Guard military units moved westward from Soviet Ukraine, while Bolshevik activists within the territory controlled by the Directory sought to usurp power from the inside by encouraging revolutionary insurrections among workers, soldiers, and peasants. The threat of Bolshevik agitators turning military garrisons and factories Red led to widespread fear of internal enemies seeking to overthrow the state from within.

These fears were often directed against the Jews, a people who made up about 12 percent of the population of Ukraine, but had largely lived apart and in urban enclaves, where they practiced their own religion, spoke their own language, and dominated certain occupations, chiefly handcrafts and trade. Several of the most visible Bolshevik leaders, most prominently Leon Trotsky, were also of Jewish heritage, which helped solidify popular suspicions of Jews. In a part of the world where ethnicity often closely overlapped with sociological standing and ideology, it was easy for ordinary folk to mistakenly conflate the Jews and the Bolsheviks.

Symon Petliura, the inexperienced journalist who was put in charge of the army of the Ukrainian People's Republic, had neither the skills, the wherewithal, nor the time to decisively put down these allegations, let alone the desire to do so. He relied mostly on recruits from the local peasantry and demobilized soldiers from the tsarist army. Many were exhausted from five years of fighting and, with few reliable sources of news, were receptive to conspiracies, rumors, and baseless allegations. The notion that the Jews were behind the tumult that had overthrown the tsar, the

Symon Petliura, the military leader of the Ukrainian People's Republic,
who was widely blamed for allowing the Proskuriv pogrom to
take place.
Courtesy of Tsentralnyi derzhavnyi kinofotofonoarkhiv Ukrainy

kaiser, and the emperor provided an easy explanation for what was, in reality, the
result of a complex set of circumstances. For his officer corps, Petliura was forced to
call upon a handful of officers with disparate goals, often contrary to the multicul-
tural socialism of the Directory.

Among these was the twenty-five-year-old agronomist Ivan Semosenko, who had
already gained a reputation as an unreliable drunkard whose talk of law and order
barely concealed his corruption before he arrived in Proskuriv. But he had military
experience, and that was enough to give him command of a brigade. The "Cossack"
brigade he commanded was, in truth, a brigade comprising predominantly peasant

soldiers hastily recruited from the neighboring countryside; it was named after the Cossacks who founded the eighteenth-century state that was regarded as the progenitor of the Ukrainian People's Republic. Similarly, the Third Haidamak Regiment that arrived with Semosenko's brigade was a peasant unit named after the Haidamak fighters of Ukrainian lore. Semosenko's soldiers emulated their commander, presenting themselves as tough guys who refused to play by the rules.

Semosenko's "Cossacks" and the Third Haidamak Regiment entered Proskuriv on February 5 at the invitation of Yuri Kiverchuk, recently appointed military commandant of the city by the Directory. Kiverchuk feared the city would fall to Bolshevik agitators, and trusted neither the city council, the soldiers of the local garrisons, nor the civilian ward guards to protect it. Hillerson's report found that there was, in fact, a conspiracy underway to carry out an insurrection, but it was poorly planned and doomed to failure. The situation, Hillerson argued, could easily have been contained by the existing civilian government, its capable city councilors, and its ward guard of mixed nationality. But Semosenko's men were dismissive of the local government and its institutions. Throughout his report, Hillerson shows how the local government, the city councilors, and the ward guards worked to defuse the tension that the presence of Semosenko's military created in the city. He shows, for instance, how Ilya Joffe, the head of the socialist bloc in the city, sought to dissuade the Bolshevik agitators from igniting an insurrection in Proskuriv, and how Shenkman, one of the leaders of the ward guard, worked with his Christian counterpart to protect the city. Despite their warnings, however, the Bolsheviks attempted to stage an insurrection in the city early on the morning of Saturday, February 14.

The uprising itself failed spectacularly within hours, as the civilian administration had predicted it would. The local garrisons, which the insurrectionists had hoped would lead the revolution, lacked the resolve to fight. Anticipated reinforcements never arrived. By late morning, it was apparent to all that the uprising had failed to spread beyond a narrow group of zealots, and that the Bolsheviks lacked sufficient strength in the city. The whole affair could have been over before most of the population awoke. And, in fact, as Hillerson points out, many Jews, who were attending religious services at synagogue that Saturday morning, had no idea of what was going on in the marketplace while they prayed.

The failed uprising, though, provided a pretext for Semosenko and his soldiers to carry out a massacre of the civilian Jewish population. As Hillerson points out, the uprising had already been decisively defeated by the time the first massacres occurred. Instead, the violence took place as soldiers celebrated their easy victory by going amok, taking vengeance on innocent Jewish civilians who did not even know there had been an attempted uprising. Despite Semosenko's reported instructions to kill and not to rob, Hillerson documents ample instances of soldiers looting Jewish shops and houses. With the military's inability to adequately pay its soldiers, it was not uncommon for victorious units to plunder, both as their reward and for sustenance. But the biggest windfall the soldiers received was after the worst of the bloodshed had ended and the Jewish community presented them with a bribe to stave off further violence. Hillerson emphasizes, though, that the massacre was not motivated by pecuniary gain, but rather by anti-Jewish hatred. The peasant soldiers targeted not only Jews who could have been involved in the failed insurrection, but also children, Jews at prayer, and families asleep in their homes, convinced that the Jews were responsible for the revolutionary unrest and were hoarding wealth that should belong to the peasantry.

Within several hours the worst of the pogrom was over, as Semosenko gave his marauding soldiers an order to cease the killing. Hillerson estimates the death toll at over 1,500 people: 1,200 who were killed immediately and another 300 who subsequently perished of their wounds. Other estimates at the time put the number closer to 3,000 or even 4,500. A detailed list of the dead documents the names of 911 victims, a figure that can be taken as the most conservative estimate.

In May 1919, Petliura had Semosenko arrested, but it is unclear whether the charge was related to the massacre in Proskuriv. One of his cellmates reported that Semosenko boasted of having murdered eleven thousand Jews and claimed that he was imprisoned for having embezzled the money he stole rather than for committing the atrocities. Regardless, by the time of his arrest, the Ukrainian People's Republic had virtually been annihilated, squeezed between Poland in the west, the Whites in the south, and the Bolsheviks in the east. Petliura's motivation in cracking down on pogrom mongers at the time may well have been to secure European aid rather than to punish the perpetrators. But the pogrom that he unleashed represented a new stage in anti-Jewish violence. As Hillerson noted in the conclusion of his report, "Proskuriv has acquired the sad privilege of having opened a new style of pogrom-making. The previous pogroms had for their main purpose the looting of Jewish property. [. . .] But with Proskuriv, the main purpose of the Ukrainian pogroms was the extermination of the Jewish population."

Document 6.1. The Proskuriv Pogrom,
February 15, 1919

Proskuriv and Its Residents

Proskuriv is the liveliest city in Podilia province. Its population approaches fifty thousand, of whom twenty-five thousand are Jews. Its democratically elected city council comprised fifty members: twenty-six Christians and twenty-four Jews. Of the Jewish members, eighteen were chosen from parochial Jewish party lists, whereas the others represent general socialist parties. The leaders of Proskuriv's Duma are Polish, as is the case almost everywhere in Podilia and Volhynia. The city's mayor was a Pole named Sikora, and the speaker of the city council was a Polish doctor, Stavinsky. Administratively, Proskuriv was managed by the military commandant Kiverchuk and Commissar Taranovich. The former was a career military officer from back in tsarist times, and the latter was a former schoolteacher.

The city was protected by a militia that was primarily subordinate to the commandant. The city's self-governing body, which did not entirely trust the militia, organized its own security force, referred to as ward guards. This force was led by a central bureau, chaired by a Christian named Gursky, with a Jew named Shenkman serving as his deputy. Since the ward guards were primarily Jewish, they were generally looked down upon by Commandant Kiverchuk, who made the existence of the guards difficult in all sorts of ways.

Back when the tsar was in power, Proskuriv not only had all the legal parties, but illegal ones as well. It goes without saying that Proskuriv's civic and political life became particularly active after tsarism fell. During the Hetmanate, repressions in Proskuriv repeatedly targeted members of socialist parties, the Bolsheviks in particular. After the Hetman was deposed and Petliura's reign began, Bolshevik cells continued to operate in Proskuriv, but did so illegally. In general, all the socialist factions, Bolsheviks included, presented a unified front in Proskuriv, headed by a Bundist named Joffe. About three weeks before the slaughter in Proskuriv, the following event took place, which proved to be fateful for the city.

Bolshevik Congress in Vinnytsia

Vinnytsia, where Petliura himself was based, hosted a congress of Podilia province Bolsheviks. This congress lasted two days, and its sessions were held without impediment. The congress passed resolutions to organize a Bolshevik revolt across Podilia province, and February 15 was chosen as the date to hold it. The fact that the congress was held without impediment gave certain persons reason to claim that the congress was called with the knowledge of Petliura's regime, as a provocation.

Objective study, however, leads to the conclusion that in this case there was no prov-ocation, and the congress was held successfully only due to Petliura's regime being poorly organized and therefore not very aware. People point out that Proskuriv was the only place where Bolsheviks took action, while in other places in Podilia province—including Zhmerynka station, home to up to seven thousand railroad workers—no action was attempted. This is also seen as [an argument] in favor of the claim that in other places there was no revolt because the Bolshevik organizations were headed by more mature people who recognized that it was not an appropriate time for one.

In Proskuriv, on the other hand, the Bolshevik cell was headed by people who were too young and insufficiently conscientious. But besides that, another signifi-cant circumstance spurred the Proskuriv Bolsheviks to take action. Two regiments were quartered in Proskuriv, specifically the Fifteenth Belgorod and Eighth Podolsk, which were definitely pro-Bolshevik. The first regiment had about 340 people in it, the other had a bit more.

Ataman Semosenko's Arrival in Proskuriv

About ten days before the pogrom, the Zaporozhian Cossack Brigade of Chief Otaman Petliura's Army of the Ukrainian Republic arrived in Proskuriv under the command of ataman Semosenko. The Third Haidamak Regiment also arrived with the brigade. According to Semosenko's announcement, both the brigade and the regiment had come from the front to rest and serve as Proskuriv's garrison. On February 6, Semosenko ordered the printing house to print an announcement that he was assuming the responsibilities of garrison chief, and in that capacity he was banning all unapproved gatherings and rallies within the city. He warned that any campaigning against the existing regime would be punished under martial law. Any calls for pogroms were similarly banned, and anyone identified as making such calls would be shot on sight.

At the same time, Semosenko sent a message to the city council, stating that he had begun serving as garrison chief, that he was committed to prosecuting anyone who violated public order, and also that at one of the stations he had ordered an of-ficer shot for attempted theft.

Word of this message reached Shenkman, the deputy chair of the ward guard's central bureau, who headed to see Semosenko, to meet him in person. Semosenko received him cordially and promised to supply the ward guard with weapons and assist as necessary with preventing pogroms. This conversation with Shenkman, as well as the fact that Semosenko had sent the aforementioned announcement for printing, became known to certain members of the city council, and they, according to the city council speaker Dr. Stavinsky, went to see Commandant Kiverchuk to find out what legal authority Semosenko had and who granted it to him. Kiverchuk responded that he knew nothing about it and at the same time ordered that the announcement, which had already been typeset at the printing house, not be published.

It should be mentioned that the Third Haidamak Regiment appearing in the city caused a state of alarm among the Jews. The regiment acted provocatively, and it was said with certainty that it had perpetrated pogroms in the past. Nobody in the city knew that a Bolshevik revolt was planned. It was not until two days before February 15 that the militia chief Kara-Zheleznyakov informed Joffe that he had heard that a coup was being planned in Proskuriv and that people in the commandant's office were asserting that there would be a Bolshevik regime in the future with Joffe at its head.

Concerned, Joffe called together representatives of the socialist factions, including the Bolsheviks. The two Communist Party representatives who came stated that, indeed, a revolt was being prepared and that the future regime was already being staffed. In response to protests from representatives of the other factions and the assertion that this revolt would lead to their ruin and the Jews' complete destruction, they said that the revolt would take place simultaneously in all of Podilia province and that in Proskuriv the rebels would find support among part of the garrison, with sixteen villages ready to come to their aid. They did not say when the revolt would take place.

In the evening on Friday, February 14, two young men from the Bolshevik faction came to the ward guard's central bureau and announced that a Bolshevik revolt was planned for midnight. They asked Chairman Rudnitsky and Deputy Shenkman what the ward guard's position would be toward them. They were told that the ward guard was, by nature, a nonpartisan organization whose sole purpose was the protection of residents. Therefore, it would be completely neutral in this case. Shenkman also mentioned the poor timing of the revolt and that it would definitely result in a Jewish pogrom. But he was similarly told that the revolt would sweep the whole province and that its success was guaranteed. Later another communist organization member appeared and announced that, by resolution of the already formed revolutionary committee, he had been appointed commissar of the ward guards and that Shenkman had been appointed as liaison to the already formed Bolshevik command center. He told Shenkman the password for command center access. According to Shenkman's testimony, he and Rudnitsky gathered together all the ward guards present and told them that they were completely free to do as they wished and demanded that they immediately remove any outward signs of belonging to the ward guards, which was done. Everyone who was asked confirmed that they would not be taking any part in the political demonstration. With the password he had been given, Shenkman headed to the Bolshevik revolutionary committee, then to the command center. Seeing that the Bolsheviks' operations were not in order and that the proposed action was going to be, as he put it, a sham, he went to speak with the most senior Bolshevik to point out that it was not a good time for this revolt. The Bolshevik, in turn, told him that he would take steps to ensure that it would be delayed until a different, more suitable time. Indeed, when

Shenkman returned to the Central Bureau after this conversation, the Bolshevik revolutionary committee commissar who had remained there informed him that he had received a message by phone that the revolt was being called off. Shenkman then went around the city to make sure that security officers were at their posts. And when he returned to the bureau, the same commissar informed him that there was a new change and the revolt was scheduled to start after six in the morning, which would be signaled by gunshots.

Indeed, at 6:45 in the morning shots were fired, and the revolt began. First the Bolsheviks took over the post office and telegraph and arrested Commandant Kiverchuk, believing him, not without reason, to be a black-hundredist and pogrom instigator. They set up their command center in the very center of town, in one of the apartments in Trakhtenberg's building on Aleksandrovskaya Street. Some of them headed to the barracks of the Fifteenth Belgorod and Eight Podolsk Regiments. There they roused the sleeping soldiers and announced to them that the revolt had begun and that the executive bodies of the Bolshevik regime were already being formed. They suggested that the soldiers attack Petliura's troops, which were concentrated in the railcars behind the train depot. When the soldiers pointed out that they had no machine guns, they were told that the peasants who were already on their way to the city to take part in the revolt had them. Then the pro-Bolshevik soldiers arrested their officers, as well as the soldiers who were against the revolt. They confiscated the regiment's weapons and headed toward the depot. There they began firing at the railcars housing the Haidamaks and other Cossacks. But when the latter emerged from the railcars, and the attacking soldiers realized how numerous they were, they retreated to their barracks. The Cossacks followed them and began firing on the barracks. Then the soldiers retreated to Felshtin and Yarmolintsy, where some of them had previously been sent to raise a Bolshevik revolt, and after that they dispersed to various places, thereby evading capture.

After the soldiers retreated, it was clear that the revolt had failed. The shots heard early in the morning alarmed the city's representatives, and they began gathering at City Hall. The mayor and city council speaker visited the commandant's office several times, but they were given no information there.

Finally, they saw Kiverchuk pulling up to the commandant's office and found out from him that he had been arrested. When asked who had arrested him, he responded, "The Yids of the ward guard."

Commander Semosenko, this time with Kiverchuk's complete consent, acceded to the office of garrison chief. He marked his accession with a lavish buffet for the Haidamaks and Cossacks, treating them to vodka and brandy with lunch. Once the feast had come to an end, he addressed the Haidamaks, describing the grave situation in Ukraine and their efforts on the battlefield, and added that the most dangerous enemies of the Ukrainian people and the Cossacks are the Yids, whom the Cossacks need to slaughter to save Ukraine and themselves. He demanded that the Cossacks swear an oath that they would perform their holy duty and butcher the Jewish population, but at the same time they had to swear that they would not loot any of the Yids' property. The Cossacks were brought to the standard, and they swore that they would kill, but not loot.

Slaughter

Almost none of the Jews were aware of the attempted Bolshevik revolt. Having become accustomed in recent times to all sorts of gunfire, they did not give much thought to the shots that rang out that morning. It was a Saturday, and in the morning Orthodox Jews headed to the synagogue to pray and then, when they got home, sat down to a meal. Many, following established tradition, laid down for a nap after the Saturday lunch.

The Cossacks who had dispersed through the Jewish streets in groups of five to fifteen people would enter homes and, their expressions completely calm, pull out their sabers and slaughter the Jews inside, noticing neither age nor gender. They killed old men, women, and even infants. They not only cut but also used their bayonets to stab. Firearms were resorted to only if individuals managed to escape to the street, in which case a bullet would be sent after them.

When news of the slaughter spread among the Jews, they began hiding in attics and cellars, but the Cossacks would drag them down from the attics and kill them and throw hand grenades into the cellars.

According to the previously mentioned witness, Shenkman, Cossacks killed his younger brother in the street near his home, then broke in and split his mother's skull. The other family members had hidden under the beds, but when his little brother saw his mother die, he got out from under the bed and began kissing her corpse. The Cossacks began hacking at the child. Then his father couldn't take it and also got out from under the bed, and one of the Cossacks killed him with two gunshots. After that they approached the beds and began stabbing those lying underneath. Shenkman himself was lucky to survive.

Witness Grinfeld says that from the window of her apartment she saw a group of about twenty Haidamaks stop by the Haseev house across the way, with four of them splitting off and walking into Shifman's house, where they remained for a very brief time. When they came out, they wiped the blood off their sabers in the snow. Eight people were slaughtered in that apartment. The others from that group entered the adjoining Hotel France; the old man who owned it ran out, and they chased after him, with the old man's children running after them, begging for mercy.

[...]

In the Zemelman house, twenty-one people were killed and two wounded. Haidamaks approached the house marching in even lines, with two machine guns. They were accompanied by a nurse and someone with a Red Cross armband, later identified as Dr. Skornik, who headed the medical detachment.

In the Blehman house, six people were killed: one was killed by a blow to the head that split the skull in half. A girl was wounded on her backside, for which her dress was lifted up. In the Zazulya house, the daughter was killed after being tormented for a while. The boy in that house was wounded several times and pretended to be dead. The mother offered the killers money, but they responded, "We only came for their souls."

The slaughter continued from two o'clock to five-thirty. It would probably have lasted late into the night, but Commissar Taranovich, who was not privy to all of Semosenko's and Kiverchuk's plans, was horrified by the bloody debauchery unfolding across the city. He ran to see Semosenko and began insistently demanding that he end the slaughter, but Semosenko paid no heed to his words. Taranovich headed to the telegraph and sent a direct line to the provincial authorities in Kamyanets about what was happening in Proskuriv. They informed him of the location of army commander Shapoval, and Taranovich, again via direct line, called him up and reported what was happening, as well as his own conversation with Semosenko. Konovalov [sic; correctly Shapoval] immediately telegraphed over an order for Semosenko to stop the slaughter at once. Taranovich took this order to Semosenko, who then announced, "Very well, enough slaughter for today." A horn blast let the Haidamaks know to stop what they were doing. The Haidamaks then gathered at a prearranged location and marched, singing and in formation, from there to their camp behind the train depot.

Information on Commissar Taranovich's actions was given by the witness Verkhola and was also recorded in the course of the investigation conducted by the Bolshevik authorities into Taranovich's actions. I personally reviewed the investigative file.

To give credit where credit is due, it should be noted that the Haidamaks scrupulously held to their oath: they killed without mercy, but did not loot. In a few houses they were offered money, and they would rip the bills to shreds. Where there were individual cases of looting, they were the exception. But besides the Haidamaks, other Cossacks also took part in cutting up Jews, primarily from Kiverchuk's unit, as did militiamen. Not bound by the oath, these did not just kill, but also looted. The stealing, however, primarily took place at night, after the slaughter was already over. This was not stealing in the strictest sense of the word, but rather looting of property that had no owner, so to speak, as entire families had been butchered. This looting was effected by Cossacks, militiamen, and criminals who had been released from jail, by all accounts, by an order from Kiverchuk, who apparently did so to be able to blame them for what happened if the need arose. It was also under Kiverchuk's orders that the militia was disarmed, and only the militiamen assisting the Haidamaks retained their weapons.

By a fateful irony, when everyone living in a home had been butchered, it was made apparent by the brightly illuminated windows. The reason for this was that all homes are illuminated by electricity in Proskuriv, where it is quite easily obtained. Religious Jews, who are in the majority in Proskuriv, in accordance with their laws, do not extinguish the lights on Saturday, or, rather, Friday to Saturday night, and they remain lit until the morning, when they [the lights] turn off because the current is shut off; then, on Saturday evening, when the current is restored, they turn on by themselves. After the terrible day of Saturday, February 15, Jews did not turn on any lights. That made the lights in the windows of houses where Jewish families had been completely slaughtered appear even brighter. That was the light that attracted looters. There were, of course, some misunderstandings, where they would end up in Christian homes. That was the reason for the occasional attacks on Christian apartments Saturday to Sunday night mentioned in the testimony from witness Verkhola and Dr. Stavinsky.

According to witness Verkhola and city council speaker Dr. Stavinsky, it was not until late in the evening that they heard of the slaughter that had occurred, and they set out to walk the streets. They saw many corpses lying about; they, too, entered the illuminated apartments, where the slaughtered people lay; they entered a few pharmacies with the intention of setting up a first-aid station, but there they met the previously mentioned Dr. Skornik, who requisitioned all the dressings on behalf of the Cossacks, claiming that among them were many wounded from the front, which was not found to be true when verified.

This same Dr. Skornik, along with a nurse and two orderlies, actively participated in the slaughter. Dr. Skornik was particularly zealous. When another nurse, appalled at his behavior, yelled at him: "What are you doing, you are wearing a Red Cross armband!" He ripped the armband off and threw it to her, then continued killing. According to testimony from three schoolboys the Haidamaks had commandeered in Elisavetgrad to serve in the medical detachment, when Skornik returned to his railcar after the slaughter, he boasted that in one of the houses they had found a girl so beautiful not a single Haidamak dared to cut her, and he stabbed her to death himself. Indeed, witnesses say that among the bodies at the cemetery was one of an extraordinarily beautiful young woman who had been stabbed to death.

Since all the staff in Dr. Skornik's medical detachment had come down with typhus, none of them had time to evacuate as Petliura's forces retreated. The detachment fell into the Bolsheviks' hands in its entirety, and as a result of the investigation, those incriminated were sent to Odessa without trial. I reviewed the investigative file and must note that Dr. Skornik was undoubtedly incriminated as an active participant. It was determined, by the way, that he was a morphine addict, and in general made a strange impression on people.

Sporadic killings of Jews, whether in the streets or in homes, continued the following morning. The Jews continued to hide and very few of them ventured outside. According to witness Tsatskis, on Sunday morning he dressed in peasant clothing, headed toward Aleksandrovskaya Street, and approached a group of Haidamaks chatting with local residents. He heard the Haidamaks say that until two o'clock they would be killing Jews individually, then from two o'clock on they would reprise the previous day's slaughter.

Dr. Stavinsky, in his capacity as the city council speaker, went to the commandant's office along with the mayor and others to seek an end to the slaughter. Witness Verkhola also went there and was very insistent in asking for the same. There, at the commandant's office, it was decided to call the city council into session, which Semosenko and Kiverchuk promised to attend. When Verkhola and Stavinsky headed to the Duma, along the way they were forced to witness several instances where Jews were killed or wounded. One Jew was shot before their very eyes next to the Duma. Very few representatives gathered at City Hall. The only Jewish member to appear was Raygorodsky. Other Jews had to turn back along the way, as there were attempts on their lives.

The city council began its session immediately after Semosenko and Kiverchuk arrived. After declaring the session open, Dr. Stavinsky briefly described the situation as it stood. Semosenko took the floor and explained in his statement that the Jews were exclusively to blame for what had happened, since, all of them being Bolsheviks, they had plotted to slaughter the Haidamaks and other Cossacks. He would do the same in the future, as he believed it to be his holy duty.

Kiverchuk made a statement to the same effect. Then Verkhola took the floor. Verkhola was of humble origins and self-educated. He graduated from art school, taught in village schools, and attended university. In his political beliefs he was a social democrat and Ukrainian patriot. Taking the floor after Semosenko and Kiverchuk, he delivered a long speech to the Duma, in which he called what happened in Proskuriv a disgrace for Ukraine. After giving credit to the Cossacks of the past, he argued that in this case Semosenko had dressed highwaymen in Cossack uniforms and taken their lead as commander. Addressing Semosenko, he said, "You are fighting the Bolsheviks, but are the children and elders your Haidamaks slaughtered Bolsheviks? Do you not know that there are Bolsheviks among other races, including Ukrainians?" He appealed to Semosenko, in the name of Ukraine's honor, to order an immediate end to the horrors under way.

Semosenko countered Verkhola in the same terms as in his opening statement. He stated that he was fighting not against elders, women, and children, but against Bolsheviks exclusively. With his eyes fixed on Verkhola, he said that, indeed, he did not doubt that, unfortunately, there were Bolsheviks among Ukrainians as well, but he would not spare them, either. He expressed his willingness to give an order to cease what was happening, so that the bodies of those killed could be buried without delay. He also believed it necessary to reprimand the city council for not warning him of the upcoming Bolshevik revolt, despite knowing of it.

Verkhola's testimony, as well as that of other witnesses, indicates that the killings lasted three days. After the city council session, however, the mass slaughter was stopped. Even so, all day Sunday and Monday there were many instances of sporadic killings of Jews, both in their homes and on the streets. There were also beatings of Jews in nearby villages, where the Haidamaks ventured of their own accord or by invitation from the peasants. The Jews dashed every which way, seeking a way out of the situation. Above all they placed their faith in Verkhola.

As was previously mentioned, Saturday's slaughter was supposed to repeat on Sunday. Three Haidamaks who appeared on Sunday morning at the municipal administration stated in passing, in Verkhola's presence, that they were instructed to slaughter Jews for three days. But after the Sunday session of the city council, Semosenko did, in fact, order an end to the slaughter, and it did not resume on a mass scale. Killings of individual Jews, however, continued on Sunday and Monday, as was stated previously. These killings were numerous.

Under Semosenko's orders, the victims of Saturday's slaughter were supposed to be buried on Monday. For this reason, bodies remained in homes and lay about in the streets from Saturday until Monday. Many bodies were chewed on by pigs.

Starting Monday morning, numerous peasant carts piled high with bodies made their way to the Jewish cemetery. Bodies were brought in throughout the day and filled up the entire cemetery. According to witness Finkel, while at the cemetery himself he counted over a thousand bodies. Hired peasants dug a giant pit at the cemetery, intended as a mass grave for victims of the slaughter. Again according to Finkel, looters appeared at the cemetery, approaching the bodies under various pretenses, feeling around and stealing from them. Relatives of the dead also came to look for their bodies and take valuables from their pockets, in some cases of very high value, but a great many bodies were found to have already been looted. Women were found with fingers cut off, presumably those on which they wore rings.

The burial was handled by overseer Dobrovolsky, who had been ordered to ensure that not a single body was left unburied by nightfall. However, it was not until four in the morning on Tuesday that all the bodies were buried. I should add that in addition to the common mass grave, another four smaller graves were dug, which were also filled with bodies. A few managed to bury their relatives in separate graves.

As was already stated, individual killings of Jews continued the next few days, both in Proskuriv and its environs. Many people were killed on the roads to nearby towns, in fields, and in the woods; Jews were also killed in nearby villages.

In addition to the Jews killed by the ravaging Haidamak mob, the authorities themselves arrested many Jews on the pretense that they were Bolsheviks, and then had them shot. One of the more notable perpetrators of this was one of Kiverchuk's assistants, one Kovalevsky, the son of a local landlord, an extremely spoiled and cruel young man.

I should say that, starting on Wednesday, February 19, a relative calm took hold in the city. It goes without saying that the Jews did not open their stores, as they were preoccupied. Semosenko, however, issued an order for the stores to be opened immediately.

On February 22, Semosenko issued a directive stating that according to information he possessed, there were many Bolshevik agitators in Proskuriv, for which reason he demanded that the population turn all these Bolshevik agitators in to the authorities by eight o'clock that same day, otherwise he would take decisive action. In the same directive he once again demanded that all the stores be opened immediately, otherwise each merchant would face a fine of 6,000 rubles.

The Jews took this directive as yet more chicanery and still another threat. To curry favor with Semosenko, they all pitched in to raise 300,000 rubles and decided to donate it through the city government for the garrison's needs. Mayor Sikora took on the task of handing over this money, and made such a mess of it that when Semosenko received the stated amount, despite knowing that it had been raised exclusively by Jews, he saw fit to issue a directive in which he wrote that he had received 300,000 rubles, not from the Jews, but "from the entire population of Proskuriv," whom he thanked for duly appreciating his Cossacks' efforts. He informed the central authorities, in turn, that Proskuriv's residents, as gratitude for maintaining order in the city and keeping it free of Bolsheviks, had donated 300,000 rubles to be put toward the garrison's needs.

Indeed, the Jews remained in a panicked, fearful state. They discussed with Commissar Verkhola all possible measures that could be taken to get rid of Semosenko. [. . .] Verkhola also found support in this matter from Kiverchuk, who resented that all the authority rested with Semosenko, of whom he was undoubtedly jealous. Furthermore, Kiverchuk believed that Semosenko, in slaughtering a large portion of the Jewish population, had done his job, and that there was no more need of him. [. . .] Verkhola headed to the command center [. . .] and managed to obtain an order for Semosenko to relinquish his authority as garrison chief and return to the front. Kiverchuk, in turn, was also soon forced to resign as commandant of Proskuriv and remained commandant only of the surrounding district.

According to witness descriptions, this Semosenko, who flooded the homes and streets of Proskuriv with Jewish blood, was a sickly young man of about twenty-two or twenty-three who had begun his military service as a volunteer back in tsarist times. With a forced serious expression on his face, he left everyone with the impression that he was less than intelligent, anxious, and unstable. I should admit, however, that based on some of his resolutions on reports that I saw, he was at the same time a person of great acumen and extremely decisive.

By my estimate count, over 1,200 people were killed in total in Proskuriv and its environs. In addition, out of the 600-some wounded, over 300 people died.

Recalling that in his first directive Semosenko threatened that anyone inciting a pogrom would be shot and that this directive was not published thanks to Kiverchuk, who was at the time generally standing in the way of authority being transferred to Semosenko, and recalling that Kiverchuk gladly offered him this authority when he expressed a willingness to slaughter the Jewish population, I arrive at the conclusion that Semosenko was primarily the physical executor of the bloody horrors that played out in Proskuriv. The main driving force behind this bloody page in Proskuriv's history was, in my opinion, Colonel Kiverchuk, that old tsarist hand, unquestionably a pogrom instigator and black-hundredist.

Proskuriv has the dubious honor of heralding a new era in pogrom execution. Prior pogroms had looting as their primary goal, meaning the pilfering of Jewish property; killings would follow the looting, but nonetheless remained secondary. The Cossacks viewed the looting as a just reward for their loyal service, and the killing of unarmed civilians as a demonstration of their valor and individual bravado. From Proskuriv on, the primary goal of pogroms in Ukraine was the wholesale slaughter of the Jewish population.

Source: "Doklad upolnomochennogo otdela pomoshchi pogromlennym pri ROKK na Ukraine A. I. Gillersona o pogromakh, ustroennykh voinskimi chastiami armii UNR v g. Proskurove," State Archive of the Russian Federation (GARF), f. r-1318, op. 24, d. 17, ll. 30–46. Translated from the Russian by Eugenia Tietz-Sokolskaya.

7

The Female Dimension of Pogrom Violence, 1917–1921

Elissa Bemporad

In May 1919, at the height of the Russian Civil War, armed bands dashed through the small towns of Ukraine, on the western banks of the river Dnipro. Led by the warlord Sokolovski, peasant insurgents entered Kornin—a town with a prewar Jewish population of approximately eight hundred—and in the course of one day, raped one hundred Jewish women and girls.[1] This information was collected by the members of the Kyiv (Kiev) branch of the Jewish Public Committee to Aid Pogrom Victims, an organization established in 1920 to gather data about the violence and to provide assistance to the victims. For each locality and pogrom, the aid workers compiled surveys with casualty figures, extent of material damage, and number of children orphaned in the violence. One entry in particular, with the number of rapes, captures a defining feature of the civil war pogroms, namely, the pervasiveness of sexual violence against Jewish women and girls. Rape marked the female experience of the pogroms and produced long-term consequences for the Jewish community as a whole.

During the civil war, sexual violence might have been as common as murder: perhaps as many as 100,000—or 1 in 12 Jewish women and girls—were raped in Ukraine alone, where the intra-ethnic clashes and paramilitary conflict reached a peak in 1919.[2] The information assembled by the aid workers reveals how the progressive intensification of violence was accompanied by an ensuing rise in the number of rapes. In the shtetl of Borshagovka (Kyiv province), where 1,850 Jews lived before the war, more than 25 women were raped in June 1919; one month later, during a second pogrom, 50 women were raped.[3] The inhabitants of the shtetl of Volodarka (Kyiv province), where approximately 2,000 Jews lived before the war, also experienced the escalation of violence through rape: on June 8, 1919, 10 women were

---

[1] See State Archive of Kyiv Oblast (GAKO), f. 3050, op. 1, d. 452, l. 8.
[2] On rape during the civil war, see Irina Astashkevich, *Gendered Violence: Jewish Women in the Pogroms of 1917 to 1921* (Boston: Academic Studies Press, 2018); and Thomas Chopard, "La guerre aux civils: Les violences contre les populations juives d'Ukraine, 1917–1924" (PhD diss., EHESS, 2015); esp. chap. 4, 309–26.
[3] GAKO, F. 3050, op. 1, d. 452, ll. 22–23.

Elissa Bemporad, *The Female Dimension of Pogrom Violence, 1917–1921* In: *Pogroms.* Edited by: Eugene M. Avrutin and Elissa Bemporad, Oxford University Press. © Oxford University Press 2021. DOI: 10.1093/oso/9780190060084.003.0008

raped; on July 3, 50 women were raped; and on July 8, during a third pogrom, 500 women were raped.[4]

While rape occurred during the earlier waves of pogroms of the late nineteenth and early twentieth centuries, it lay mostly at the periphery of the violence.[5] It increased in frequency during World War I, in the context of the mass expulsions of minority populations branded by the Russian imperial army as dangerous enemy aliens. Even then, though, wartime rape was more often than not perpetrated as an individual rather than as a collective crime, and did not single out Jewish women, but targeted other minority groups as well, Germans and Poles in particular.[6] During the civil war, rape of Jewish women and girls reached massive proportions in the pogrom economy. Perpetrators divested Jews of their goods and money and stripped them of "their" women. Rape became a form of plunder, especially in those impoverished communities in which, following multiple raids, no other form of ransom was available. All combatant troops in the civil war committed sexual violence against Jewish women and girls. Anti-Bolshevik forces, in particular, employed rape as an instrument of war and ethnic cleansing, to punish an imagined Jewish enemy that threatened Ukrainian, Polish, or Russian national aspirations.[7] The public dimension of mass rape became a way to enforce the national-political supremacy over the Jewish community and its purported alliance with Bolshevism. Thus, sexual violence targeted Jewish men as well: as a way of degrading and chastising them, men were forced to witness the rape of daughters and wives. Furthermore, the extreme violation of female symbols of motherhood—the cutting off of breasts or the slitting of a pregnant woman's stomach—demonstratively tested the Jews' right to procreate.[8] Women's bodies were turned into public spaces to eradicate the "political pollution" produced by the alleged Jewish-Bolshevik enemy group.

The allegation of Judeo-Bolshevism targeted Jewish men more than it did women. The imagined politicized enemy group, which sabotaged through Bolshevism the national dream of independence of Ukrainians, Poles, and Russians, was highly gendered. Acting on the widespread (and partly true) assumption that men were more likely to be the object of violence, many husbands and fathers fled as the invading troops approached, leaving behind wives and daughters. On the night of June 15, 1919, more women than men were killed in

[4] GAKO, F. 3050, op. 1, d. 452, ll. 28–30.

[5] Gur Alroey, "Sexual Violence, Rape, and Pogroms, 1903–1920," *Jewish Culture and History* 18, no. 3 (2017): 313–30.

[6] On rape during World War I, see Eric Lohr, "The Russian Army and the Jews: Mass Deportation, Hostages, and Violence during World War I," *Russian Review* 60, no. 3 (2001): 404–19; esp. 416–17.

[7] Mass rape of Jewish women and girls was so widespread that in several instances, non-Jewish neighbors in southern Ukraine complained to the military authorities. See Nokhem I. Shtif, *Pogromen in Ukrayne: di tsayt fun der frayviliker armey* (Berlin: Vostok, 1923).

[8] Photographic evidence of sexual crimes against Jewish women was put on display in a 1925 Moscow exhibit on the pogroms of the civil war, and was included in the ensuing publication: Z. Ostrovskii, *Evreiskie pogromy* (Moscow: Shkola i kniga, 1925), 117, 125.

Kytaihorod (in Russian, Kitay-gorod): as the pogrom began, many men had already fled the town.[9]

When mass rape was carried out in the shtetl, where most residents knew each other through proximity and familiarity, it became intimately public and anonymity was hardly a choice. And yet in its aftermath, the victims and their families shrouded sexual violence in silence. Humiliated and traumatized, victims were understandably unforthcoming in discussing rape, which in turn made it impossible to pinpoint the precise number of victims.[10] Besides the natural shame associated with rape, victims from a traditional background knew that sexual violence would affect their marriage market value and thus rarely discussed it. Similarly, family members hardly ever related the rape of daughters, sisters, or wives unless murder followed sexual violence. Chaim Dayter described the harrowing moment when, on February 15, 1919, fifteen members of the Ukrainian troops broke into his home in Proskuriv and one after the other, raped his eighteen-year-old daughter Bella—in front of him and his wife.[11] He disclosed the victim's identity because the rapists killed her. Finally, not unlike other genocidal contexts, sexual violence could appear as secondary in the eyes of the victims and their families, and perhaps even seem irrelevant compared to the widespread horrific torture and murder, all too common during the pogroms of the civil war. The perception of a hierarchy of crimes and suffering might have silenced the victims and discouraged them from sharing their experience. Murder eclipsed sexual violence.

The medical records that doctors and midwives compiled in the aftermath of the violence provide a comprehensive picture of the scale of sexual violence. While they rarely mention the victims' names, they do provide information about age, marital and social status, the number of perpetrators who gang-raped each victim, where the violence took place, as well as statistics about illnesses, pregnancies, abortions, and suicides that followed the rape. As rare as they are, some sources do allow us to recover the victims' voices, and capture a glimpse into the emotions experienced by those targeted for rape. One such source is the diary of the Yiddish writer Malka Lee (1904–1976). At the age of fourteen she recorded her personal experience of violence in her native shtetl of Monastyryska, in western Ukraine, which Polish and Ukrainian troops repeatedly occupied. Lee conveys the female experience of terror and shows how the fear of rape could trigger or exacerbate the Jewish refugee crisis.

Rape (and the fear thereof) had a devastating impact on Jewish demography. It promoted the rush for internal and external migration, as relocation from the place of trauma became a plausible way to prevent further sexual assault. Unleashing an epidemic of venereal diseases, unwanted pregnancies, and abortions, often carried

[9] Institute for Jewish Research Archives (YIVO), RG 80, folder 360, pp. 32863–65.
[10] On rape and silence during the Holocaust, see Helene Sinnreich, "And It Was Something We Did Not Talk About: Rape of Jewish Women during the Holocaust," *Holocaust Studies: A Journal of Culture and History* 14, no. 2 (2008): 1–22.
[11] YIVO, RG 80, folder 358, pp. 32752–53.

Photo portrait of the Yiddish writer Malka Lee (1904–1976), who witnessed sexual violence during the pogroms of the civil war and chronicled her experience in a diary. She immigrated to New York in 1921.
Courtesy of the Institute for Jewish Research Archives (YIVO), New York

out in the absence of medical care, rape increased women's mortality rates. Finally, concerned demographers recorded the psychological shock and post-traumatic stress disorder caused by the violence, arguing that it triggered a dramatic plunge in Jewish women's birthrates compared to those of other ethnic groups.[12]

The experience of Jewish women during the pogroms of the civil war is not limited to victimhood. Women took part in rescue efforts, as aid workers, nurses, and midwives, they collected data about the violence, and as fighters some even participated in fending off the assault on the Jewish population by joining self-defense units.[13] Men might have been more effective in putting together historical and literary accounts of the events: compared to women, they might have been less burdened by the immediate practical needs of everyday life that followed

[12] On long-term consequences of rape during the civil war, see Elissa Bemporad, *Legacy of Blood: Jews, Pogroms, and Ritual Murder in the Lands of the Soviets* (New York: Oxford University Press, 2019), esp. chap. 1.
[13] Elias Heifetz, *The Slaughter of the Jews in the Ukraine in 1919* (New York: Thomas Seltzer, 1921), 130.

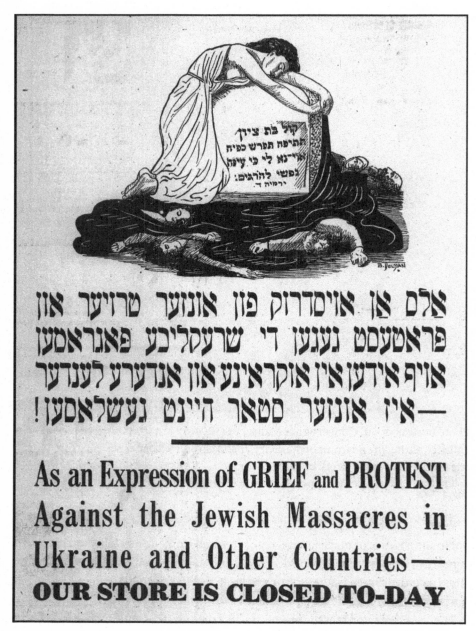

אַלס אַן אויסדרוק פון אונזער טרויער און
פּראטעסט געגען די שרעקליכע פּאנראמען
אויף אידען אין אוקראינע און אנדערע לענדער
—איז אונזער סטאר היינט געשלאסען!

As an Expression of GRIEF and PROTEST Against the Jewish Massacres in Ukraine and Other Countries— OUR STORE IS CLOSED TO-DAY

A woman with outstretched arms is mourning over a tombstone with the engraved Hebrew verse of Jeremiah 4:31, "The cry of a daughter of Zion gasping for breath, stretching out her arms, 'Woe is me! I am fainting before murderers.'" The tombstone is surrounded by a sea of blood and the bodies of Jews murdered in the pogroms. The image of the Jewish people as a woman is at the heart of the biblical poetry of lament. Below the image is the announcement in Yiddish and in English translation that stores will be closed in protest of the massacres of Jews in Ukraine during the civil war.
Forverts, November 22, 1919, 3. Courtesy of the *Forward*

The Yiddish writer Rokhl Faygnberg (1893–1976) holds her baby boy. The photo was taken after mother and son managed to flee the pogroms of the civil war in hiding.

Courtesy of Daphna Levy, the granddaughter of Faygnberg

destruction. But women too experienced the writer's calling. Rokhl Faygnberg (1885–1972) emerged as one of the most powerful chroniclers of the genocidal violence of the civil war. A native of Lyuban (a small town in Belarus), Faygnberg experienced the violence as a refugee. Her autobiographical writings capture aspects of the gender dimension of the refugee experience, and provide evidence that hiding among neighbors, disguising one's identity, or converting to Russian Orthodoxy as a measure to eschew the violence might have been easier for Jewish women than it was for men. In particular, Faygnberg's account of the destruction of one shtetl illustrates the intimacy of pogrom violence, often carried out by neighbors.

Women also became agents of violence. They too took advantage of the political and socioeconomic disarray generated by the civil war and engaged in rituals of violence. Wives of ataman leaders of the Cossack armies showed their eagerness to seize the property plundered by their husbands during the attacks on Jewish settlements. By doing so, these women encouraged them to engage in further violence and murder.[14] In some instances, Russian and Ukrainian women were emboldened to play an active role in ethnic cleansing. "Women! It is your turn to do something for the sake of our suffering Russia, boycott everything that is Jewish, and spread this idea as much and as far as you can. Remember—this will be worse for them than all other pogroms, and they will leave Russia," read a note that appeared in the streets of Kyiv during the pogroms of October 4–7,

---

[14] YIVO, RG 80, folder 450, folio 7.

1919.[15] Some women, such as Nastia Natalenko, reached an almost legendary status among other gangs of peasant insurgents and bandits.[16]

The utter turmoil of the civil war muddled the ethnic and gender identity of the actors involved, transgressing the expected polarity of Jewish victimhood and non-Jewish perpetrators.[17] Like Jewish men, Jewish women too partook in violence against other Jews. Taking advantage of the power vacuum generated by the war, they too could become complicit in the looting and murder of their fellow Jews.[18]

---

[15] YIVO, RG 80, folder 409, folio 34.

[16] YIVO, RG 80, folder 587, folio 36.

[17] On a Jewish male bandit who, in a shtetl in Cherkasy, killed a young woman and helped murder a member of the local Jewish self-defense unit, see, for example, State Archive of Kyiv Oblast (DAKO), f. 3050, op. 1, d. 128, l. 34.

[18] State Archive of Zhytomyr Oblast (DAZhO), f. 1820, op. 5, d. 97, ll. 3-5, 44, 71–74ob.

Document 7.1. Looting and Rape in Pechora

A Jewish refugee by the name of Lifschitz, who also served as an aid worker in the Kyiv branch of the Jewish Public Committee, wrote his account of the June 12, 1919, pogrom in Pechora, Podolia province. Led by Sokolovski's band, peasant insurgents engaged in looting and killing Jews—blaming them for supporting the Bolsheviks—and raped Jewish women and girls.

The pogrom in Pechora took place on June 12, 1919, at five in the morning. Sokolovski's gang, numbering five hundred people, entered Pechora, pulling along a massive supply train loaded with Jewish property from other places they had raided. Looting began immediately upon arrival, and the killing an hour later. The local priest went to the gang's headquarters, and his pleas to stop the carnage were met with, "This is the answer to the Bolsheviks for the Red Terror." The priest argued that the local Jewish population was apolitical, but his arguments did not help. Then the priest declared that he had supposedly come on behalf of Christians who demanded an end to the pogrom. That had the desired effect: a sign from the chief stopped the carnage. An hour later, at three o'clock, they headed out, accompanied by local musicians. The gang rode through streets bathed in blood. Almost all Jewish property (except the money and valuables, which the thugs took for themselves) was left to local Christians. For the bright future to come, the Jews of Pechora—like all the Jews of Ukraine—paid with the blood of their sons, the sacred blood of their infants, and the honor of their daughters.

P.S. Almost all the women thirteen years old and up were raped by the thugs. Children were raped in front of their parents, some were then killed. There were rapes in the street before a sneering audience. Many women caught venereal diseases. There were a few pregnancies. One woman whose husband was in America went insane after finding out she was pregnant five months later.

Source: State Archive of the Russian Federation (GARF), f. R-1339, op. 1, d. 423, l. 42. Translated from the Russian by Eugenia Tietz-Sokolskaya.

Document 7.2. Looting and Rape in Smila

In the fall of 1919, the troops of General Anton Denikin of the White Army, who fought against the Red Army for the reinstatement of the tsar and the return to monarchism, conquered most of Ukraine. The Cossacks formed the core of the White Army detachments. The representative of the Russian Red Cross Assistance Committee, A. D. Yuditsky, wrote a report about the pogroms carried out by the White Army troops in Smila (in Russian and Yiddish, Smela), Kyiv province, from August to December 1919. The report focuses on several instances of mass rape of Jewish women and girls. Hundreds of victims contracted venereal diseases, and some committed suicide.

In Smila, Denikin's reign began with a pogrom and ended with one. To be honest, it is challenging to determine when exactly the first pogrom ends and the second begins. The four months that the savage volunteers had their way in the town constituted one continuous pogrom. The Jewish population did not even have a moment of peace. Many military detachments passed through Smila. The Preobrazhensky Regiment passed through, as did the Izmaylovsky, Semyonovsky, Pavlovsky, and many other regiments.

As early as when the guests—the volunteers—arrived in the last ten days of August, their appearance was marked by a real, modern-style pogrom, with all the accompanying details and nuances. The pogrom feat was undertaken by General Khasov's Special Scout Division. The Second Kuban Guerrilla Regiment was particularly excellent on this mission. The drunk Cossacks set fire to the Jewish cooperative in the center of the town right off the bat. From there the flames spread rapidly to adjacent buildings, burning them to ashes. While the fire raged, the Cossacks joyfully sang, "We beat the Yids, we beat the Commune," song lyrics that have gained great fame throughout the region where pogroms occurred.

At the very same time that some enjoyed the fire, other groups of volunteers scattered across the town and took action with gusto: they looted apartments, killed and slashed people, and so on. They demonstrated particular energy in chasing down Jewish girls and women, whom they then dishonored right there in the street for everyone to see. The hapless victims' hysterical cries and sobs were heart-wrenching. Two of my wife's brothers witnessed a whole group of about twenty drunk Cossacks savagely raping one Jewish girl in a cellar. The rape was accompanied by horrific torture. Each rapist would come up with ever more terrible ways to violate his victim. I was told that the poor girl committed suicide afterward. There were many elderly women among those raped. For instance, I know of Mrs. M., a sixty-year-old woman. The public is embarrassed to talk about this and often sweeps such grievous facts under the rug. Doctors, however, attest that a large number of women came to see them after the pogrom, particularly young women. And to their great misfortune, many of them have contracted venereal diseases.

During the first pogrom in August, there were twenty-two dead, about three hundred injured, and at least four hundred raped. The destruction in the town was staggering. Suffice to say that [many] Jewish homes lost even their hearths and chimneys. Floors everywhere were torn up and ruined, the dirt in cellars dug up, often up to fifteen feet down. In general, the gangs wreaked havoc primarily in the town's poorest quarters, such as on Kovalevka and similar streets. The thugs inflicted horrific suffering on their victims. Wherever they broke into they typically beat everyone present with ramrods, prodded them with burning candles, pulled nooses tight around their necks, and jeered at their victims. [. . .]

But the worst of it began at the send-off, when the White Guard cutthroats began retreating toward Rostov in December from the front lines stretching between Kyiv and Fastiv and between Grebenka and Cherkasy. The entire Volunteer Army was routed through Smila. The Jews of Smila didn't wait for an invitation: they left their homes and hid wherever they could. Many laid low in the cellars or attics of Christians they knew. Some of the Jews gathered in synagogues and awaited their fate as a community. [. . .] The great tragedy did not take place until Friday (this was in the last few days of December). The last military detachment was passing through, made up of Chechens and Ossetians. They stopped in the town for no more than 1.5–2 hours. But during that short time they managed to get so much done and worked so zealously that the next day 107 casualties were brought to the Jewish cemetery. Around 600 were wounded. The number of rape victims was terribly high (according to some local doctors, the figure is over a thousand). Two-thirds of the victims have contracted syphilis. This time Kovalevka, the town's poorest area, again suffered the most. The Ossetians and Chechens surrounded the street, prevented anyone from leaving, and set the houses on fire. The frightened residents ran out into the street in terror, but the executioners would immediately shoot them or hack at them with sabers. Two little tots were ripped in half.... That Friday would have turned into a St. Bartholomew's Day massacre for Smila if the Cossacks had remained another hour or two. But the Cossack "heroes" heard the first cannon fire from the Red insurgents in the nearby villages of Popovka and Turnovka. That sent them into such a frenzy that they left their work unfinished and fled to Bobrinskaia to load onto their train.

Source: State Archive of the Russian Federation (GARF), f. R-1339, op. 1, d. 438, ll. 25–26. Translated from the Russian by Eugenia Tietz-Sokolskaya.

Document 7.3. Denikin's Forces Depart from Smila

Doctor Sara Margolina described what happened in December 1919, as Denikin's White Army troops withdrew from Smila, pushed back by the approaching Red Army. White Army soldiers broke into her home and carried out acts of violence against family members and refugees, who were there hiding. In her report, which she sent to the Editorial Board for Collecting and Publishing Materials on Pogroms in Ukraine, Margolina provides extensive evidence of sexual violence against women and girls.

For eight days, Denikin's cavalry was in retreat nonstop past our house. The street was dark with thousands, tens of thousands of riders. It seemed the passing troops would never end. An endless chain of carts formed their long supply train. The heavy carts were piled high with all sorts of provisions. Many of the carts carried piles of clearly stolen items: suitcases, baskets, down mattresses, samovars, pillows, blankets. [. . .] Our house was on the main street and, strangely, during the entire time the "heroes" were retreating it was never attacked. The miracle was ascribed to the two doctors' signs hanging on the main entrance to our home. Counting on the "well-being" of our dwelling, several of the families that had faced looting came to live with us. There were children and young women among them. Our niece, sick with typhus, was brought over, but, besides her, my husband and tenant were already lying sick with typhus. Our mother was also sick. And all of us, the sick and the healthy, watched this retreat with racing hearts and boundless worry. [. . .]

By the Julian calendar, it was December 20. While caring for the sick, I happened to look out the window, and to my horror saw a group of riders split off and head straight toward our house. I had a glimmer of hope that maybe they would pass farther on, but alas, a knock on the door dispelled any doubts. At the same time, a few Cossacks ran in from the courtyard, went straight to the wardrobes and hangers, and after cleaning out everyone's pockets, ran off. The knocking on the front door intensified. Our tenant—a Russian telephone operator, [who lived with us along with] her friend, who was also Russian—ran in, breathless, and took the keys to open the gates. They came into the courtyard on their horses. About ten people came into the house, two of them officers. One had a very intelligent face, reminiscent of Nikolay Chernyshevsky, and the other had an actor's shaved head and well-fed face. The guests declared that they could only stay for forty-five minutes, so [we should] quickly put the samovar on and offer something to eat. My brother began getting the samovar ready, while I stayed with the guests. They sat down in the dining room; rather, only the officers sat, whereas the privates could not sit without permission, so they stood the whole time. However, one of the soldiers, in a tall white hat, decided not to waste time and went through all the rooms, putting everything to his liking in his pockets. [. . .]

The officer turned to me with various questions about my relatives, my material wealth and theirs, assuming and trying to convince me that we had huge stores of all sorts of stuff. All this was said with much mockery and irony. With pain in my heart, I fell silent. The tea was ready, and we served bread, crackers, everything we had. The smitten operators brought jam. Another ten people came in and also had tea and snacks. I was constantly pouring tea; when the talkative officer had satisfied his appetite, he got up from the table and instead of the word "thanks" he said something else: "Make it happen." Right away several Cossacks ran over to my brother-in-law, who was lying in bed, dragged him off, took off his boots, and to loud laughter all around forced him to dance the Kozachok, whipping his bare feet with horsewhips. This was in the bedroom of our sick mother, who looked on in wordless despair. Then came the most terrible looting. They turned everything over, took shoes and clothes, and demanded money, gold rings, and earrings, drawing their sabers and whipping with horsewhips as they did so. My brother-in-law's cries as he was beaten ran together with the noise of falling furniture, upended wardrobes, pulled-out drawers, and breaking dishware. Everywhere around us there were only animal-like faces, red, sweaty from the tea they had just had, burning with hatred toward us. It was the first time in our lives that we saw such misanthropy, such disdain and heartlessness toward Jews, as would be difficult to imagine toward even the most harmful of animals.

At that moment I heard that I was being called for help from the room where the girls were. Upon running there, I saw, to my horror, Cossacks leading three girls who were fighting back with all their might. The youngest one was only fourteen, almost a child. In her despair she broke free of the miscreants and threw herself into the bed where [my] typhus-stricken husband lay. She was left behind. They locked the other two unfortunate girls in the study after first chasing me out of there, and stood at the door to keep me from going in. In extreme despair I rushed to the officers, pleading with them, in the name of all that was sacred to them, to defend the innocent children. The untalkative [officer] who looked like Chernyshevsky didn't even want to look at me; the other one said he would come soon, but both remained in the courtyard and continued peacefully chatting about something. When I again ran up to the higher-ups with pleas and unbeknownst [to myself] unwittingly touched the "actor's" sleeve with my hand, he gave the spot a shake and said not to touch him, because I could get him dirty. Despairing, I ran back into the house; the screams of a girl being raped sounded from the study. A Cossack stood at the door, guarding the booty, waiting his turn. [. . .] She was calling to me for help, and I was losing my mind with despair. I darted to and fro through the rooms like a caged animal, seeking some way to save the poor girls, but the entrances and exits were blocked by Cossacks who would beat me with horsewhips as I approached the door. Suddenly, I noticed an unguarded door from the dining room to the garden. Hoping for a miracle, I wanted to go through this door to reach the street through the garden, but I was noticed and hit hard on the back of the head with a horsewhip. The hand with the horsewhip rose again, but one of the Cossacks, like a knight, uttered, "We don't touch women . . ."

I ran into the dining room, where a crimson-faced Cossack had his bare saber to my sister's neck, demanding money and rings. I rushed toward her and was thrown back toward my mother's bedroom. I heard her moan and ran toward her room. There, a Cossack was attaching a rope to the lamp hook and getting a noose ready for my brother-in-law. He was still being beaten all over with horsewhips, and by now he was lying almost unconscious behind an upended wardrobe. I ran up to the Cossack and grabbed the rope from his hands. He hit me with a horsewhip and went to another room. Meanwhile, they started beating my nephew, still a boy, on my sick mother's bed. They took the blanket off my typhus-stricken niece and carried it away, and poured some kind of powder in my mother's eyes. At the same time, everything was being carried out of the house—food, linens—while the rape of the girls carried on. One girl, a university student, was raped by five Cossacks. The sixth started to lead her from the study to the kitchen, but suddenly left her and ran away. The other girl, a high school student of about fifteen, was raped by three miscreants. Before that the poor girls wanted to hide in the room of our tenant, the telephone operator, but she chased them out of her room. The other girls were able to hide in the courtyard.

The officers waited patiently for everything to wrap up and remained in the courtyard, then came into our apartment, and that's when the former polytechnical student began looting quite thoroughly. When he saw me, he showed me that he had a lot of gold and silver in his pocket, and at the same time kept putting lots of trinkets and various items from the cupboard into his pocket. I reminded him that he had said that his being in our house guaranteed safety, for us and for our property. He responded, "Things have taken a different turn now," and continued looting my room, which had not been ripped apart yet. Suddenly, he turned to me and declared that he had chopped up plenty of people already, that he is a wonderful surgeon when it comes to cleanly chopping off heads and does so better than a doctor, and that he was a sure candidate for [medical school]. He took all the medical instruments, medications, and bandages. [. . .] In almost every house girls, women, and even children had been raped, and their number turned out to be enormous. Finally, at noon on Saturday, December 21 by the Julian calendar, the Bolsheviks entered the mutilated city.

Source: State Archive of the Russian Federation (GARF), f. R-1339, op. 1, d. 438, ll. 25–26. Translated from the Russian by Eugenia Tietz-Sokolskaya.

Document 7.4. The Doctors Speak

These medical records illustrate the experience and condition of rape victims, who were brutalized by the White Army forces during the pogroms in Cherkasy, Kyiv province, in December 1919. Many of the soldiers belonged to the White Army's Cossack detachments. Compiled by physicians, gynecologists, and midwives, and sent to the Editorial Board for the study of pogroms, these documents provide painstaking evidence of the physical and emotional cost of sexual violence.

1. March 28, 1920. Survey of gynecologist Dr. Goldman, chief physician at the Jewish hospital.

The doctor has recorded about 120 instances of rape.
Age range of the victims.
Victims range from thirteen to forty-five years old. Six to seven cases involving minors (thirteen–fourteen years old). A small percentage also involved the elderly. The majority are fifteen years old and up. There were about ten married women among the victims, the remainder were unmarried.
Characterization of the rapes.
These were gang rapes, involving for the most part three to four rapists. There were cases of up to ten to twelve rapists per woman. Cases of individual rape, involving one person, were extremely rare.
Particularly terrible cases.
There were many of these. For instance, one poor woman was raped by twelve people. After that the miscreants forced the victim's husband, in turn, to engage in sexual intercourse with the unfortunate victim, while a Cossack made certain

they were not faking it. Often several girls were raped simultaneously in the same house: one group would rape one girl in one room, another group raped another one in the next room, and so on. The victims' cries and screams came from all sides and merged into a unified chorus. The parents and heads of the household were typically beaten during this time. Often, the parents would flee as it happened.

When the rapes were observed.

1. The largest number of rapes took place as Denikin's forces entered Cherkasy. This was the work of the advance guard.
2. In the middle period there were isolated cases.
3. As Denikin's forces left, the number of rapes again grew rapidly. There were, however, fewer than at the beginning.
4. During the Grigoriev uprising, the doctor observed a relatively small number of rapes.

Instances of infection.

The doctor recorded eight cases of infection with venereal disease. All were gonorrhea cases. The disease was identified in a timely fashion and successfully treated. There were no fatalities.

Pregnancies and abortions.

Many girls lost their periods. This was not, however, due to pregnancy. This was apparently the result of nervous shock or other causes. Preventative measures were, however, taken to put a stop to fertilization in case it had taken place.

Suicides as a result of rape.

The doctor is aware of one suicide. The exact reason for the suicide is not known. Some believe that it was the result of rape and terrible suffering. The victim's surname was Sambur. The girl was about twenty years old.

2. Survey of Dr. Shendarevsky, infectious disease doctor for the first district and former director of the outpatient facility of the city's medical benefit fund.

Dr. Shendarevsky saw about fifty victims personally. Many of the victims had been raped several times, as Denikin's forces entered and left the city and during their stay [in the city]. Overall it should be noted that the rapes took place over the entire time that Denikin's forces were present. During the winter evenings, attacks would begin at three o'clock, accompanied by looting and mass rapes.

Makeup of the victims.

Since the district this doctor was responsible for was industrial (tobacco and match factories), the majority of victims were workers. There were, however, many housewives. There were also educated girls (such as the high school student Vernik). As for age, there were many minors who were ten and eleven years old and a smaller number of elderly women who were around fifty years old. One ten-year-old girl (a refugee from Moshe) died of excessive blood loss after being gang raped.

Instances of infection.

The doctor is aware of about five syphilis cases, about five cancroid cases, and up to ten cases of gonorrhea. In two instances the husband and children were also infected. In one family, consisting of eight people, everyone has eyelid inflammation (blepharitis) due to gonorrhea.

Pregnancies, abortions.

Pregnancies were widespread. There were pregnancies among the deaf (Butovetskaya) and the mentally unsound (Vorobeychik). There were fifteen pregnancies among the doctor's patients. In general it would be fair to say that a good half of the victims became pregnant. There were very many abortions. Doctors facilitate[d] them. Unfortunately, some sought a doctor's aid too late, whereas others, being too self-conscious, did it at home (using all sorts of methods) or with help from midwives, healer women, and so on. In the latter case, there were fatalities. That was how two of the doctor's patients died: Schlief, age nineteen, and Panorova, age eighteen. Both were extraordinarily beautiful.

In general, the majority of the victims hide their ill fate even now (especially those who did not get pregnant). The doctor saw evidence of this in his own practice. When treating typhus and other illnesses, in tracing the progression of the disease he would also find out about their misfortune. Some would ask, as a by the way, "Doctor, is it all right that I haven't had a period in six weeks?" The doctor would respond with a question: "Did the Cossacks do anything to you?" And the patient would typically turn out to be a victim. Two sisters, university students living on Nikolaevskaia Street, contracted typhus; it turned out that one of them, the more attractive one, had also been raped.

Total number of rapes in the city.

As the volunteers arrived, they committed up to sixty-six rapes. That is the official figure recorded by doctors. When Denikin's forces left, the doctors estimate there were at least two hundred cases.

3. Survey of Dr. Shendarevskaia (a female doctor).

Dr. Shendarevskaia recorded about twenty instances. These were victims who did not want publicity and did not go to the hospital for that reason, and others. These were the easiest cases, not requiring surgical intervention. The majority of victims were workers, with a lot of high school students. In terms of age, the victims were very young, with the most common age being sixteen. [. . .]

The rapes were primarily gang rapes, with eight to ten people per victim. There were instances of infection with syphilis and gonorrhea. One woman of about fifty (Volodarskaia) who was infected with gonorrhea passed the disease on to her husband. On one victim the doctor discovered syphilis by chance. She was treating the patient for typhus and besides the typhus rash discovered syphilitic sores on her chest and neck. Such cases were frequent. Even now, the victims' emotional state is extremely dismal. They are trying to leave the places tied to terrible memories.

4. Survey of the midwife Ruvinskaia.

Fifteen to twenty affected women sought help. Two victims came to Ruvinskaia from nearby towns. The majority of the victims were girls aged fifteen to twenty. One girl was thirteen. Many of the rapes were gang rapes (two to three people in a row). There were also unnatural, barbaric rapes. One girl, a seventeen-year-old worker at a candy factory, was raped in the mouth. During the rape the monsters yelled, "Don't scream, Yid girl. We'll kill you." Her mouth was disfigured. For a long time afterward, the girl suffered terrible vomiting. Merely recalling the incident caused her to vomit horrendously and left her in a sickly state.

Instances of infection.

There were several gonorrhea cases. When the disease was discovered early, it was for the most part effectively treated, but many remain infected even now. Mrs. Ruvinskaia had few abortions, because the embryo was forced out early.

5. Testimony from Mrs. Lipkova, a midwife, March 24, 1920.

Two victims sought out Mrs. Lipkova. One victim was raped as Denikin's forces arrived. She was a young woman, sixteen to seventeen years old, a refugee from Moshe, from an educated family. The other victim was a thirty-five-year-old widow. In both cases they were raped by groups of people. The first victim tried to buy off the rapists. They took the money and then went ahead with the rape. Throughout the rape the girl was completely unconscious and unaware of anything. She had an abortion. After she recovered, she left this area forever.

Mrs. Lipkova is also aware of a case where one of her colleagues, another midwife, was raped. Cossacks attacked the house of Mrs. Lipkova's father (a very religious person). There was looting. Two girls from the neighbor's family on the other side of the house were raped in front of Lipkov [the father]. The terrible sight of the rape and the girls' screams had an awful effect on the old man. He began ripping out his hair, clawing his skin, and moaning terribly. Denikin's men killed him. Jews who were hiding in the neighboring garden [heard] the brief, tragic dialogue that preceded the killing. They demanded the old man's money and (valuables, but he had nothing). Then a shot rang out and (the old man fell dead. "What a good shot," one of Denikin's men said, and the group left).

Source: State Archive of the Russian Federation (GARF), f. R-1339, op. 1, d. 438, ll. 81–82 ob. Translated from the Russian by Eugenia Tietz-Sokolskaya.

Document 7.5. A Mother and Daughter Understanding

These excerpts from the diary of fourteen-year-old Malka Lee illustrate how the threat of sexual violence weighed on the family institution, how mothers and daughters bonded through the experience of imminent danger, and how the expectation of rape became one of the leading forces promoting the refugee crisis. Lee, who was eventually rescued from rape by a local prostitute, brings to life the terror experienced by women in the wake of the violence perpetrated by Symon Petliura's Ukrainian forces.

News spread across the city: Petliura's men were going from house to house looking for dishes and bread for the soldiers. We had a few dried-out loaves of bread. So the children went up to the attic to hide them. Mother went out to buy something. I sat in the shadowy house, my eyes restless, like the minute hand of a restless clock, looking for anything we had forgotten to hide in the attic, because then the ladder was to be removed, and it would not occur to anyone to go into the hiding place without a ladder.

Suddenly fists hammered at the door and a voice thundered: "Open up!" Paralyzed, I was silent. So the door began to shake, bayonets twisted in the crevices. All alone, I was terrified of the shaking door and I burst into tears of despair saying: "My mother will come soon." That excited them even more and they knocked open the door by force. In despair, I opened the front door which led to the burned-out porch. The Petliurite, hearing me jump out onto the porch, went back outside away from the door. I saw before me a giant of a man. His fur hat was tilted to the side, a tuft of hair peeped out from one side and waved. At the back of the hat hung a long woolen braid. His jacket unbuttoned, his naked chest was exposed like armor and singed my eyes like red glowing iron. White teeth like an aroused animal, and eyes—black and terrifying. He stood down below on the pavement and I up above on the porch, my hands entwined over my heart like a cross.

He mocked my standing and shivering. He bent down—my dress enveloped me modestly like a gust of wind. My mouth open and terrified, I gaped as eyes swallowed my legs from below the porch, and teeth bared like an animal's. I was quaking and trembling like quicksilver. The sky above my head was covered with a black fur. The twilight split open. Suddenly in the distance there appeared a prostitute from our city. I called out to the strange, rejected woman: "Zosya! Zosya!" She approached and at my signaling took away the Petliurite.

My mother came running. The children jumped down from the attic like kittens. They had heard how I had cried and they had been silent so that no one would hear them and take away the dried-up loaves of bread. Children do not know of any other danger. The twilight melted like wax. Shadows stalked across the room. Terror ate into our faces like deep pockmarks. We sat in the dark and the night came swimming like a black hearse. Fists—hammering logs—again knocked. Shining spears stabbed through the cracks in the door. The door began to move and tremble like a living creature. We recognized the same shouts and a triumphant laughter: they had returned. With desolate eyes my mother poured all of our fear into our father's eyes. . . . She quickly grabbed two gray military blankets and threw one onto me, the other onto herself, stuffed rags behind her back in order to look hunchbacked, and smeared her face with ashes. We ran into the empty next room, jumped up to the open black windows. Black mouths swallowed us, spit us out into the black night onto the empty streets. We ran like ghosts. We felt behind us footsteps were racing, no not footsteps—in the blank night they echoed like gangs of marauders. We ran and were silent.

For the first time I felt such understanding for my mother throughout my limbs, and my mother felt the same for me. We ran and were silent. Thoughts danced like spinning wheels; we felt like sacrificing ourselves for each other, we ran through strange back alleys and did not speak. On the other side of the street soldiers were sitting over red lit torches and roasting potatoes, soldiers were singing, it seemed to us: red torches were lit in the night, shining a path for terrified wanderers—shadows who want to hide somewhere.

We ran by another street. Soldiers were lying, sleeping on the cold ground, on garbage. Rifles were snuggling with their heads, as if they were already tired of the bullets coming out of their throats. They wanted to rest at night just like us. To hide somewhere. It was dark in all the houses. We knocked at the doors, tried the locks. Everyone was scared to open because of the danger to themselves. That is how we wandered exhausted into a derelict house. We hid among burned-out pieces of iron, collapsed half fainting. Only then did tears roll down from our eyes. Our sacred tears mixed together in a silver river that fused us together in a mother and daughter understanding.

All the Girls Run Away from the City

There came a terrible evening. The air was flashing behind a wall of darkness. The danger moved like an armored car across the city. The city gasped in a deep stupor as if before a storm. The Bolsheviks fought with Petliura's men. The latter—foreseeing their defeat—began to destroy the half-dead city. The mothers could sense it: their daughters had to be saved from the terrible night coming.

All the girls of the city came together and ran to the train station to save themselves and escape. I was unable to tear myself away from my mother, as if I had grown into her. When I went out into the dark street, my mother's crying blocked my way. I saw blindness before me. With the piece of bread in my hand I ran to the train, where hordes of girls were already sitting on the floor, like herds packed into freight cars. The train did not move. It seemed to me: it's just a story that grandmother used to tell. A black bear swallowed all the children into its belly. In the distance the forest was black, like herds of black bears. The forest brought from its darkness disconnected cries of tortured hoarse throats. The night moaned in pain and the train did not move.

All the girls were sitting on the steely floor. Tears washed our faces. It seemed to us that we ourselves had brought our lives toward the danger. The terror hammered like drumming footsteps in our hearts. We sat all night snuggled up to each other, swallowing the darkness of the woods. A red sea came swimming into the sky. Night took off its dirty shirt behind the mountains. In the sky hung the moon—a pale rose. The day began to dawn. The train did not move. In the golden-blue morning I so wanted to run back home into the city, to look once more at my mother. Like lightning I tore myself from the train, left the girls and ran back to my mother. The streets shuddered with a deathly breath. On the hilly road up to my house there ran a ribbon of blood like a gutter. Behind my steps strange black gangrenous bones stuck out from the streets. I went over the bloody roads into my house. My mother spotted me—she wandered toward me like a night wanderer. She touched me and still did not believe it: it's me. Or my shadow. The deadness vanished from her face and she held me with her mother-hands. She recounted: the whole night voices had rocked the darkness, as if all the dead were moaning from their graves. And it had seemed to her that all the girls from the trains were tearing the night and screaming. Somebody had screamed over the city with thousands of voices. She clung to me as if for the last time and pushed me out of the house toward the train station.

I stood paralyzed, swallowed the brightest face in the whole world: my mother's face. . . . In her faithfulness I lost my way like a sinking ship, I was not sure whether to remain by my mother or to run away against my will. My mother pushed me out of the house by force. I ran back over the bloody streets to the waiting girls. I told them about the bloody rivulets from the night of slaughter in the streets. Then we were all paralyzed by a picture: Zosya, the prostitute who had saved me that time behind the porch from the Petliurite, was running covered in blood, her hands cut up. When she saw me she started crying so pitifully, showed her hands, her body. A gang of Petliura's men invaded her home at night. When her father, the wood-cutter, wanted to protect her from the band, they hacked him to pieces with the axe, threw him out onto the street. They tormented her on top of her father's mutilated body. Cut up her hands and her body. She showed her hands again. She looked like a wounded cat carrying in its paws bloody pieces of meat. She was hiding in her shame. Such pity for her enveloped me; I became so close to her in her pain and I could not help her at all.

When she entered the train with us, she lamented to someone, showing her tortured, cut-up hands: now she would never be beautiful. Never. And she was in such pain. We became cleaner thanks to her shame. Were we, in our pure maid-enhood, perhaps the guilty ones? A martyr. Perhaps she had redeemed us? I felt her pain in my body, I embraced her and started crying out loud: "Mama!! Mama! Whose fault is it? Whose fault is it?" The train finally started moving. Like a scared animal the train roars into the distance. Fields disappear, stones fly, striking girlish thoughts. Fall back down dejected. It seemed as if suddenly Petliura's men would come flying, stop the train cars, pull us away to somewhere in the fields. We were flying somewhere, somewhere in eternity where the train would bring us. None of us knew where.

Source: Malka Lee, *Durkh kindershe oygn* (Buenos Aires: Yidbukh, 1955), 121–26. Translated from the Yiddish by Leyzer Burko.

Document 7.6. *A Writer's Calling*

The autobiographical recollection of the Yiddish writer Rokhl Faygenberg brings to life the gendered experience of refugees during the bloody pogroms carried out by Ataman Nikifor Grigoriev's troops, who fought on behalf of the Ukrainian People's Republic. Here Faygnberg also reminisces about how, encouraged by the words of the prominent writer and editor Mordkhe Spektor, she decided to become a chronicler of destruction.

It happened during the fall of 1919. After the dreadful summer of the Jewish massacres, when I went into hiding among the peasants of the nearby villages holding my child in my arms, and eventually reached Odessa. I went to see Spektor at once and told him about my Ukrainian scroll of agony, about my fine small-town home with its acacia trees below its windows, which was destroyed. I told him how I managed to reach the city at the risk of death, of how a goodhearted Bulgarian peasant gave me her holiday dress with the national colors for the journey, and how I put a little cross around my child's neck: not only were Jew-murderers still roaming around the Balta roads, but signposts by General Grigoriev were still hanging from the telephone poles, calling on people to kill all little Jewish boys, because when they grow up they will all be communists. He listened to everything I said, without making a sound. Then he invited me into the building of the Odessa Jewish community, so that I could hear the stories of the Uman refugees, about how entire families were buried alive, so that I would soon forget about my own trivial problems. "But bring with you a notebook and pencil," he added, "everything, everything must be recorded." From then on, every day, we used to stop by the *kehile* building and hear out the stories of the refugees of the Ukrainian Jewish *khurbn*, destruction. There were several writers among us there. Jews would tell us their stories and we would write them down, and then we would discuss the terrifying details that had been conveyed to us, which caused our blood to freeze in our veins.

Source: David Kassel, ed., *Spektor-bukh* (Warsaw: Ahisefer, 1929), 132–33. Translated from the Yiddish by Elissa Bemporad. Originally published in *Pakn Treger*, the Yiddish Book Center's English-language magazine.

Document 7.7. *Chronicle of a Dead City*

Rokhl Faygnberg became the only woman to collaborate with the historian Elias Tcherikower (besides his wife Riva Tcherikower) in his effort to record the anti-Jewish violence of the civil war. Based on her interviews with survivors, this account about the pogroms in Dubovo, which Faygnberg sent to Tcherikower in Berlin in July 1922, was later published as an expanded chronicle into Yiddish, Russian, and Hebrew. The account was also used as evidence at the famous 1927 Schwartzbard trial against the Jewish anarchist Scholem Schwartzbard, who assassinated Petliura in revenge for the pogroms.

Markela Brishko was the son of a wealthy peasant. He graduated from the Zemski school in Dubovo district. Then he gave private lessons in Jewish homes and for the past few years he was a clerk in Dubovo. Brishko considered himself an intellectual and was a fervent Ukrainian nationalist. In the national Ukrainian pogrom movement he was a very capable worker. In the first peasant uprising in Uman the pogrom chief Klimenko made him the commander over Dubovo and the surrounding villages. He entered the town with twenty horsemen, and the next day, following predetermined signal shots, the peasants burst into Dubovo from the non-Jewish neighborhood in the surrounding villages, with axes and pitchforks. The massacre lasted two days and two nights. After the massacre Brishko married a Jewish girl from Dubovo. Her father was a cantor in Dubovo and her grandfather had struck it rich, was a member of the Jewish community leadership and a tax farmer. The girl graduated from the gymnasium in Uman and was also a fervent Ukrainian nationalist (her name was Feyge-Vitele Kalika). [. . .]

All those murdered in Dubovo during the first massacre on Pesach Sheni in 1919 were buried in a mass grave in the Dubovo cemetery. Lying on top of the mass grave is a tombstone which has toppled over. That was the sign. The burial took place Saturday morning. The rabbi of Dubovo, Moses Aaron Berdichevsky, called for that because it was very hot and the corpses could not lie there any longer.

Facts: Sonye Soshkes—Victim No. 22

She was an orphan. Together with her mother she had a little store in the non-Jewish quarter. When the massacre started, she ran away to hide in a garden that belonged to a peasant she knew, a customer and a good friend. His eight-year-old boy spotted her in the garden and told his father. The peasant took an axe and killed her, chopping off her limbs, and with each limb that he chopped off he would say: "That's for your matches! That's for your tobacco! That's for your sugar!" Her bones were gathered into a sack, which was buried just like that. [. . .]

Kozakov's Small Massacre, Dubovo, the Twentieth of Sivan 1919

The second massacre in Dubovo was the work of the band of the bandit leader Kozakov.

Kozakov and his band burst into Dubovo after several battles with Brishko's volunteer soldiers from the surrounding villages. After the first massacre, which Brishko himself organized through the local peasants on Passover Sheni in 1919, he and his Ukrainian bandit soldiers terrorized and plundered the town, but no foreign bandits were allowed into Dubovo. The Dubovo Jews paid him and his detachment for that and it was said that they were protecting the town. This protection cost the Dubovo Jews dearly. Birshko's stubbornness caused a tremendous victory for the bandit leader Kozakov. At the time he was freely robbing and murdering in the Jewish towns of the Uman region and Brishko was blocking his way to Dubovo.

Then Kozakov wanted to enter Dubovo, of all places. The war between Brishko and Kozakov over the Dubovo Jews lasted for several weeks and the winner was Kozakov. At the critical moment, Kozakov had good friends in Dubovo who supported him. The Russian telephone operator Yelena Vasilyevna and the Dubovo shoemaker Dimitro Shabolinski, in whose house the telephone station was located, helped Kozakov in the difficult moment, and the Dubovo Jews were his. That is why he honestly shared Jewish property with the local Dubovo peasants. [...]

This time Kozakov entered Dubovo with red and Ukrainian flags. He had with him about five hundred men. The massacre lasted two hours. All the victims were driven into the "headquarters" where the caravan of bandits had stopped. It was the house with the large courtyard and good horse stalls for the horse post in Dubovo. On the bottom floor the victims were murdered and thrown into the basement, and on the upper floors young Jewish girls were dragged by their braids to cook lunch for the bandits, to get drunk with them, and to make merry. [...]

Kozakov's Great Massacre: The Tenth, Eleventh, and Twelfth of Av 1919

This time Kozakov burst into Dubovo with a large band of about three thousand men. Before summer, when he had pillaged and murdered in the towns of the Uman region, many peasant youths from the surrounding villages had joined him. They were mainly armed horsemen. Their naked swords gleamed like mirrors against the sun and this time they also carried high above their heads red and Ukrainian flags. Music played. The residents of the non-Jewish neighborhood rejoiced at the guests and the murdering began immediately. It was the day after Tisha B'av in 1919. The massacre lasted for three days. The whole town was put to death. For those three days there was a celebration in the non-Jewish neighborhood, in the houses the tables were set day and night. The young people played on accordions and danced with the bandits in the streets. Everyone ate and drank their fill together with their wives and children. The property of the Jewish town was brought to the non-Jewish neighborhood. A festive mood prevailed in the peasant courtyards of Dubovo, but they were already more than satiated.

On the third day of the massacre the Dubovo peasants rang [the bells] in the church for everyone to gather in the market for a meeting. The peasants assembled next to the church and demanded of Kozakov that he stop slaughtering women and children. Kozakov acquiesced. For the Jewish women and children, one made a hiding place at the home of the shoemaker Dimitro Shabolinski, and the men were still killed with all sorts of violent deaths and thrown into the "clay" [pit]. After the great massacre there remained in Dubovo only 110 widows and orphans and 32 men who had hidden out with honorable, good gentiles in the surrounding villages.

Dubovo's four Jewish blacksmiths also remained alive. For all three days of the massacre they hammered horseshoes for the bandits and sharpened their swords. The blacksmiths of Dubovo were the only Jewish witnesses to all the violent deaths met by the Jews who were killed. The "clay" in Dubovo were pits behind the hill where the Dubovo peasants used to dispose of the carcasses of their horses and cattle. There the ground is marshy and everything sinks into the depths. The Jews of Dubovo also sank without a trace after Kozakov's great massacre. The Dubovo peasants did not allow them to be taken out of there and to be given a Jewish burial, and there was no possibility of doing so either. The great massacre of Dubovo lasted three days and three nights, the tenth, eleventh, and twelfth of Av 1919. [. . .]

Zalman Molodovnik's Wife—Victim No. 15

She was nineteen years old and was a beauty. She was born and raised in Golovanevsk to poor and kind parents. At sixteen she finished high school and at eighteen she was a pharmacist.

She married Zalman Molodovnik out of love. They were a young and happy couple. It was only six months after their wedding. He was killed first, and right in front of her. Then the bandits started with her. They exulted in her beauty and tore off her clothes and she was pulled from one hand to another. A group of red-hot excited bandits surrounded her and each one threw himself onto her to rape her, but she calmed them all down. She smiled at them and gently stroked their heads. She called them all into her husband's pharmacy so that she could give them scented soaps and douse herself with perfumes and then she would go with them to the "headquarters." The bandits allowed themselves to go with her into the pharmacy and there right in front of them all she poisoned herself with carbolic acid. The bandits were enraged and they carried her on a spear out onto the street, but she was already dead. [. . .]

The End of the Jewish Community in Dubovo

After Kozakov's last massacre, the Dubovo peasants adopted a resolution in the district that all Jews should leave Dubovo; they only made an exception for the blacksmiths. The blacksmiths with their families were allowed to remain living in Dubovo as before, but the widows and orphans yearned to escape from the devastated town anyway. However, the way to Uman was still dangerous. Several times they tried to go and had to turn back. All around bandits were running wild. The Dubovo widows and orphans had pieces of bread to eat which the Dubovo peasants used to give them out of pity. Two or three times bread was brought to them from Pokovilov [?] and from Talne. Twice the Dubovo shoemaker Dimitro Shabolinski also traveled for their sake to Uman and brought a little money for the Dubovo widows and orphans from the committees there. He, a personal friend of Kozakov, also had pity on them. Really he fell in love with the Jews. Whoever had a penny gave it to him to hide, and his home became an exhibit of Jewish furniture and objects. The widows and orphans stayed in his house—in the same house where he and the telephone operator Yelena Vasilyevna had hidden Kozakov so that Markela Brishko would not harm him. Then the Dubovo peasants called Dimitro Shabolinski "the Jewish Batko [father]."

In the end, the widows and orphans left Dubovo. Whoever had money from selling their houses gave it to Dimitro for him to bring to Uman, because they were scared to carry it themselves. And Dimitro Shabolinski served the Jewish widows and orphans honorably. He brought the money to them in Uman right on time. The Uman Bolsheviks already knew about his honesty and kindness and he had absolutely no fear of any Red detachment returning to Dubovo in search of the guilty. The blacksmiths and their families also did not all remain in Dubovo. Out of fear they then escaped to Golovanevsk.

During the holiday season, when the widows and orphans had left Dubovo, the Dubovo peasants dismantled and destroyed the Jewish houses. Afterward they broke all the tombstones in the Jewish cemetery, and they plowed the place over and planted grain. The Dubovo synagogue with the broken windows and doors was sold to the Dubovo peasants by the contractor Isaac Kortshun for 11,000 rubles, and the Dubovo study house, which was a complete wreck, was sold to the peasants by the Dubovo blacksmith Moses Rabinovitsh for 2,500 rubles. They took the money for themselves. For that the homeless [Jews] in Uman summoned them to a rabbinical court, to the Uman rabbi Kontorshtsik, but right then the Denikin government arrested the rabbi and the heinous act with the Dubovo synagogues remained as it was. That was the winter of 1921. The holy books from the Dubovo synagogues were sent before the holidays to Talne. Now the Jewish settlement of Dubovo has been completely erased. The location of the Jewish ruins has been plowed over by the peasants and planted with fields and gardens. Nevertheless, every week Dubovo Jews travel from Uman to the fair in Dubovo.

Rokhl Faygnberg collected and recorded this account in the winter of 1921. The twelve homeless families from Dubovo who fled to Odessa compiled the lists of the victims. The lists do not include those who drowned in the river, those who were lost in the woods and on the roads and paths, and the children who died of hunger in the fields where they were fed the grains from the green ears of corn. Nobody can remember them. Nobody can say when, where, and how many of them died.

Source: Institute for Jewish Research Archives (YIVO), Tcherikower Collection, RG 80, folder 235, ll. 21708–801, "Khurbn Dubove, a pinkes fun a toyter shtot." Translated from the Yiddish by Leyzer Burko.

Document 7.8. Women as Agents of Violence

In the aftermath of the civil war, Soviet authorities set up investigative commissions to punish those who participated as counterrevolutionaries in the pogroms. What follows is the indictment of a Jewish woman who was accused of collaborating with Petliura's troops during the pogroms in Zhytomyr. Not only did she engage in looting Jewish property; on behalf of the perpetrators she also identified Jews, who were then murdered.

Indictment concerning Sura (Sonya) Yankelevna Margulian, accused of participating in both Zhytomyr pogroms. In April of this year, in accordance with an order issued by the Volhynia provincial Extraordinary Commission (EC) for Combating Counterrevolution, Sura Yankelevna Margulian, known as "Sonya," staying at the Hotel Russia at 4 Bolshaia Chudnovskaia Street, was arrested as a participant of both Zhytomyr pogroms (April 26, 1919, letter to the EC Counterintelligence Department).

On April 26 of this year, the EC received a statement signed by several persons that during the pogroms the aforementioned "Sonya"/Sura Margulian had indicated who was to be killed. The investigation conducted by the EC procured materials allowing it to conclude that Sura Margulian did indeed participate in both Zhytomyr pogroms in 1919, as someone who directly indicated which Jewish apartments to destroy, as well as specific Jewish individuals to kill.

In addition, the same investigative material exposed Sura Margulian as a person who hid property looted during the pogroms and who used that property for her own personal benefit. For example, witnesses questioned by the EC, including Nuhim Franz, Isaac Kagan, Maria Streltsova, Abram Shaposhnikov, Shlema Naiberg, and Nadezhda Kruchinskaia, testified that they saw Sonya during the second pogrom (and one witness, Isaac Kopel, saw the same during the first as well) walking around the city with the looters and pointing out who to kill and loot, and also splitting the looted money and items with the pogrom perpetrators and fencing items.

During a search conducted at the Gitelman residence at 13 Moskovskaia Street, where Margulian had taken her things, fifteen different items were found, although it has not been established that they were improperly obtained. Upon being questioned by the Extraordinary Commission, Sura Margulian did not plead guilty to participating in the pogroms, explaining that the witness testimony accusing her was the result of a desire for revenge and hostility between her and the witnesses, and that by citing other witnesses she could prove she had not been involved in the pogroms. Given the existence of such material, the EC transferred Sonya's case to the Investigative Commission handling the pogroms.

On May 17 of this year, on the basis of the materials gathered by the EC, the Investigative Commission charged Sura Margulian with direct participation in both pogroms. In light of the explanations Margulian had given, the Investigative Commission conducted repeat questioning of all the witnesses and questioned new ones. The information gathered by the investigation established the following.

During the first pogrom, groups of Petliura's soldiers would come to see Sura Margulian, and she would go with them into the city. This happened several times. Upon Margulian's return from the city, where she had gone with Petliura's men, she would be carrying something, trying to hide it (witness Fuksman); after the pogrom Margulian had a lot of different items (witness Franz). During the second pogrom, Sura Margulian walked along Chudnovskaia Street with a group of soldiers and pointed to various houses (witness Naiberg and witness Franz); one time Margulian left the Hotel Russia, where she lived, with soldiers who had come there, after which she returned carrying a piece of red silk, which she later offered for sale, and upon her return she was dividing up some money with the soldiers (witness Kruchinskaia); in addition, Margulian returned to her room at the hotel with some bundles, wore a cross on her chest, and carried various items with her (witness Shaposhnikov). During the same pogrom, soldiers stayed with Sura Margulian at the hotel, and after the pogrom she bought items from Petliura's soldiers that had intentionally been looted for her during the pogrom (witness Shanskaia).

On the basis of the foregoing, the Revolutionary Tribunal, in the order prepared at its meeting on July 15, 1919, resolved: to bring Sura Yankelevna Margulian, a citizen of Cherniakhov, Volhynia province, forty years old, to trial before the Revolutionary Tribunal, on charges of participating in both pogroms that took place in Zhytomyr, in January and March 1919, which participation involved her, along with other persons not identified by the investigation, engaging in January and March 1919 in the theft of various property from persons not identified by the investigation, accompanied by armed assault on the homes and stores of Zhytomyr residents, and after said pogroms engaging in the concealment of stolen goods and the purchase and sale of items intentionally looted for her during the pogroms.

Source: State Archives of Zhytomyr Oblast (DAZhO), f. 1820, op. 5, d. 97, ll. 3–5, 44, 71–74 ob. Translated from the Russian by Eugenia Tietz-Sokolskaya.

8

Documentary Fiction of the Pogroms
of the Civil War

Harriet Murav

Itsik Kipnis's Yiddish novel *Months and Days: A Chronicle* (*Khadoshim un teg*) was first published in 1926. The novel is an example of a wider impulse at the time to document the events and experiences of the pogroms of the Russian Civil War. Other Yiddish and Russian literary authors wrote fictionalized and factual accounts of the pogroms, and relief agencies gathered first-person testimonies and compiled extensive data on the death, injuries, property damage, and dislocation inflicted on Jewish populations in Eastern Europe and Russia in this period. Some of the most important literary responses include lengthy poem cycles; Kipnis's novel was praised by critics at the time for its apparent simplicity and accessibility. In *Months and Days*, Kipnis intertwines two stories and two kinds of emotion that do not belong together: the joy and delight of the first few months of his marriage, on the one side, and the terror, sorrow, and rage he experienced during the July 1919 pogrom in Slovechno, in northern Ukraine, on the other. "Buzi" and "Ayzik" are the names of the newly married couple in the novel.

Kipnis was born in Slovechno in 1896.[1] He worked as a leather tanner until 1920, when the Leather Workers Union sent him to Kiev (Kyiv) to study. Sulphuric acid, which appears in the opening of the excerpted chapter from *Months and Days*, was used to process animal hides. The novel drew the attention of Yiddish critics at the time of its publication, mostly because of the naivete of the narration. It was translated and published in Russian in 1930. In contrast to Kipnis's novel/chronicle, the most important literary works about the civil war pogroms were primarily works of poetry, written in a deliberately fragmentary, difficult style. These include, for example, David Hofshteyn's *Troyer* (Sorrow), Perets Markish's "Di kupe" (The Mound), and Leyb Kvitko's *1919*. Kipnis's appeal largely stemmed from his apparent directness and simplicity. He became widely known as a children's author in Yiddish and Russian translation.[2] He returned to the theme of the pogrom in Slovechno

---

[1] I base my account on Mordechai Altshuler, "Itsik Kipnis: The 'White Crow' of Soviet Yiddish Literature," *Jews in Russia and Eastern Europe* 52/53 (2004): 68–167.

[2] Another discussion of *Months and Days* can be found in Mikhail Krutikov, "Rediscovering the Shtetl as a New Reality," in *The Shtetl: New Evaluations*, ed. Steven T. Katz (New York: New York University Press, 2007), 211–32.

Harriet Murav, *Documentary Fiction of the Pogroms of the Civil War* In: *Pogroms*. Edited by: Eugene M. Avrutin and Elissa Bemporad, Oxford University Press. © Oxford University Press 2021. DOI: 10.1093/oso/9780190060084.003.0009

and to its consequences in later work. After World War II, he wrote a fictionalized memoir about his native shtetl and short stories about Babi Yar and postwar Jewish life in Kiev. His praise of the Jewish star as an object of pride and the general anti-Jewish turn in the Soviet Union led to his arrest in 1949. His interrogators also used the allegedly "nationalistic" qualities of *Months and Days* as another mark against him. Kipnis spent seven years in the gulag, and was rehabilitated in 1956. He died in Kiev in 1974.[3]

The anti-Jewish violence of the Russian Civil War was carried out by warring state and nonstate armies, insurgent groups, paramilitary forces, and individual warlords. In the case of Slovechno, where *Months and Days* takes place, the perpetrators were locals. Kipnis blames the eruption of violence in his native shtetl on his neighbor Marko Lukhtans, the chief of police, and an individual named Kosenko, in addition to peasants from the town and the surrounding region. Kipnis describes Lukhtans, who was a veteran of World War I, as a "liar, a gypsy, and a beggar."[4] The names Lukhtan(s) and Kosenko with the variant Kosinko appear in both the archival documents and in *Months and Days*.[5] One of the distinguishing features of Kipnis's novel is the use of real names both of Jews and non-Jews; his novel is one of the first works of prose fiction to document Jewish catastrophe.

Kosenko was a young man of the age of nineteen or twenty. He was literate and worked for a time as a clerk for the Food Board; in the period before July 1919, he had no definite occupation, but then joined the local police and, together with the police chief, began an anti-Jewish agitation campaign in nearby villages and settlements. The main points of his speeches were that Jews were going to seize churches and transform them into synagogues, force peasants to register marriage, births, and divorces with rabbis, and also, that Jews hoarded manufactured goods, particularly, salt, in order to fleece peasants.[6] In a word, Jews, all of whom were allegedly Bolsheviks, were about to take power and impose Judeo-Bolshevism on the local population. Kipnis attributes his neighbors' turn to violence to this sort of provocation and incitement.

Rumors about an outbreak of anti-Jewish violence prompted Jews to seek assistance and protection from Lukhtan, the chief of police. However, testimony from one of the Jewish survivors, Isaak Goldberg, suggests that Lukhtan had made a prior arrangement with a group of what the text calls "bandits" to storm the town on his signal. Itsko-Mordakovich Pashkovskii, another inhabitant of Slovechno, also testified that he heard the cry "Begin!" in Russian ("Nachinai!") around 2:30 in the morning of July 15, 1919.[7] The excerpt from *Months and Days* that follows recounts

---

[3] For more on Kipnis, see Harriet Murav, *Music from a Speeding Train: Jewish Literature in Post-Revolutionary Russia* (Stanford, CA: Stanford University Press, 2011), 248–58.

[4] Itsik Kipnis, *Khadoshim un teg: A khronik* (Kiev: Kiev Kultur-Lige, 1926), 41.

[5] Testimony from L. Kaplan, in "Kievskaia raionnaia komissiia evreiskogo obshchestvennogo komiteta po okazaniiu pomoshchi postradavshim ot pogromov," State Archive of Kyiv Oblast (DAKO), f. 3050, op. 1, d. 225, ll. 17-ob.

[6] DAKO, f. 3050, op. 1, d. 225, ll. 17-ob.

[7] Tsentral'nyi derzhavnyi arkhiv vyshchykh orhaniv vlady (TsDAVO), "Pokazanie Itsko-Mordakovich Pashkovskii," f. 2497, op. 3, d. 154.

the onset of violence: Kipnis and his wife go to sleep in their clothes; awakened by the sound of shooting, the couple flee through their neighbors' gardens. The next day they learn that one Jew was severely beaten, another killed, and that shops and houses were ransacked. Kipnis remarks with bitter irony, "Each family celebrated the holiday their own way."[8] The killing and destruction continued for two more days. Kipnis writes, "All our streets were crisscrossed with filaments of dread."[9] One eyewitness reported sixty-eight killed and forty-five wounded in Slovechno; other reports give slightly different numbers, "more than sixty" killed and more than a hundred wounded.[10] Kipnis's mother-in-law and two of her children were killed in the pogrom; his first wife, pregnant at the time, later died of typhus, after giving birth to their daughter.

Salt was a flash point in the neighborly violence in Slovechno. Kipnis's account of pre-pogrom interethnic interaction stresses this point. Instead of dishes and bowls, his mother-in-law started to take salt to the neighboring villages, because "for salt you can get everything." "Everything was upside down at the market," Kipnis goes on to say. Peasants would exchange a wagonload of wood for "a bit of salt," which was frequently adulterated with chalk, flour, saccharine, paint, or dye.[11] In the excerpt from Chapter 8 of *Months and Days* that follows, a nameless peasant woman comes out of her house to talk to Ayzik about the looting and violence and accuses Jews of hoarding salt. The woman's outburst, however, takes a surprising turn. She brings out food for the Jewish children sheltering in the courtyard, providing a moment of care in the ongoing terror.

Kipnis's style is more complex and artful than it may at first appear. Even though "Ayzik" is the first-person narrator, he hands over the narrative microphone, so to speak, to other characters who tell the story in their own way. The thoughts and utterances of particular characters merge into the narrator's account, and it is sometimes difficult to tell who is thinking and saying what. The names of individual characters are not identified, and we hear only voices speaking, as if to express commonly held emotions. "Ayzik's" voice varies across a range of emotions that include affection, love, bitter sarcasm, resentment, and anger. He is full of affection and love for his wife, mother, and mother-in-law. In contrast, he belittles his own fellow Jews for their indecision after the violence began, calling them "geese." He is angry at his father for his failure to provide shelter for the family during the pogrom. He unleashes venomous bitterness against non-Jews, asking, for example, "And you, *goyim*, my faithful neighbors, did you at least wash the blood from your scythes and your knives?"[12] Kipnis expresses his own desire for revenge; he wonders at one

---

[8] Kipnis, *Khadoshim un teg*, 89.
[9] Kipnis, *Khadoshim un teg*, 103.
[10] L. B. Miliakova, *Kniga pogromov: Pogromy na Ukraine, v Belorussii, i evropeiskoi chasti Rossii v period grazhdanskoi voiny 1918–1922 gg.* (Moscow: Rosspen, 2007), 179.
[11] Kipnis, *Khadoshim un teg*, 67–68. Jews in Eastern Europe traditionally held a state-granted monopoly on salt, and in the aftermath of World War I and during the civil war, there were shortages of manufactured goods, including salt.
[12] Kipnis, *Khadoshim un teg*, 138.

point, for example, when Jews will go out and murder non-Jewish women (*shikses*), and it is likely that this dream of revenge also includes other forms of violence against non-Jewish women. It bothers him that non-Jewish children (whom he describes with the derogatory term *shkotsim*) are, as he says, treading on the bodies of his dead.[13]

The "months and days" of the title indicate the different qualities of "Ayzik's" experience: the "months" are the calm, peaceful, and joyous time of his daily life as a newly married man.[14] As the author puts it in the epigraph, this was "summer with blossoming days like poppies in June." Life in Slovechno before July 15, 1919, the day the pogrom started—was not, however, free from hardship or personal and ethnic and religious animosity. Kipnis describes the hardships faced by his mother-in-law, whose husband had already emigrated to the United States; wives left behind by their husbands struggled to provide an income for themselves and their children. Jewish aid organizations who helped Jews after the pogroms noted in their records the particular difficulties for women already separated from their husbands. Kipnis describes his own constant conflict with his father, who was angry because his son refused to work for him. The entire town disapproved of Kipnis's failure to observe the Sabbath and other Jewish holidays. Even though Jews and non-Jews lived in close proximity, and participated in a common economic life, they experienced interethnic tension nonetheless. In contrast to the "months" of normal life, the word "days" in the novel's title refers to the outbreak of violence that took place, as the following chapter title reveals, on "Wednesday, Thursday, and Friday."

There is little graphic description of violence in the excerpt that follows or in the novel as a whole. No one is ennobled by the experience of the pogrom; the common suffering makes no one better; the antagonisms within Kipnis's family are not diminished but increased. The violence makes neighbors into strangers. In the midst of chaos, however, perfect strangers offer care, as in the episode of the strange old woman who cries, admonishes Kipnis, yet gives the Jewish children food. The excerpt reveals the uncertainty, fear, and anguish that is the experience of those fleeing violence no matter who, where, and when—whether in Ukraine in 1919 or across the world today.

---

[13] Kipnis, *Khadoshim un teg*, 136.

[14] For a discussion of this point and the novel as a whole, see David Roskies, *Against the Apocalypse: Responses to Catastrophe in Modern Jewish Culture* (Cambridge, MA: Harvard University Press, 1984), 84–106.

Document 8.1. Itsik Kipnis's *Months and Days*

Wednesday, Thursday, and Friday

"What do you think, Buzele, will we go to sleep and wake up in the morning to find that nothing happened?"

And Buzele nodded her head in agreement with me.

"Only you know what, sweetheart? Sleep in your clothes. Just take off your shoes and stockings."

"But can we put out the light?"

"Yes, we can."

We did. And things were good for Buzi and me, in our house. Maybe in the morning there wouldn't be any holiday, and I would have to go to work at Hershke's very early in the morning, like always. Anyway, I knew so little about pogroms! Once, however, when I was a child (I must have been five when it happened) I dreamed that there was a pogrom in our town: it was winter, the shopkeepers had built themselves white inner doors, and their wives, masked and with revolvers in their hands, stood on the other side of those doors. They knew how to shoot. It was in the middle of the marketplace, in winter. The place was full of frozen, bloody clods, so full that you couldn't get through. The lumps, smeared over with snot, consisted of frozen blood. It looked as if a big pogrom had taken place. I wandered around alone the whole night and couldn't escape the labyrinth of bloody lumps. At home my father, armed with bottles of sulfuric acid, stood over Timukh and Pavel and wouldn't release them, because they wanted to carry out a pogrom against us.

It was a moonlight night in winter. The horror stretched from heaven to earth! . . . When I woke up thick lumps of snow were falling in the gloomy morning outside. As soon as I managed to free myself from my nightmare, I felt good again. That was then.

"Maybe when we wake up tomorrow, Buzele, it'll be like after a bad dream. As long as we get through the night."

"When will it be like after a bad dream? Tomorrow morning?"

"Yes, tomorrow morning. Go to sleep, sweetheart."

"You, too!"

And we put out the light, and everything was fine in our room, only our thoughts raced a bit. . . . Goodnight!

* * *

I woke up first. I thought it was raining outside—an irksome rain. The mechanism that made the thunder wasn't working properly, and the thunder didn't come off well! I heard screams, and crowbars clattering on tin, and there was shooting, too.

"Buzele, get up, quickly!"

"Buzele, sweetie, wake up, get up, now!"

"What is it, what's going on?"

"It's nothing, sweetie, nothing. Get dressed, here are your stockings. Put on your shoes, we have to go."

And Buzi obeyed me, I asked her not to hurry, so that she wouldn't drop anything.

The mistress of the house, shocked and mute, was dressed. She wrung her hands. It was as if there were a fire in the middle of the night. We headed out.

"We have to go through the neighbors' gardens to get to the grove; our family won't know anything."

"How are we going?"

"Through the gardens."

And we were off, trying to get out of the nightmare any way we could. Climbing over a water pit, we landed in the first garden. As we went along, our careless steps disturbed everything growing along our path. I stumbled on a vein of watermelon. That was the end of the watermelon! The plants were soaked with dew. We crawled over a second fence. One garden after another. Buzi's teeth were chattering, perhaps from the cold, or from fear and the suddenness of it all. We arrived in a patch of tall hemp, up to our necks. Two children, and it seemed we had saved ourselves: amid the hemp, we were hidden from the whole world.

Nonetheless, we kept going, and made a lot of mistakes. We had to be careful not to wake the dogs in the courtyards nearby, even though we could hear dogs barking somewhere far away at the other end of town. Over there, behind us, axes and crowbars clanked, and voices cried out, and they seemed to be human voices. Maybe some kind of competition was going on there? Heavy stones being pulled from the earth, perhaps?

"Who's faster? Who's going to be first?"

There it was light and you could hear voices of victory.

"Where are you off to, Buzele? We have to rouse our family!"

"Right, let's go."

We arrived at my father's house. Two confused children in the middle of the night. We didn't find anyone there. How did they get away?

What's the matter, you don't know how they did it? Right here, through the window, and then to the grove, and they abandoned their trusty house, leaving it to the abuse and the caprices of others.

"Let's keep going, sweetheart."

And we set off for the grove.

And there we heard hushed voices. There was nothing to be afraid about, however, they were Yiddish. They were talking quietly and shushing each other like a flock of geese spooked in the middle of the night. You keep your eyes peeled, you're frightened, you look for something to grasp on to.

Buzi cheered up a little. We joined the flock.

"Is that you, Khine?"

"Yeah. Who's that? It's Ayzik! Where's Buzi?"

"Here, of course."

"Right, there she is, indeed. The times we live in, what misery! Where are we supposed to go and what are we supposed to do in a misfortune like this?"

"What's going on in town?"

"In town? They're breaking in, beating people, robbing them."

Khine was carrying several children at once. One in her arms, one on her shoulders, and one in her womb. She was Shloyme the shoemaker's wife; Shloyme was also there somewhere in the flock. It was in the middle of the night; there were twenty of us walking one by one, like geese in a row. We went along not knowing where we were going, we went where we could. Buzi didn't want anyone to talk.

"You have to keep quiet."

Soon we were out of the grove and into the rye, and we kept going. But someone starting shouting at us from somewhere in the rye—to drive us back. Maybe it was only a young boy? It was dangerous to stop, however, at a time like that. We took a moment to confer and then the geese decided to go back.

Back where? To town?

Not worth it.

Then let's stay here, but split up into little bunches.

But Buzi was afraid to separate from other people.

"What a child you are! Me, you're afraid to believe me? This is my grove, I know it like the back of my hand!"

And we convinced Buzi. We went off to the side and climbed over a fence, which I knew led to a family of trees, and sat down there, Buzi and I, two lost children. Even though it was beloved summer, it was chilly, and it was good to be just the two of us in a completely unfamiliar garden. We should have been thinking about our people, mine and Buzi's. Where were they headed now? Soon dawn would come. After all, it was summer, and a summertime night is short.

From a distance we could see other people sitting in pairs under the trees. We had nothing to be ashamed about.

No, it was better not to talk in the meantime, in around an hour, we would get up; in about an hour, it would be daytime, and we would go see what was happening in town.

* * *

"It burned up. But there was no smoke and no fire!"

This was my father's neighbor speaking in a group of people standing near my father's house, and now we joined them, Buzi and I.

She had nothing but a light dress over her body; her legs were bare except for her shoes, and she was sprinkled with dew from spending the night in Slovechno's fields. I was also just barely covered.

At another time our town wouldn't have tolerated this, but now we were greeted almost joyfully.

"Good morning, good morning! Where did you spend the night, children?"

"In Lev's field." We answered cheerfully, in good spirits. It's not for nothing that people say the day is cleverer than the night, cleverer and more cheerful. Blessed is daytime!

Soon two messengers arrived, Meylekh and Yosele, to see whether we were there.

"Yes, we're here, children. And where did you end up? Home? Where did you spend the night? . . . Good, we'll soon be over."

And we were all satisfied with something—blessed be the day!

And the neighbors, the peasants? What are the neighbors doing around father's house? The neighbors—they're returning a few pillows to their neighbors, the Jews.

One said, "Here are your pillows, dearie, we thought to keep them so robbers wouldn't carry them off!" And she grew red as she spoke.

Another neighbor added, "Come, Leah, here are your dishes. How was I supposed to know? I saw them taking everything, and it just so happened that I needed a few dishes. Take them off my hands. Look, our neighbor, the tall one, yeah, him, he's the one who robbed your place, Leah, go to him, let him give you all the flour he's got; it'll be nothing to him, he's not sick! You shouldn't take other people's things."

A third neighbor let on that she knew certain secrets.

"Mat, I know, I saw with my own eyes who broke in through your window. He's a devil. I'll tell you who, I'll tell you his name, only not now."

And another neighbor pointed out this same good friend, the neighbor who was whispering secrets in Mat's ear, that this was the one who spent the whole night dragging away leather from Mat's storeroom. Go and try to figure out who did what! But the Jews, not yet accustomed to pogroms, thought they were owed something. They persisted:

"Of course, the neighbors have to return everything they took."

And also, "Wouldn't they die of shame anyway?"

The Jews rigidly stuck to their opinions of non-Jews. "There's no telling what can happen. Goys are goys: thieves with thick heads!"

They started packing up and returning the accursed pillows and the stolen bedding. Windows were shuttered up. Women saw to the animals and drove them off to pasture. People stood on guard in front of their houses even though it was early morning. It was as if every house were its own village, and every village had suffered a robbery. Everyone was dying to know what happened, but it seemed that everything was just about over without a problem, although, well, that's not quite right:

"Last night they beat the hatmaker very severely."

"Who? Yankel-Leyb the hatmaker?"

"Oy oy oy, he isn't a well man. But how is he? How is he doing, the poor man, Yankel-Leyb?"

"And Gedalye-Yeshue's son, he was running down the Antonovich road, near old Zalmen's tannery; he wanted to run away, and they shot him."

"And?"

"He suffered until daylight and then it was over. They're sobbing so hard at his house, it's like the walls are crying. The funeral is probably soon."

"Wait a minute! How did this happen? What about the police chief?"

"You mean Kublinets? People are saying he's mixed up in the whole business."

"Meaning what?"

"Meaning that he promised to give twenty rifles to us to defend the town, and then push came to shove, he played dead."

"So how did it start?"

"Like this. At eleven o'clock that policeman strapped on five rifles and told the young people they could go around in the meantime with sticks. Around twelve o'clock, someone signaled with a shot and they came from running from every corner, and the town was darkened with them. The police divided up the rifles among the non-Jews, and the Jewish patrol scattered."

"And the police chief?"

"That piece of crap? He organized the whole thing! Him, and Kosenko, and your neighbor, Marko Lukhtans! They say he's not around, but it's a lie. He's got one of our local scum to lend him some clothes and he's hiding at one of their houses on the other side of the river."

"Then there's no hope of spending tonight at home?"

"Who knows? We'll see. In the meantime, it's quiet in town, they've scurried back to their holes. A lot of shops were smashed, and the goys' little kids are rummaging in the dirt for loot."

"Then maybe let's go to town?"

"Let's go."

* * *

Our mother was delighted to see us. She smiled at us with her usual good smile, and asked whether we wanted breakfast.

She'd already milked the cows.

"And where are Meylekh and Rokhl?"

"But I sent them to you! I've been to your place three times today, but you weren't there."

And we told her where and how we spent the night. Mama gave us her own account, and wanted to know what was happening at our place.

"Nothing in particular, things were thrown about a bit, but tenderly."

"Is the landlady here?"

"Yes, she's home. Do you want a glass of milk, children?"

"No, we'd rather go home."

The streets had that after-the-fair look, but the kind of austere pre-Passover fair. Dust and dirt in front of every door. Bits of paper strewn with broken glass. What the hell! Each house celebrated the holiday in its own way, each busy with its own affairs! You could hear crying coming from Yeshue-Gedalye's street. At the club, which Basya ran, everything was broken, torn up, stuck through, and smashed, so there would be no sign of any "commune"!

Buzi and I walked around in a pair, as if we were joined at the hip, and we listened to what people were saying.

That's how we were since yesterday, and we must have been pretty tightly bound together, because no one bothered to separate us. And we both concluded it would be good to find out what was going on at our house, in our room, although by now we didn't care that much.

The doors were unscrewed and flung open a bit inelegantly as if in preparation for a rushed wedding. But things were quiet in the house. The landlady was leaning on her nightstand. She was looking through the window and talking to herself. You might think she was praying, but you'd be wrong. She was cursing her Mordechai! According to her way of thinking, he should know what was going on here, and should be home at a time like this. And also, she felt sorry for her furniture and the house. She felt every scratch, whether it was on the cupboard, or the painted floor— as if someone had taken a burning nail and scraped her own flesh. The scum had tossed around and scratched all her furniture, and rummaged in her things.

In the kitchen we found an old goy up on the oven, creeping around, muttering and searching for something.

"Serhey, what do you need? Something of yours get lost there?"

I took a burning piece of kindling from the stove and raised it over Serhey.

He was a healthy old man from a village nearby, old but without a single gray hair on his head.

Things were getting uncomfortable for him, but he wasn't too happy about leaving without anything.

I shoved the stick in Serhey's direction.

"You're not coming down?"

"Don't hit me, young man. I'm coming down. I'm looking for some salt, I thought there'd be some salt, but people took it already."

I threatened him with the stick, and he stuck to his guns, until I dragged him down from the oven and tossed him to the ground.

He started protesting.

"What are you doing—I thought there was salt!"

And he slunk away, his tail between his legs, without even looking back.

At first, Buzi didn't let me deal with him, but now she laughed. The landlady was very pleased, because the door to the attic was right above the oven, and don't ask what went on there. Although she was already thinking it would have been good to have taken all her stuff and dragged it over to Khantsheke, the daughter of the rabbi's wife, who lived right next door. She was also a snake, but they say it's better to keep your keys with a thief.

And where were our teacups? The nice ones I bought for Buzi a week ago—that we kept on the buffet?

The buffet had been pried open and the beds and bedding tossed this way and that!

"Timofeyko," the landlady said, "Timofeyko took your cups. No one else but him was hanging around here."

"If it was Timofeyko, then I know him, he's a neighbor, my age."

He too was a young man, he too had been married for just a year, and also had a beautiful young wife. He was building himself a house in his father's courtyard. Taking our cups was for when he would move into his new house, so his wife could decorate her buffet just like we did with ours! Well, he was right, Timofeyko. It could be that he also took a look at something else in our room, for his own house-to-be. He was right, of course. It didn't matter that he was a very pious young man, and that he and his wife belonged to a godly sect. If I'm not mistaken, it's called "Shtundists." Such young people with such deep devotion! What use would God-fearing people like that have for Buzi's cups?

Now our room was more like a public bath than our room. Of course, it still was our room, but we didn't feel connected to it. If we were bound up with something, it was to our mothers and families, but each family was celebrating the holiday on its own!

But then our mother Khaytshik, Buzi's mom, came over.

"Will you eat something, children? You suffered the whole night long. Now you have to gather your strength, the whole thing could start up again."

She smiled.

She was right! Wisdom was on her side. It was time to do what she said, we had to eat something. But what could we do if we couldn't swallow? The food wouldn't go down. We couldn't even open our mouths to take a bite.

"Eat, Buzi."

"You too."

We started to laugh at all our troubles.

"Then lie down, children, and rest."

Now you're talking. Let's lie down for however long we can and rest.

* * *

At around noon, the plan was to go to Buzi's mother Khaytshik, and then from there on to the little woods, to my mother's. We met Khaytshik already standing at the threshold. She was holding a bowl of milk for us. And she wanted some advice.

She wanted to take Nokhem, and Aunt Freydl, and set out on the road to Behun. First they would go to Aunt Rosla at the mill, and then, if something were to happen, they would keep going!

"Why, what's the matter?"

"I don't know." Khaytshik's face was earnest and thoughtful, like the time when we used to talk about how we would get all the things we needed for our wedding, and I got annoyed, because she gave me too many responsibilities. Now she had the same face; she had three small children, and at the mill it was certainly calmer. But what should she do with us, her two grown children, was it better to keep us with her, or with my people, who lived near the wood?

"I don't know," she repeated. "People are saying it won't be so good here this evening, and if we're going to leave, we have to start on time, and that's why I was coming to you, so we could talk it over."

"Mama, where are the children?"

"I already sent them to Nakhmen's.

And we all set off toward the woods to talk with my folks about what to do.

And the way things stood (who could know in advance whether it was wise or foolish), was that we weren't going to go with Buzi's mother. The woods drew us.

We reluctantly parted with her, our mother, and with a barely noticeable tear in her eye, she left us first to God's and then to my family's care. She was a lot less worried about herself than about us.

This was on Wednesday, Wednesday during the day, and our mother, together with several other families, was going to spend the night at Aunt Rosla's, at the mill—that is, of course, if the roads weren't blocked. And if they had to, they would keep going.

* * *

Did they already have Gedalye's funeral?

People said yes. In the meantime, the day slowly turned, and it was afternoon, two or three o'clock.

There was hardly any news from the shtetl, and as far as the neighbors were concerned, it was as if they regretted their excessive goodness to us from the morning. Now they seemed more hostile; they had looks that could kill. Never mind, the hell with them! We had to think about where to spend the night. On a normal day, we would have eaten supper at this time. But now we were like creatures, who would in the evening become helpless and ownerless. Animals usually provide themselves in advance with a place to rest at night.

The previous night a mix-up had taken place: my father had stolen away from the family without telling anyone, and holed up in a shed at the tannery (it turns out that hiding had the following quality: the more deeply you hid, the more frightened you were!). Tonight we had to make sure the same thing wouldn't happen again. Wherever we were going to be, our father had to be there, too. We were planning to spend the night in Shmoylo's barn.

Should we bring the children now?

Yes, this could be done, and the grown-ups would come later, when it began to get dark. Mother had gathered some cloth and rags and led the first group of guests to Shmoylo's barn for the night. Shmoylo, however, was a good friend and advised against it.

"He was not certain himself about the safety of his house and his livestock."

"Tonight," he said, "all hell's going to break loose in the shtetl." He was wheeling out his wagon, that one, over there, the one without steps. He was greasing the wheels. We could do as we pleased, but he would not advise us to remain in town for the slaughter.

Shmoylo could also have a fire lit under him; now his eyes had daggers in them. His old, withered, religious mother, who for years stunk of incense—had given him a hard time. Last night our people in the barn heard her screaming at him and his wife: "How lazy can you get! Corpses would do more. Everyone else is going and getting all the good stuff, and you just lie there. You just can't be bothered to get off your backsides!"

No one could have expected such a strange outpouring from her. That an old, pious witch, who for ten years now had a foot in the grave, would open her rotting mouth when she heard that people were taking their neighbors' things. If you talked to her, she wouldn't touch a fly on the wall, and her refinement knew no limit. Now her son had a look that could kill, and we were stuck without a place to stay for the night:

"Shmoylo says that the town's going to be on fire tonight, and that anyone who shelters Jews will be killed together with them."

Well that's another kettle of fish. In that case, let's harness the horse and set off for Petrashi.

Ovdey had been hiding our horse since yesterday. With the wagon, with the harness, with everything (it turns out that a ring is easier to hide than a horse). Fairy tales weren't going to help us, there was nothing to be done except harness the horse!

And we were off to Petrashi. On the way, as we were going up the hill, we saw a lot of other Jews also going, men, women, girls, and boys—also to Petrashi. Old and young, they seemed so calm and carefree, without bundles in their arms, like the peasants I used to see going to celebrate a holiday in this or that village. They too went, old and young, with their wives and sweethearts. They too didn't carry anything more than a kerchief or a bottle, so they could bring back holy water, but the difference was only that they were going all dressed up and had the intention of returning home again at night, and we were going in our ordinary clothes, and were preoccupied with where we were going to spend the night.

I felt ashamed that my father had his wagon. It should have been that all of us, together—were going on foot. That's how Jews traveled, after all!

And in the fields we met groups of kids, Christians; they seemed a little strange, we hadn't seen them like this before. How would we answer them, if they started asking questions as we were making our way?

But they didn't ask anything.

They were taking the paths along the fields, it seemed, going somewhere.

They were ashamed of something.

Something out of the ordinary. Perhaps for the first time in their lives they were going to play some kind of trick, because someone had incited them to do it, or because they were envious of other places that had gotten ahead of them.

Ashamed and gray, a bit crestfallen, their heads drooping, they were coming from all sides, like a flock of hungry ravens—in the direction of our poor Slovechno.

And we were coming from the exact opposite direction—to them in Petrashi. Look, they didn't hinder us. Maybe they'd let us stay overnight in Petrashi. We were, after all, Slovechno Jews, but it wasn't true that they nurtured any particular feeling for us. We never heard anything like that from them. And yet my father was going to see someone allegedly devoted to him, who brought hides to his tannery.

"He's going to receive us in style. Arkhip is his name, and he'll treat us to everything from soup to nuts!" said father.

I would like every Jew to have such a good friend in Petrashi. Someone who would welcome them warmly.

Father was boasting about his good friend, but as our wagon entered Petrashi, the locals started circling it.

"Oy, they're staring at us!"

We were sitting there in the wagon with our families, but other Jews had already arrived before us. We were a new group. And others were still coming.

There were some Jews who smoked, and they asked for cigarettes, and as they smoked their faces assumed a carefree expression, like someone smoking on a fast day.

Avram the Petrashi Jew already had a lot of Jewish refugees (I had once seen his house full of Jews from the town—but that time it was different. That time he was marrying off his eldest son, and the whole shtetl had come to celebrate the occasion). Wasn't there a watchman at Avram's?

"In a Jewish house!"

Standing at the fence across from the house, the priest was talking to Avram about the Jews and Slovechno.

The Petrashi priest was a good-looking man, around thirty years old, with a stately appearance. He smacked his lips and was surprised that so many Jews suddenly up and left Slovechno—"a pity, a pity."

Maybe he was sincere. It's entirely possible that there's one priest out of a hundred who didn't dirty his hands with this business.

The visor on Avram's cap was a little to the side as he spoke.

"So many guests may no evil eye befall them." And also, "God should at least make sure it goes smoothly."

Avram was a great guy. Tall and broad-shouldered, chubby, with a reddish-greenish beard like freshly dried young grass, a soft face sprinkled with freckles, and big expressive eyes. He wore an alpaca jacket and was everyone's buddy. He had friendships with boys, even though he was the father of five grown sons. And when he talked, he wasn't ashamed to speak in his loud, village voice. That's who Avram from Petrashi was.

Father got down from the wagon, and almost whispering in Avram's ear, asked him where such-and-such Arkhip lived. Avram answered that he knew and would take us there. Behind us there were two families with small children, a cat, and pots of milk.

The milk was for stopping up mouths of little ones who started making a racket at night.

There was, however, nothing necessarily keeping Arkhip home all the time; he could be in the forest, or somewhere, or on a trip; it was just our luck not to find him, and we spoke instead to one of his sons, a fourteen-year-old, a shepherd.

"I'm not letting you stay without my father's permission."

"Don't be such a child! Your father always brings hides to my tannery, every year. We're on the best of terms! Just try not letting us in, and you'll see how he'll yell at you!"

"Without father, I don't know anything about this!"

"When is he coming, your father?"

"I don't know, maybe in the evening."

"In that case, there's no problem! Just let us into the barn until he comes! Look what this idiot is up to."

And whether he wanted to or not, the young shepherd brought out a wooden key and unlocked the barn for us. We unharnessed the horse (the other families had rented wagons, so they sent them back), spread out some cloths and rugs for bedding and lay down. There were three families in that barn, and each had a small addition.

And as soon as a child made a peep, we gave him some milk. There was a boy we didn't know; he was sick and didn't want anything, and as soon as the grownups had nothing more to say, they fell silent.

I went out to cover the horse with a blanket and to give it some fresh hay, when an old lady came up to the wagon. She was from the neighboring house. She was barefoot and was wearing a shift and two aprons, one in back and one in front—for a dress.

And she was crying!

She was crying, because she had had to see with her own eyes: "How is it possible that a such a desolate and bitter generation has arisen? One that takes other people's things? It used to be that you never would have heard of such a thing! Could it be that the damn war made them so depraved?"

After a little while, she wiped her eyes, took a piece of straw from the wagon and tried it on her old, rotten teeth and remembered something:

"There's just one thing that makes you a bit guilty, my dear. You shouldn't have held back the salt! You should know, dearie, how much people suffer without salt.

I'm not going to ask you anymore why you had to go and do such a thing. There's nothing worse than food without salt! Even a cow won't take a drink of water unless you give it salt. What other proof do you need? Even a cow! Oy, my dear, how we suffered without salt! It could be that's the reason people are so angry—they've gone to look for salt!"

"Yeah," I say to the old lady, "people are angry; they've gone to look for salt."

"God protect us from such things. Wait a minute, dearie, I'll be right back."

And in two minutes she had gone back and forth twice through the gates and brought out ten baked potatoes in a wooden tub.

"Give these to the little children; let them eat. Give them, my dear." And she wiped her old eyes with her apron.

It took about an hour for the daylight to be extinguished in every corner of the sky. Evening's ashy pebbles rubbed against every eye that wanted to stay open. From outside the barn it smelled of grass—green grass. Outside the barn green gardens grew. The gardens were resting now in their voluptuous languor and each blade of grass nestled in the fresh, cool dew, unashamed and undisturbed. Inside our barn the floor was flat and dry, and there were places for three families. Buzi was tired and already falling asleep, and I wanted to take off her shoes before she dozed off, although I didn't want to wake her. Mother and the children were asleep. But it seemed that father couldn't fall asleep. He didn't want to disturb anyone and lay still. It was quiet all around; you only heard the horse chewing monotonously over and over again. I had already removed one sticky, sweaty sock, and was getting ready to take off the other one. Someone opened the door. Barn doors were broad and in the countryside the moon was low and visible, and the whole barn was suffused with moonlight. But who could it be coming to us so late, it was nighttime, time for sleep! I soon saw who it was. It was our shepherd:

"Jews! Jews! Get out of here! I don't want you here; I'm afraid!"

"Who are you afraid of?"

And the young shepherd didn't know who and what he feared, he was still little, "he was afraid they'd set the whole place on fire." He didn't want this to happen, and he was crying.

It seemed that there was nothing to be done. The matter was clear—we had to get out of there. But where to?

Little by little, everyone got up; we started looking at each other with a question in our eyes. The grownups scowled at each other; just as you were beginning to get warm and cozy, you had to wake up! But soon everyone came to; the situation was clear, although no one wanted to give an opinion about what to do, as if it were none of their business! A couple of the men began thinking about it and talking it over. It would be their decision. They would figure it out and everyone would do what they said.

And here was the problem. The men didn't know what to do:

"Maybe leave and return back to town?"

"Maybe harness the horse and sneak out of the village on the quiet (which would be hard) and spend the night under the open sky, somewhere in the fields (but wouldn't that be too frightening)?"

Source: Itsik Kipnis, *Khadoshim un teg: A khronik* (Kiev: Kiev Kultur-Lige, 1926), 82–98. Translated from the Yiddish by Harriet Murav.

9

Pogroms in Modern Poland, 1918–1946

Anna Cichopek-Gajraj and Glenn Dynner

Jewish communities in interwar Poland endured two major waves of collective violence. The first occurred in the aftermath of World War I as Poland achieved statehood; the second followed the death of Poland's benign authoritarian leader, Marshal Józef Piłsudski (1867–1935). Both waves of violence were products of not only anti-Jewish animus but also reigning economic resentment and a weakened state apparatus. Both proved far less lethal than those in Ukrainian lands in 1918–1921. Yet over 130 collective attacks on Jews occurred on Polish territories from 1918 to 1921, resulting in as many as 300 deaths; and over 100 occurred between 1935 and 1937, with dozens of casualties.[1] Many attacks were conceived as reprisals against supposed Jewish economic power and "Judeo-Bolshevism," involved carnivalesque mob violence, and were unquestionably pogroms.[2] Together, they served as brutal reminders of the limits on inclusiveness in the newly born, multiethnic Polish state.

The Jewish-Christian economic symbiosis that had prevailed in the noble manorial economy for centuries and largely kept violence in check had declined by the end of the nineteenth century as a result of peasant emancipation, noble impoverishment, and the rise of both exclusionary Polish nationalism and racial antisemitism. Peasants and nobles, animated by anti-Jewish hostility and in search of new economic opportunities, found themselves on a veritable collision course with Jews, and some participated in anti-Jewish boycotts. In the immediate aftermath of World War I, urban populations joined peasants in acts of anti-Jewish violence. Hunger and rage over perceived Jewish control of food supplies and prices, as well as perceptions of Jewish disloyalty and treason—namely, their alleged anti-Polish and pro-German or pro-Bolshevik sympathies—amplified the existing anti-Jewish sentiments and fueled pogroms throughout the Polish lands. Polish Legionaries perpetrated even more deadly pogroms after conquering eastern territories for the new Polish state.

---

[1] Estimates of casualties vary from 14 to 118. See William W. Hagen, *Anti-Jewish Violence in Poland, 1914–1920* (Cambridge: Cambridge University Press, 2018); Sławomir Buryła, Kamil Kijek, Artur Markowski, and Konrad Zieliński, eds., *Pogromy Żydów na ziemiach polskich w XIX i XX wieku: Studia przypadków (do 1939 roku), tom 2* (Warsaw: Instytut Historii PAN, 2019)..

[2] Historians have often employed euphemisms for Polish pogroms ("incident," "excess"); however, this is beginning to change. See Hagen, *Anti-Jewish Violence in Poland* and Buryła et al., *Pogromy Żydów na ziemiach polskich, 4 vols.*

Anna Cichopek-Gajraj and Glenn Dynner, *Pogroms in Modern Poland, 1918–1946* In: *Pogroms*. Edited by: Eugene M. Avrutin and Elissa Bemporad, Oxford University Press. © Oxford University Press 2021. DOI: 10.1093/oso/9780190060084.003.0010

Sites of pogroms on Polish territories between 1918 and 1946.
Public Domain, Wikimedia Commons

One of the first pogroms occurred in Kraków in April 1918, after bread rations were reduced and prices for black-market flour began to surge. The city's Polish Catholic majority blamed the prices on the Jewish traders, who dealt disproportionately in flour and other foodstuffs. Ethnic Poles were further enraged by rumors of alleged Jewish war treason. On April 16, a market day, mobs of adolescent youths and women entered the city center, beat Jewish passersby, and plundered Jewish-owned stores. Two days later they moved on to the Kazimierz Jewish district, casting Jewish goods onto the street for easy plunder. Demobilized Polish soldiers and Habsburg imperial-royal policemen refused to protect victims and even joined in the violence. This seemed to legitimize the pogrom: if authorities were not interfering, many assumed, beating the Jews must be legal. Sporadic violence continued for days, resulting in one to two deaths.

Over the next two years, Galicia (Austrian Poland)—ruled in turn by several military regimes, coveted by both Polish and Ukrainian nationalists, and nearly partitioned—was engulfed by pogroms carried out by Polish soldiers and civilians, many of whom suspected Jews of being in league with virtually all of their enemies. The most lethal occurred in Lwów (formerly Lemberg, currently L'viv) on November 22–24, 1918, in the wake of a Polish–Ukrainian military conflict. Ethnic tensions had long simmered in this city, essentially a Polish and Jewish enclave within a predominantly ethnic Ukrainian region. Poles sought Lwów for a newly independent Poland, whereas Ukrainians sought it as the capital of their prospective West Ukrainian republic. Jews opted for neutrality. Yet as soon as the conflict ended, victorious Polish troops disarmed a Jewish self-defense unit, thereby giving a green light to the plunder. Together with civilians, they proceeded to sack the Jewish quarter, killing as many as 150 people, raping scores of women, and looting over 500 shops. The perpetrators seemed to relish the opportunity to exact retribution for supposed Jewish disloyalty and wealth, sometimes committing their gruesome acts to the accompaniment of feasting, drinking, and music.

Victorious Polish troops also assaulted Jewish communities in historical Lithuania (present-day Belarus and Lithuania). On April 5, 1919, they summarily executed thirty-four Jews mistakenly identified as Bolsheviks. On April 17, they entered the town of Lida, looted Jewish-owned stores, and beat, publicly humiliated, and murdered Jews, a total

Aftermath of the pogrom in Lwów that occurred November 22–2421–23, 1918. The original caption reads: "These four children, whose parents were murdered in the pogrom in Lemberg, were taken in by refugees."
Courtesy of the Institute for Jewish Research Archives (YIVO), Thousand Towns Photo Collection

of thirty-eight. On April 19, they commenced a three-day, slow-motion pogrom against Vilna's Jews. Soldiers burst into Jewish homes pointed out by non-Jewish neighbors, robbed, arrested, beat, and tortured Jewish inhabitants, executed at least seventy-five, and looted and desecrated Vilna's two main synagogues—all well after the Polish–Bolshevik fighting had ceased. Prime Minister Ignacy Jan Paderewski (1860–1941), after initial public denials, warned that those guilty of "assault, violence or robbery, or any other transgression against the security of life or property of Jews or Christians, will be arrested and punished with all severity of law."[3] Such pronouncements carried more weight in territories that were firmly under state control.

By the 1920s, virtually all that was left of the old interethnic economic system was the predominantly Jewish markets and fairs, to which peasants flowed from surrounding rural areas in a weekly, monthly, and annual rhythm. Despite the younger generation of peasants' increased educational and economic ambitions, and increased nationalist sentiments, Piłsudski managed to keep collective anti-Jewish violence largely in check. Piłsudski's death on May 12, 1935, occasioned a sharp rise in violent picketing of Jewish-owned stores and stalls, as well as assaults on Jews, their customers, and occasionally police. Leaders of the ethno-nationalist "Endecja" movement promised: "The current regime will collapse, a nationalist regime is coming, the new regime will expel Jews from Poland, there will accordingly be no more unemployment, and Polish workers will at last find work."[4] The purge of Jews from the economy that Hitler had achieved in neighboring Germany, they claimed, could happen in Poland too.

The ensuing wave of violent boycotts, assaults, property destruction, and pogroms—possibly the first occurring in Grodno on June 7, 1935—resulted in about two thousand serious injuries and roughly sixty deaths, though estimates vary widely. In November 1935, police killed thirteen armed anti-Jewish assailants in Odrzywół (near Radom). Endecja activists, who instigated the violence, construed the incident as proof that the government was in Jewish hands.[5] Violent picketers, some paid by Endecja, now regularly attacked Jewish merchants and their non-Jewish customers throughout central, western, and northeastern Poland, where Endecja's influence was strongest. Some unemployed Polish Christian men, who joined in pogroms, found the presence of Jewish women working at stalls and stores particularly troubling: among the listed evils for which Jews were held responsible was "trade conducted by women."[6]

The most notorious pogrom occurred in Przytyk (near Radom), a hotbed of anti-Jewish activism. Two days before the pogrom, Jewish communal leaders had taken

---

[3] Isaac Lewin, *A History of Polish Jewry during the Revival of Poland* (New York: Shengold, 1990), 178–79.

[4] Archiwum Państwowe w Lublinie, *Urząd Wojewódzki Lubelski-Wydział Społeczno-Polityczny, s. 1897* (1935), 193. Endecja at this time was represented by the Stronnictwo Narodowe party.

[5] In Grodno, after a Pole died in a fight with a Jew, mob vengeance resulted in sixty wounded; two later died. Thanks to Josh Zimmerman for suggesting how to properly categorize this event. A clash near Zagórów on February 5, 1936, similar to the Odrzywół incident, resulted in five casualties.

[6] "Report on Visit to Truskolasy," 1–3, American Jewish Joint Distribution Committee (JDC) Archives, Poland, 1933/44/89; United States Holocaust Memorial Museum (USHMM) Archives, Kielce, 15.427 sign. 54, p. 168.

Funeral for Jewish victims of the Przytyk pogrom. The original caption reads: "The funeral of Chaya Minkowski, one of the Jews killed in a pogrom in Przytyk on March 9, 1936. The funeral was held in Radom."
Courtesy of The Ghetto Fighters' House Museum, Photo Archive Collection, Israel

preventive measures. They sent a delegation to the district governor to convince him that the numerous anti-Jewish attacks of prior months were a common threat to public order, since non-Jewish customers were being assaulted too. The governor agreed to supply police reinforcements, but they proved insufficient. On March 9, 1936, a market day, a mob prevented a police officer from arresting a picketer who was physically harassing a Jewish baker's customers, and then began attacking Jews. A local Zionist self-defense group's resort to guns escalated the violence. Stanisław Wieśniak was shot to death, allegedly by Sholom Lesko.[7] Wieśniak's death triggered a furious rampage through the Jewish suburbs with cries of "Kill them; don't forgive them for what they have done to our brother."[8] Around one hundred apartments and shops were destroyed and twenty-five Jews seriously injured. Joseph and Hayya Minkowski were bludgeoned to death. In the trial that followed, Jewish self-defense fighters received heavy sentences, while Polish perpetrators were acquitted or given light or suspended sentences. Police were now ordered to avoid confronting hostile crowds in order to protect Jews.

Over the next two years, violent picketing, assaults, and pogroms proliferated in the country's more ethnically Polish areas, in particular. While older peasants tended to resent Endecja activists for impeding their access to cheaper, Jewish-sold goods, their sons—often frustrated in their attempt to break into urban occupations—were

[7] Several testimonies argue for Lesko's innocence. See Institute for Jewish Research Archives (YIVO), Poland I., RG 116, box 13.2; and JDC Archives, 1933/44/790, p. 588.
[8] Adam Penkalla, "'The Przytyk Incidents' of 9 March 1936 from Archival Documents," *Polin* 5 (1990), docs. 3–5, pp. 334–56.

more willing recruits. Pogroms usually followed a "trigger" event. In Mińsk Mazowiecki (near Warsaw), in June 1936, a mentally ill army veteran named Judah Leib Chaskielewicz killed his former officer, Sergeant Jan Bujak, sparking a rampage in which sixty Jews were wounded. In Brześć nad Bugiem (currently Brest in western Belarus), in May 1937, a butcher named Ajzik Szczerbowski stabbed the kosher meat inspector Stefan Kędziora as he attempted to confiscate his unauthorized meat, setting off a pogrom that was virtually unimpeded by police. Although only the latter of those two pogroms proved lethal (two victims died from their wounds), in both cases the obliterated Jewish stores and stalls were replaced by Christian ones. Pogroms had become a blunt instrument for Jewish economic displacement.

Mordecai Gebirtig's 1938 protest song "It's Burning" warns that "our poor town's on fire" and urges Jews to quench the fire "even with your blood," suggesting a call to arms. However, some of the most effective Jewish responses to pogroms were those coordinated with ethnic Poles of goodwill, including joint protest strikes and self-defense initiatives organized with the Polish Socialist Party. American Jews, for their part, demonstrated before the Polish embassy in Washington DC, alerted antifascist groups and the press, threatened international boycotts, and helped pay to retrain pogrom victims in the crafts, a less resented occupation. Anti-Jewish violence began to die down during the last two years before the war.

The more than 200 pogroms that broke out in the Polish eastern borderlands during World War II in the summer of 1941 might be considered sui generis in light of their immediate context of Nazi–Soviet military conflict. However, the pogroms that

Aftermath of the Mińsk Mazowiecki pogrom. The original caption reads: "Victims of a pogrom in Mińsk Mazowiecki in June 1936."
Public Domain, Wikimedia Commons

occurred in the wake of the war (1945–1946) fell into the more familiar patterns of urban anti-Jewish violence described in this volume.[9] As in 1918–1921, post–World War II Poland was beset by lawlessness, displacement, banditry, poverty, rampant food shortages, and hunger. And as in 1918–1921, Jews were accused of profiteering, disloyalty, and Bolshevism, while demobilized soldiers and militiamen joined civilians in killing, beating, and robbing them. Each postwar pogrom was, moreover, sparked by a rumor of ritual murder, reminiscent of accusations in the Russian past.

In 1945–1946, attacks on Holocaust survivors were almost daily affairs, resulting in hundreds of deaths.[10] At least three of those outbreaks—in Kielce, Kraków, and Rzeszów—should be classified as pogroms. The bloodiest took place in Kielce on July 4, 1946, after a missing boy turned up and accused Jews of having kidnapped him. Local women in particular, some barely literate, believed that Jews were snatching their kids for ritual purposes—a bizarre twist on the very real wartime mass murder of Jewish children and the postwar rise in crimes against all children, Jewish and Christian alike. In the ensuing bloodbath, Jews were plundered, shot, bludgeoned, and thrown out of windows. By the end of the day, forty-three Holocaust survivors had been killed. The ritual murder myth also played a role in Kraków where, on August 11, 1945, a pogrom began when a young boy ran out of a synagogue screaming "People, help! They want to murder me!" [11] In response, a Polish mob proceeded to demolish the synagogue's interior and trample sacred objects. Rioters dragged Jews out of their apartments to the streets to be beaten or, in the case of Róża Berger, killed. In Rzeszów, on June 12, 1945, large crowds gathered on the streets, cursed Jews as militia escorted them to their station, threw stones, plundered Jewish apartments, and beat up their residents.

What differentiated the post–World War II pogroms was their context of recent Nazi occupation, genocide, and communist takeover. Polish society was gripped by a social crisis caused by years of German occupation and a need to survive outside and against the occupier's law.[12] Relentless antisemitic propaganda during the war amplified established tropes of alleged Jewish inhumanity and danger, and the postwar communist takeover enabled the myth of Judeo-Bolshevism to resurface with new force. Polish witnessing and participation in the genocide during the war often determined postwar behavior— some participants in postwar pogroms were the very men who had robbed, denounced, or murdered Jews during the Holocaust. Finally, fears over Jewish property restitution produced lethal resentment towards Holocaust survivors as they attempted to return to their homes. The poet Czesław Miłosz's prediction that Poles would one day be counted "among the helpers of death" thus came to pass in ways he may not have imagined.[13]

---

[9] Among the worst cases, on June 30–July 2, 1941, Ukrainian nationalists (OUN), German death squads, and local Ukrainians and Poles staged a pogrom in Lviv, killing several thousand Jews. In Jedwabne on July 10, Poles killed up to 1,600 Jewish neighbors (the estimates are still debated).

[10] Estimates of casualties vary from a few hundred to over a thousand.

[11] Institute of National Memory (IPN) in Kraków, BU 829/1255, Bill of indictment, September 5, 1945.

[12] Kazimierz Wyka, "The Excluded Economy," in *The Unplanned Society: Poland during and after Communism*, ed. Janine R. Wedel (New York: Columbia University Press, 1992), 41.

[13] Czesław Miłosz, "A Poor Christian Looks at the Ghetto (1943)," in *Postwar Polish Poetry*, ed. Czesław Miłosz (Berkeley: University of California Press, 1983), 75–76.

Document 9.1. Police Report about the Incidents Involving Policemen in Kraków on April 16, 1918

On April 16, 1918, a market day, mobs entered Kraków's center, beat Jewish passersby, and plundered Jewish-owned stores. Many assailants were demobilized Polish soldiers; and Habsburg imperial-royal policemen—mainly ethnic Poles—often refused to protect victims. This report describes cases where police tolerated or actively joined in the violence, which continued for a few days and resulted in property destruction, injuries, and one to two deaths.

Salomea F. (address: Jakób Street, age eight) testified that when she walked down Grodzka Street near St. Peter and Paul Church, she saw people beat a Jew without mercy in the entrance of an apartment house; so she asked mounted policemen no. 11 and no. 25 to intervene. To that, one of them responded, "This does not concern you at all," and these policemen kept watching without emotion as the assailants bullied and mercilessly beat a defenseless human being. [. . .]

Second lieutenant Dr. Karz, a military doctor, and Dr. Zygmunt Ehrenpreis, an attorney, called on policeman no. 27, who stood on Starowiślna Street in front of the post office, to intervene as Jews were beaten there. The policeman refused, saying that he had no order to intervene.

Zygmunt R. was a witness to police corporal no. 80 beating a Jew at the corner of Grodzka Street and Dominikański Square.

On April 16, at 4:30 in the afternoon, a store with mixed goods and spirits owned by Jakób Goldstein, age sixty-seven, at Krowoderska Street was completely plundered. The policeman on duty was staring idly. Goldstein reported to the police what damage he suffered and gave names and addresses of the culprits who robbed his property, asking that the policeman immediately conduct a search in their apartment, where he would surely find his stolen goods. [The report then includes a follow-up question:] Has the immediate search been conducted?

In the grocery store of Joachim Messer at Krowoderska Street everything has been robbed and the mounted police supposedly just watched idly. [The report then anticipates further testimonies:] The store's owner Messer will probably give more details.

Junior officer Dr. Józef B. saw from a window of the Military Headquarters at Gertrudy Street that in the *planty* [park around the old town] a Jew was beaten while a patrolling soldier watched idly.

Source: Police report April 19, 1918, in Akta Prezydialne [Presidium Acts]: Kommando der K. K. Militarpolizeiwachabteilung in Krakau, April 19, 1918, National Archives in Kraków, C. K. Dyrekcja Policji w Krakowie, 29/247/118, pp. 1085–86. Translated from the Polish by Anna Cichopek-Gajraj.

Document 9.2. "The Lemberg Horrors," by Joseph Bendrow

In the wake of World War I, Galicia (Austrian Poland) changed hands frequently and was the scene of numerous pogroms carried out by Polish soldiers and civilians. The most lethal occurred in multiethnic Lwów (formerly Lemberg, currently Lviv) on November 22–24, 1918, in the wake of a Polish–Ukrainian military conflict. Victorious Polish Legionaries and civilians looted over 500 shops, raped at least twelve Jewish women, and murdered as many as 150 Jews.

There were scenes which have not been witnessed for many a century. For three weeks, beginning with the 1st of November, every child in the Jewish section knew that the Poles were making ready for a pogrom against the Jews. The Polish newspaper *Pobudka* called openly for such a pogrom and the Polish soldiers talked about it quite frequently, picturing how they would begin the bloody work in the Jewish streets as soon as Lemberg would be captured from the Ukrainians. In the Polish section of Lemberg there were only two subjects of discussion: the battle with the Ukrainians and the pogrom that threatened. One week preceding the pogrom, when the Polish women gathered around the stores and stands, a municipal officer consoled them in the following words: "Be easy, children!"—these were his very words—"Have patience. Soon we shall get to the Kraków Square. We will then begin to tackle the Jews and you shall have all that you need. You just wait and see!"

The soldiers made a little song: "General Roya with his brave little boys is coming and he will make a wedding feast for the Jews."

Roya was then the Polish commander. Following the pogrom he became demented and he is to this very day confined in a lunatic asylum.

As you see, the Jews had it borne in upon them from all sides that the Poles were getting ready for them. They expected a pogrom. But the murderous massacre that actually took place was even beyond their expectations.

On November 22nd, early in the morning, the Polish soldiery marched into Lemberg, accompanied by martial music, and immediately after, the Jewish section began to hum with the strains of mouth harmonicas, songs, and profanity against Jews. Here and there shots fired on Jewish houses were heard.

We have a great number of depositions of Jewish witnesses, who were told by the soldiers that they had been promised two free days to massacre and plunder to their heart's content in the Jewish streets. A Jewish Legionary, that is, a Jew who had volunteered in the Polish Army and fought to liberate Lemberg for the Poles (and of such Jews there were many, and many of them laid down their lives for Poland), pleaded with the Polish commander that he should send aid to his family, because they were plundering his parents' home. The commander met his request with the declaration that the Jews were to be plundered, that this was the command from on high, and the Jewish solider received no aid for his family.

When one studies the details of the pogrom, one sees clearly that this was an organized and carefully prepared attack. The plunderings on a large scale began toward six o'clock in the evening. One large pogrom horde gathered around the theater (which stands at the boundary line of the Jewish quarter) and from there smaller groups of marauders were dispatched, every group under the command of a leader. Every group was sent into a territory of its own, in order that it might not compete with the other groups. Later on the groups exchanged their scenes of operation, so that every spot was visited by one group after another. These groups were equipped with guns, hand grenades, knives, and steel helmets, as if getting ready for a front-line attack. From twenty to thirty soldiers thus equipped would attack the Jewish houses, break through doors, enter the rooms, and begin the "work." Some would torture the inhabitants, searching their pockets, beating and insulting them—old and young, men and women—outrage the girls, while others would rob and carry with them everything they could lay their hands on. All that could not be taken was broken, ripped open, and thrown into the street. They stripped women to make sure that they had not hidden any money in their clothes. Sick women were dragged by their hair from their beds; children were thrown out of their cradles, and all the time they would curse in the most abominable fashion, and would conduct themselves like real devils.

Sentries were stationed in front of doors in order to take care that no one escaped, and in order that no one should escape from the Jewish section of the city they stationed at the end of the streets machine guns and armored automobiles. Anyone who dared show his face in the street was fired upon.

For further protection the entire Jewish section was surrounded with a cordon of soldiers, thus taking care that no one could leave or enter the Jewish streets. Simultaneously with the attack on the Jewish houses, attacks were also made on the Jewish stores.

In the course of two hours all Jewish shops were pried into, the merchandise dragged into the streets, the fixtures broken, and everything annihilated. The jewelry house of Tisfer, situated in the very heart of the city, a few steps from the place where the Polish military command then had its headquarters, was plundered in the light of day. This is only one instance out of many hundreds.

And thus it went on for two days and two nights; for forty-eight hours the Jewish populace had not one minute's respite.

The soldiers were also accompanied by civilian marauders. Many of them are well known to us by name. We also know quite a number of the soldiers and their officers who participated in the pogrom. Among them were many men of high standing: important officials, school teachers, students, etc. Many of education behaved worse than the most ignorant. And in many cases an educated marauder would sit down with his bloody hands at a piano, play a beautiful composition, and then break the piano.

Nearly 11,000,000 crowns was stolen in cash. The total damage amounted to about 30,000,000 crowns, and the majority of those affected are the poorest of the poor.

From the depositions the Committee compiled various figures regarding the number of marauders.

Robberies by ordinary soldiers without officers numbered 1,918. Robberies by organized pogrom groups in which officers participated together with soldiers are estimated at 494; robberies of the military with an admixture of civilians, 391; officers in their own right, 6; civilians by themselves, 6. The total is 2,815 various cases of pillage, and that is only a fraction of the actual sum total. [. . .]

Mrs. M. A. Neuer adds this to the deposition:

"On the 23rd of November, nine o'clock in the morning, three Legionaries came into our house. One [of] them wore on his arm the white and red band (the Polish national colors). He was a tall, strong man. It was he who killed my brother. I remembered him very well. A short time ago I met him once more. I have met him on the Zigmuntowska [Zygmuntowska] Street. He was at that time on duty; however, as soon as he spotted me he disappeared.

"On the 23rd of November three Legionaries burst open the door of our house with hand grenades and went up to the first floor of the apartment of a woman, N. Greier by name. They asked her to open her safe for them. She told them that she did not have the key. They beat her in the most murderous fashion and then came up to the apartment of my brother, beat him up and demanded gold and silver. My brother gave them all he had. One of them began manhandling my sister-in-law and knocked out several of her teeth; then they began to beat her mother, a very old woman. One of them leveled a revolver toward my brother and killed him. My brother still had time to signal to his children to leave the room and soon after he departed this life.

"The bandits trampled on the dead body and beat the children in order to stifle their cries. One threatened to shoot my sister-in-law if she did not give him money. My fourteen-year-old niece took his hands, led him around the rooms, and showed him everything, asking him to take all only to leave Mama alive. She said to him: 'The mother of your God would surely have had pity on us, and have you no pity on us?' A second soldier who was stationed near the door was touched by these words and called off the other fellow. They took along well stuffed bags. Before departing they exclaimed: 'Now you can keep watch over your dead!'"

"In another apartment in the same house a Legionary was sitting at an open piano and playing while his comrades danced. This was followed by robbery and beating. They wanted to shoot an old Jew, but his daughter warded them off. Then they forced a gun into her mouth and tantalized her for a long time, threatening every minute to fire the gun. The three Legionaries who plundered and murdered in our apartment afterward joined the others and participated in those scenes; then they returned to us and again trampled the dead body under their feet. I also want to add the following fact: Before they shot my brother he pleaded with them to be left alive for the sake of tortures which he had stood so long, because he was just recently released from a prisoners' camp in Russia. He said that he had not yet seen enough of his children and he pleaded with them to be left alive for the sake of his children. One Legionary answered him thus: 'It is a pity to let a strong Jew like you live, we must kill you.'"

During the two days that the pogrom lasted, Jewish deputations went to the supreme commander, Captain Manchinski, and pleaded with him to send aid. It was all in vain. This Captain, who is looked upon by the Poles as a national hero, told the deputations that the Jews were firing on Legionaries, and similar wild goose stories. He, more than anyone else, is responsible for the pogrom. But the civilian officers of the city have not behaved much better. They also dismissed the Jewish deputations with all sorts of far-fetched accusations. We were exposed and sentenced to pillage, murder, fire, and violations, and there was no one to come to our aid. [. . .]

For the present, at the time when I left Lemberg, about a month ago, we had the following summaries:

In two pogrom days (the 22nd and 23rd of November) there were killed thirty-six Jewish merchants, eleven artisans, two of liberal occupations, and 24 unskilled laborers—in all 73. As a matter of fact, the number of those murdered and burned outright during these two days is much larger. Many of our dead were dragged away by the soldiers and buried [in] the Christian Cemetery. We have only listed the dead that we knew by name, and these are only a small number of the actual victims. Aside from this: Out of the 5,000 depositions only 3,000 were perfected. The same holds true about the wounded, and about those who have suffered in other ways. For the present we have a list of 443 wounded ones. A great number of those were very severely wounded and died several days later, but these have not been included in the list of the dead. The Committee has also compiled tables, showing the damage to property caused the Jews by the pogrom. But also these tables are far from complete.

On November 22nd toward evening, after the Jewish households were already plundered and everything was destroyed, the marauders began the burning of Jewish houses.

And here we again see the hand of systematic preparation. They brought automobiles loaded with petroleum and benzene, and after a short while the entire Jewish section was enveloped in flames.

Special arson patrols rushed through the streets equipped with all the prerequisites for firing houses. They walked from house to house and put them on fire.

They did not burn houses only—they burned men too! In many places they stationed soldiers to not permit anyone to escape from the burning houses. Some of the Jews who ran out of the houses to escape the fire were shot down on the spot. Many jumped from windows and from roofs, and whoever could, saved himself.

Many, however, were burned alive.

The yells of the unfortunates were heard throughout the entire city, but the marauders only laughed. Their cultured co-murderers yelled: "Keep yourselves warm, children!" And the burning and the killing continued.

The Jewish inhabitants of a certain burning house, seeing that there was no escape, gathered into one room which was not burning yet; the men put on their shrouds and in a wailing voice began to recite the confessional (the prayer of the last rites). A Christian who passed by was touched and saved them.

The bandits searched out all the synagogues and small chapels, burned and destroyed the holy scrolls, and demolished all the furnishings. In this fashion they burned the Suburban Synagogue, an edifice 400 years old, of great artistic value. The Jewish temple (the place of worship for the more progressive element) was also fired by the marauders and plundered. But the temple was saved.

Two young men, David Rubenfeldt and Israel Feigenbaum, who made an attempt to save the holy scrolls from the burning synagogue, were shot down on the threshold by the Polish Legionaries. A Jewish student who lifted up the holy scroll was found dead near the synagogue with the scroll closely pressed in his arms.

In the Hadashim Synagogue nearly seventy Jewish souls took refuge. They thought there they would find sanctuary against the soldiers. Soon, however, a band of marauders arrived. They asked of these seventy souls a ransom of 2,000 crowns. The poor Jews could not scrape together more than a few hundred crowns. This was not enough for the bandits, so they erected a gibbet in the center of the synagogue. They called over the first victim and ordered him to put the noose around his neck. The unfortunate ones began to plead that they would rather be shot. Then they were released and ordered to bring together all the holy scrolls and the books. These the bandits soaked in kerosene and ignited. The door of the synagogue was fastened and a sentry placed outside, so that none of the Jews should escape. Fortunately the Jews knew of a little straggling street in the rear, of which the Poles knew nothing. In this fashion they escaped.

Source: Joseph Bendrow, "The Lemberg Horrors" [excerpt], in Evidence of Pogroms in Poland and Ukrainia: Documents, Accounts of Eye-witnesses, Proceedings in Polish Parliament, Local Press Reports, Etc. (New York: Information Bureau of the Committee for the Defense of Jews in Poland and Other East European Countries, n.d.), 27–34. Original: Joseph Bendrow [pseud. for Joseph Tenenbaum], Der Lemberger Judenpogrom, November 1918–Jänner 1919 (Vienna: Hickl, 1919). Anonymous translation.

Document 9.3. Testimony from the Vilna Pogrom, 1919

Victorious Polish Legionaries also terrorized Jewish communities in historical Lithuania (present-day Belarus and Lithuania). On April 19, 1919 soldiers burst into numerous Jewish homes in Vilna, robbed, beat, and tortured inhabitants, executed at least seventy-five, and looted and desecrated synagogues well after the Polish–Bolshevik fighting had ceased. Before his death, Meir Steinman managed to write, "I burn, but cannot be consumed," probably alluding to a classical rabbinical analogy between the biblical burning bush and the Jewish people, who are similarly burned but never consumed.

Steinman, Meir, forty years old, a merchant, Soltanishki Street.

On Monday, April 21, legionaries came to Steinman several times and demanded money. The third time they came they planted a grenade, placing it in an oven. Afterward they came back, went to the oven, found the grenade, took Steinman with them, and accused him of possessing a weapon. Steinman's daughter forcefully defended her father and declared that she had *found* the grenade in the street, believing that this claim would save her father. The legionaries would hear nothing of it, and dragged Steinman several *versts* [about 0.66 mile] from Soltanishki Street—and several days later people found him dead and unburied, far from home. Steinman had been horribly beaten. People found a note in his pocket upon which was written: *I burn, but cannot be consumed.*

According to Christian neighbors, Steinman was forced to dig his own grave. Afterward, they shot and fatally wounded him. Before his death they tormented him horribly.

Steinman had been a very distinguished man, beloved throughout the region.

Source: Herman Bernstein Collection, Institute for Jewish Research Archives (YIVO), RG 713, 12, box 46, folder 851. For the burning-bush interpretation, see Midrash Rabbah Shemot, 2:5, Moshe Aryeh Mirkin, ed., *Midrash Rabbah: Shemot Rabbah*, 1:63–64. Translated from the Yiddish by Glenn Dynner.

Document 9.4. Report about the Incidents of March 9, 1936, in Przytyk

After Marshal Piłsudski's death on May 12, 1935, there was a sharp rise in assaults on Jews, their customers, and occasionally police by ethnonationalist Endecja activists. In Przytyk on March 9, 1936, a mob prevented a police officer from arresting a violent picketer and then began attacking local Jews. The local Zionist self-defense group resorted to guns. Stanisław Wieśniak was shot to death, allegedly by Sholem Lesko; and Joseph and Hayya Minkowski were bludgeoned to death. In the ensuing trial, Jewish self-defense fighters received heavy sentences, while Polish perpetrators were given light or suspended sentences.

I have to report the following on the fair and the incidents on March 9, 1936, in the town of Przytyk. Around 10.00 hours wagons from the neighboring villages started to arrive as usual in Przytyk, and by noon about 600 wagons had arrived altogether and around 4,000 people, mostly men. Although this fair was the so-called annual fair, it was no different from the normal Monday fair. I observed nothing unusual happening on the square and the market place till 14.00 hours to arouse suspicion that this market was any different from the previous one, except that the Jews had erected more stalls than at previous markets. There was no greater boycott of the Jewish shops than before. The Jewish population were ignoring the boycott of Jewish shops, and I observed that the Jews were mainly interested in the stall selling Jewish bread, which no Poles were approaching. Moreover, it was observed that the Jews were making fewer complaints to the police about the peasants boycotting them, and it would appear from their behavior as if they had become resigned to everything. About 15.00 hours a certain Strzałkowski from the village of Goszczewice, *gmina* Przytyk, standing near the Jewish bread-stall, shouted at peasants approaching the stalls and tried to stop them by force. Following a complaint by Jews who had seen this, Strzałkowski was asked to identify himself by police constable Aniołek. He refused to do so and the policeman therefore tried to take him to the state police station, but Strzałkowski categorically refused to go to the police station. Meanwhile about 100 people had gathered and shouted objections to Strzałkowski's being taken to the state police station. By surrounding police constable Aniołek, they prevented his attempt to take Strzałkowski to the police station. Police constable Aniołek left the crowd and reported the above to the station commander, and pointed out Strzałkowski, who had meanwhile climbed onto a wagon. The station commander, with five policemen, ordered Strzałkowski to identify himself. As he had no identity papers, they asked him to go to the police station. Strzałkowski categorically refused and, seeing the mob gathering around him, tore himself away from the station commander and ran into the gateway of a house. At the same time the mob became dangerous and tried to attack the police. After Strzałkowski had escaped, the police called on the mob to disperse and had to face stones, a whippletree, and a small chair being thrown at them by the mob. They had to retreat to the gateway of the police station, followed by a mob 300 strong. But the police, with fixed bayonets on their guns, prevented them approaching nearer, and the mob, persuaded by several people calling for calm, retreated from the gateway and stopped nearby.

The station commander, having contacted the Director of the Investigation Department by the telephone, acted on his orders. He collected all his thirteen policemen and started to break up the crowd. The latter would only disperse under the threat of firearms being used. But it did disperse and peace followed. As a large number of Jews, mostly youths, had at the same time gathered on the pavements to watch the police and the crowd, the police started to disperse the Jews, who ran off in all directions, and calm prevailed. Groups of police then started to patrol the square, while the station commander went back to the station to report to the Investigation Department about having restored order. At this moment, several Jews burst into the police station to report a fight in Zachęta (Przytyk District) near the church. The police went there at once and discovered that on that side of the bridge both Poles and Jews were throwing stones at each other; the Jews were throwing stones from their houses and the side streets, while Poles were throwing stones from the street. Meanwhile a considerable crowd had gathered on the bridge, trying to force their way to the square through the Jews attacking them with stones. The police charged both Jews and Poles and did not allow it. The crowd then retreated toward the church, and panic broke out among the peasants, who started to run and flee the town. This encouraged the Jews to start throwing stones and to chase the fleeing peasants, especially those running from the square. The result was that a great panic broke out among the peasants in the square, who started to flee toward the church on foot and by wagon. At the same time these appealed to the police, who were breaking up the crowd in front of the church to stop the Jews killing Poles in the square. But the police could not cope as there were only five of them.

Once the crowd in front of the church began to disperse back to their homes, the police started to move back toward the square. Here they found that Jews were indeed attacking peasants with stones and metal objects. They kept appearing suddenly from the narrow alleys and throwing stones at the peasants standing in the square and on Warszawska Street. The police tried to break up the fighting here as well. But because news spread that Jews were killing Poles, those peasants already on their way home returned to the town and tried to reach the square. The police, however, prevented this, and only individuals managed to force their way into the square. These were reinforced by the peasants who were coming back from the marketplace and they started to throw stones at the windows of the Jewish homes in the square, and especially at those on Warszawska Street. At this point the police charged the peasants, who fled in panic toward the church. Then several pistol shots were fired from the window of Leska, Moszek's [sic- Shlomo Lesko's] first-floor apartment on Warszawska Street, and these killed Wieśniak, Stanisław, from Wrzos village. Here I should add that after the Jews notified the police station that there was fighting in Zachęta near the church and the police arrived there, they found that Kubiak, Stanisław, from Słowików village had already been badly wounded, having been shot by Jews.

Separately from the above, peasants reported to the police that several Jews had used firearms. So far the exact number of peasants wounded had not been determined, and there are no exact figures over the Jews. In addition, Josek Minkowski, from Podgajek (Przytyk District), was killed, and his wife Chaja was fatally wounded, dying during the night in [the] hospital in Radom. It was not determined when Minkowski was killed, because the above events took place over a relatively short period of time, about 45 minutes, and the mob moved rapidly from place to place.

None of the police was hurt in suppressing the incidents. It has been established beyond doubt, that only Jews used firearms during the events, while peasants used mainly stones and clubs. [. . .]

Source: Radom- Report no. K.D. 172/36 from the Commander of the District (Powiat) State Police, Police Officer Munk, to the Commander of the Provincial State Police in Kielce about the incidents of March 9, 1936, in Przytyk. Dated March 14, 1936. In Adam Penkalla, " 'The Przytyk Incidents' of 9 March 1936 from

Archival Documents," *Polin* 5 (1990), 329, doc. 1. Original in Archiwum Państwowe w Kielcach, Urząd Wojewódzki Kielecki I, vol. 3533, pp. 409–11. Translated from the Polish by Adam Penkalla.

Document 9.5. Prohibition against Making Arrests at Fairs, Markets, and the Like Where the Crowd May Prevent Them

Before the Przytyk pogrom (March 9, 1936), a mob prevented a police officer from arresting a picketer and forced several officers to retreat, and then attacked Jews (see Document 9.3). In the aftermath, police were ordered to cease confronting crowds in order to protect Jews.

Kielce, July 14, 1936.

To the Chief of the Investigative Office and the County Commanders in the Kielce District.

In a town [Przytyk] in the Kielce district, there was an event in which the prosecutorial authorities ordered the police to arrest a certain individual for agitation against Jews. The commander of the police station, intending to execute the prosecutor's order, came to arrest this individual at the market during the fair, and it was at the time when the individual was calling the population to boycott the Jewish shops and stalls, pushing buyers away from them.

The commander of the station met with the active resistance of the arrested person, who was later assisted by a crowd of several hundred people who, having taken an aggressive attitude, did not allow the arrest to take place. In this situation, the policeman was forced to abandon his task.

It then follows from the aforementioned that the policeman acted unwisely, because under the conditions described above, he should not have attempted the arrest at all, due to the high probability of finding resistance both from the arrested and from the collective counteraction of the crowd; since there were about six thousand people at the fair. This probability, of course, found its confirmation, and, by giving up the arrest out of necessity, the policeman undermined the authority of the police uniform and caused the seeming impunity of the restive crowd.

From the experience described above delivers the conclusion that in cases when political, anti-Jewish, and [other such] issues are concerned, individual policemen should not make arrests during fairs, markets, and similar population gatherings when there is a suspicion that the arrested person has a number of supporters in the crowd who will then come to his aid.

Arrest in such cases can only be carried out when the police have sufficient resources necessary to break possible resistance and to suppress possible collective outbreaks. Otherwise one should wait for the right time and place when one would not expect any resistance from the crowd.

To avoid similar events in the future, the county commanders will instruct their subordinates, at briefings or during training, under what circumstances to attempt arrests, dismiss illegal meetings, and so on, so that the police activities end with a desirable effect.

Source: The Kielce District Command of the State Police No. I.0.3/9. United States Holocaust Memorial Musuem (USHMM) Archives, RG 15.456, p. 34. Translated from the Polish by Anna Cichopek-Gajraj.

Document 9.6. The Pogrom in Mińsk Mazowiecki

Polish pogroms usually followed a "trigger" event. In Mińsk Mazowiecki, in June 1936, a mentally ill army veteran named Judah Leib Chaskielewicz killed his former officer, Sergeant Jan Bujak. This act sparked a rampage in which sixty Jews were wounded.

A report then came that the funeral of the sergeant would be taking place soon, and that the Endeks [followers of Endecja] were preparing to use that occasion for another pogrom. The Bund [Jewish Socialist] Central Committee now sent Comrade Yoysef Gutgold and me down to Mińsk [Mazowiecki]. We appealed to the PPS [Polish Socialist Party], and they sent one of their party activists to go with us. Together, we were supposed to seek any means of avoiding another outbreak, and to organize a resistance group in case another pogrom did in fact break out. Gutgold went because he was Secretary of the Central Committee of the Leather Workers Union in which both Poles and Jews were members, and in Mińsk Mazowiecki there was a local of the union of Polish cobblers who knew Gutgold well because he worked on their labor issues for them, helping them with their battles and their strikes. The comrade from the PPS went with us to connect us with the PPSers there and to win their help to ward off another pogrom.

The three of us arrived together in Mińsk Mazowiecki. The city looked deserted. No living soul was to be seen on the streets. The businesses in the center of the town were boarded up (they were all Jewish businesses). All the homes were shuttered. It was so empty and sad that, walking through the silent, empty streets, we were afraid of the echo of our own footsteps. Adding to our apprehension: our PPSer, who was a real Pole, looked like a Jew.

We went over to the office of the Cobblers Union. It was closed. We stood and waited. Soon a committee member came and opened the office. We stepped inside. In the course of about a half hour, the Cobblers Union committee members gradually gathered. We sat down to talk things over. Everyone was in a somber mood. The Polish cobblers stated that they didn't believe they would be able to do anything. The antisemitic fire the Endeks had lit was so great that there was no way you could talk to a Pole and appeal to his sense of justice.

I wanted to cheer things up a bit to dispel the somber mood, so I said: "We, that is, those of us who have just come from Warsaw, have not eaten yet, and you probably haven't either. Let's all go get a bite to eat." Soon food and drink were brought in (and some whiskey as well). We all sat down to eat, but it didn't do much good. We ate in silence. No one spoke. The general mood did not improve.

Suddenly we heard the ringing of church bells. Someone went out to see what was happening and came back with the news that a house was on fire. Antisemitic hooligans had set a Jewish home on fire and the church bells were ringing to summon the firefighters to put out the fire. In many Polish towns it was the practice, in case of a fire, to ring the church bells as a signal summoning the townsfolk to come and extinguish the blaze.

We all left the union office and went to where the fire was. A crowd was standing around the burning house, silently looking on. Fortunately, the house was empty, the Jewish residents having run away beforehand. But fire and wind know no difference between Jew and Pole: the fire quickly spread to a Polish house next door. When we arrived, the flames were licking ever more fiercely at the roof of the Polish house.

The onlooking townsfolk continued to gaze quietly at the fire. In an [instant] a thought occurred to me: What if there are people, Poles, inside the house, and something tugged hard at me. In a moment, I was inside the house. Once there, I did in fact find some people in a panic. Children were being saved. Suddenly I noticed an old, paralyzed woman who, in the panic, was forgotten. I grabbed the old woman and carried her out in my arms. A kind of rescue trance overcame me. I went onto the roof, shouting out for water. Now, finally, several people in the crowd ran and brought buckets of water and handed them up to me. I stood up there and threw buckets of water at the tongues of flame. The smoke was choking me, and the tin on the roof was burning the soles of my feet. The flames almost reached me, but I stood fast, pouring water on the fire.

Our group, Yosl Gugold, the PPSer, and the cobblers, who were mixed with the crowd, quickly oriented themselves to the situation, and one of them called out, pointing at me: "Paczcie [original spelling], to Żyd! Żyd ratuje Polski dom!" ("Look, it's a Jew! A Jew is saving a Polish house!"). People in the crowd agreed: "Prawda, to Żyd!" ("True, it's a Jew!"). Our comrades became bolder and began talking and crying out to the crowd: "The Endeks will bring us nothing but misfortune. When they set a Jewish house on fire, all our houses will go up in smoke." Among the crowd, many agreed. At that point our people got up their courage still more and began crying out: "Down with the Endeks!"

The fire grew smaller and died out. I got off the roof and joined my comrades. The people in the crowd were eyeing me intensely, as if they were trying to decide if I really did look like a Jew.

Soon the news spread that a Polish home was burning and that a Jew had put out the fire and had rescued an old paralyzed Christian woman. The crowd got even bigger and each person would tell another what had happened. People began to agree with our cobblers, who, having become ever more bold, said the Endeks were guilty of all kinds of evildoings. It became more and more apparent that the mood of the Polish crowd was changing. Then our group of Polish cobblers began demonstrating in the streets, crying out against the Endeks, and some of the people in the crowd joined with them, and a real anti-Endek demonstration took place. Seeing this, the two of us, Yosl and I, went off to the Jewish neighborhood. We banged on the shutters of the Jewish homes and shouted to them in Yiddish: "Come out, don't be afraid!" Shutters and windows began to open and people came out into the street.

For the rest of the day, the three of us, Yosl, the PPSer, and I, together with a group of the Polish cobblers, walked all around the streets of the town, observing what was going on, and listening to the talk of the townspeople. There were no more assaults, and no more antisemitic incidents in the town. Later that night we traveled back home.

The funeral of the sergeant [Jan Bujak] was carried out peacefully; no further attempts were made to attack Jews in that town.

Source: "The Pogrom in Mińsk Mazowiecki" [excerpt], in Bernard Goldstein, *Twenty Years with the Jewish Labor Bund: A Memoir of Interwar Poland* (Indiana: Purdue University Press, 2016), 363–66. Translated from the Yiddish by Marvin S. Zuckerman.

Document 9.7. Interpolation of Deputy Dr. Emil Sommerstein after Brest on Bug [Brześć nad Bugiem] Pogrom, May 13–14, 1937

In Brześć, in May 1937, a butcher named Ajzik Szczerbowski stabbed the kosher meat inspector Stefan Kędziora as he attempted to confiscate the butcher's merchandise. The pogrom that followed, virtually unimpeded by the police, resulted in many wounded and two eventual casualties, widespread destruction of Jewish stores and stalls, and their replacement by Christian ones.

On the 13th of May, 1937, about 7 h. 30 min. in the morning, a police-agent Stefan Kędziora was stabbed to death by the butcher Szczerbowski while he was confiscating the meat, which, according to the latter, originated from ritual slaughter (*shechita*).

It is well known in what kind of atmosphere we are living. It is created by the constant inciting of the greater part of the press and by the antisemitic agitation. All means are equally good for the antisemites in order to attain their aim, and they are appealing to the lowest instincts of the mob. It could therefore be expected that, guided by their headquarters in Biała Podlaska, they would use this common murder for their designs, and that the mob would profit from this accident in order to have their fun at the expense of the Jewish population. It was, indeed, very easy to organize a pogrom under the slogan: "Jews slayed a policeman."

Therefore at about 9 o'clock in the morning the Governmental Commissioner of the Jewish Congregation at Brest, Dr. Kagan, rang up the Starostwo [District Administration] and signaled them the imminent danger. They answered him that Starosta [district administrator] will not receive anybody in this matter.

In one hour, maybe slightly later, but not later than in two hours, small groups formed, consisting mostly of youth and even of ten- to twelve-year-old boys and of women. Then the riots began. The groups were passing through the streets and, on their way, they were breaking windowpanes in Jewish lodgings and shops. Among the mob which was throwing stones there were even fashionable ladies, wearing hats, who were breaking the windows with their handbags.

Quite independently from these riots, the Christian stall-owners in the market took their revenge on the Jewish ones. At this opportunity, the stalls were upset and a certain number of Jewish stall-owners were beaten. The little stock of their merchandise was to a certain extent destroyed and part of it disappeared.

While this happened a Jewish delegation went to the Starosta. The delegation consisted of: the president of the Jewish Congregation, Kowartowski; physician Dr. Sarnakier; president of the Merchants' Association, Mr. Rosenberg, and Mr. Jaglom. The delegation called the attention of the Starosta to the growth of the antisemitic action and asked for an energetic intervention of the police.

The first thing the Starosta said was that the riots were caused by Jews. He [exhorted] the Jewish population to behave quietly and not to provoke the Christians.

The Jewish delegation refuted this charge, which made the whole Jewish population responsible for a crime committed by a private person. The delegation stated also that the Jewish population was behaving quietly and did not think to provoke anybody.

In the course of this interview the Starosta received a call on the phone. He said that he has just been informed that the Jewish mob is demolishing a Polish school in Sienkiewicz Street.

Later it was proved that this information was false. The school, mentioned above, was not damaged at all and the Jews did not attack anybody, nor defend themselves. Finally, the Starosta declared that he will be on guard concerning order in town.

In the meantime the groups which were breaking the windows were growing steadily. They were joined by unemployed and by the lowest classes of the population, armed with iron bars and axes. The windows were broken in all Jewish shops and lodgings. The non-Jewish shops and lodgings were carefully omitted and remained without any damage, although they were very often in the close neighborhood of the Jewish ones. This discrimination was carried out even before there appeared in the windows images of saints, crosses, and inscriptions "Christian shop."

In the afternoon, small groups were entering by force Jewish shops and lodgings. After having thrown stones, they broke the window frames and the doors. They penetrated into the Jewish lodgings, they destroyed everything and cut off the cushions. Then they threw everything on the street, and the feathers of the cushions formed a white layer on the pavements.

Late in the afternoon, and especially in the evening, the third act was performed: demolishing of the closed Jewish shops.

At about 6 o'clock in the afternoon the delegation of the Jewish population, consisting of: the vice-president of the town, Mr. Mastbaum, the president of the Jewish Congregation, Mr. Kowartowski, Dr. Sanakier, Attorney Głowiński and Jaglom, went to the Wojewoda of Polesie (Governor of the Province). They asked him to act energetically in order to master the grave situation.

The Wojewoda made the Jewish population responsible for the riots. He also reproached the Jews for tolerating illegal ritual slaughter. The delegation showed the groundlessness of these charges and asked him to energetically proceed in order to stop the dangerous riots. As the delegates remarked that the police forces ought perhaps to be reinforced, the Wojewoda declared that he is responsible for the peace and safety in town and that he will give appropriate orders.

In the meantime, the gangs carried on their destruction. They did not omit any shop. The stalls with soda water and sweets disappeared without any trace; only the dug earth showed where they were standing before.

The shops were destroyed one after one, systematically, without hurry, without fear of being disturbed. Slowly they broke iron bars, shutters, and locks, and plundered the goods, destroyed the fittings, bills of promise, documents, correspondence, telephones, and such objects as were difficult to take away or did not present any value for the assailants.

In the streets petroleum and benzine flowed, somewhere else some spirit, and in another one could smell the scent of perfumes; instead of the dust of the street there was a cloud of powder in the air.

They made pavement out of the phonograph records, on which they were cycling.

On the streets, however, no precious objects nor jewels were found.

The poor residents of Kobryńska Street were robbed even of their kitchen vessels.

In another place a wooden house where poor Jewish families were living was pulled down in 15 minutes.

The café of Szapiro, located near the office and lodging of the Wojewoda, where a police guard stands constantly, was demolished, destroyed, and plundered during the bright day.

In a factory of soda water the assailants had to work a long time breaking the machine and reservoirs of copper.

The work went on, without interruption and with great precision, in order not to leave anything in the Jewish shops.

The spirit of destruction prevailed over robbery, but was finally vanquished by the latter. Their combined effect was depriving the Jewish population of all its property, for which it had worked for several generations. It was thus deprived of its means of existence.

But the hooligans were by far not courageous, they ran away whenever they met the slightest resistance.

Such cases were recorded in quarters where workers live.

At Białostocka Street a gang was attacking a house, where in addition to Jews there were also some Christians living. The gang ran away as soon as one of the Christians discharged his gun in the air. In another place, a merchant fired a bug gun and thus saved the rest of his property.

The following case was also related: a lady-merchant alarmed the firemen. When they came, the hooligans ran away. The lady had to pay a fine, but saved her small property.

So it went on until late in the night; they plundered even drug shops (chemists).

According to official reports, there were in Brest 150 policemen from the town and its surroundings.

The reinforcements, sent from Warsaw, in spite of being sent in the afternoon and in the evening, could be deployed on the streets of Brest only in the morning of the next day, when of Jewish lodgings there remained only stones and bricks, and in the shops—broken shutters, pieces of wood, and broken furniture.

Nowhere did the police encounter the hooligans.

The events of the 13th of May were characterized by the correspondent of the "Słowo Wileńskie" in the following way: "What happened here has by far exceeded the Przytyk events." The "Wieczór Warszawski" made a large inscription: "In 16 hours the Jewish shops in Brest were completely destroyed." The "Goniec" wrote about the cancelling [of] debts in Brest; of course, they were not writing about Jewish ones. What cruel irony and horrible delight on account of the terrible tragedy of the Jewish population!

On the next morning, they tried to remove all traces of the terrible destruction from the streets. They carried away lorries of broken glass and mixed together the broken furniture, goods, and the white feathers.

In spite of the presence of 390 policemen (240 arrived from Golodzinow [Golędzinów, suburb of Warsaw] and 50 local ones from the surroundings), they plundered and demolished shops and lodgings in the suburbs until noon of the following day. The suburb of Grajewo [currently Grayevka] suffered the most of all. The police [were] concentrated in the center of the town; however, there was nothing more to guard, though the Police Headquarters were informed several times about the events in the suburbs.

In such a way the destruction and plundering of property of the Jewish population of Brest, amounting to several thousand people, [were] accomplished. They were deprived of the most necessary things: furniture, clothes, and lodgings.

An accomplished, terrible pogrom, which was made systematically and calmly.

Mention must also be made of the many people who were hit [beaten] and who were assisted either in the Jewish or in municipal hospitals or by private physicians.

The question arises: how all this was possible in the principal town of a province (*województwo*) [Polesie] in the presence of the authorities and of the police, in a town which is within four hours of travel by rail or road from Warsaw? People say unanimously that even the least number of police would do at the beginning, or even afterward, to master the situation. It was only the lack of activity of the authorities, responsible for peace and security, which caused the terrible catastrophe of the great Jewish population. They are also responsible for the shame which will never be forgotten, especially since the "reaction" of the Polish population did not follow immediately, but started about two hours after the murder of the agent Kędziora, and was growing systematically under the guidance of leaders from a known party [Stronnictwo Naradowe].

The evidence given by the victims is throwing a bright light on the attitude of the police. Szymon Sondak hid himself in the courtyard in Dąbrowska Street no. 108. This house was attacked by the assailants. The owner locked the gate and tied the hooks on the gate with a thick rope. The assailants could not open the entrance. According to Sondak, a police car then arrived with the agent no. 405. He stopped the car and cut the ropes through a gap of the gate with his bayonet. The assailants penetrated into the yard and hit Sondak. When the latter asked the policeman to assist him, he did not get any answer from him.

Szloma Blinder, defending himself from a gang which was forcing the entrance, spotted four policemen and shouted to them: "Police, help!" and was answered: "Hide yourself!" Blinder was hit with a stone in his eye and ran away. His shop was plundered and only the part of the goods that was destroyed was left.

Mordka Bluberg, after having shut his fruit shop in Dąbrowska Street no. 107, was watching from his lodging, situated over the shop, the events in the street. At 6 o'clock in the afternoon five assailants started to break the entrance of his shop by means of iron bars. Then Bluberg went out on his balcony and shouted for help. He perceived three policemen, among them the district officer Sokołowski, no. 1014. He asked him for help, and then Sokołowski took his gun, directed it toward Bluberg, and shouted: "Run away, or I will fire!" Bluberg hid himself in the lodging and the assailants broke the shutters and plundered his shop.

Jochil Szenmel related that at 11 o'clock he was attacked on Unia Lubelska Street. He related this incident to the policeman on service, Aftanuk.

The policeman replied: "First you kill a policeman, and now you demand assistance. There are no policemen in the Office."

These facts illustrate the attitude of the authorities who were supposed to oppose the violence. They also explain why the destruction and plunder lasted so many hours.

Source: "Interpolation of Deputy Dr. Emil Sommerstein to the Prime Minister, Leader of the Government, and Home Minister in the Case of the Robbery and Destroyment of Property, as well as Beating of the Jewish Population in Brest on Bug [Brześć nad Bugiem], on the 13th and 14th of May, 1937." JDC Archives,

Poland, 1933/44/890, pp. 1–8. Translated from the Polish by anonymous, adjusted for readability.

Document 9.8.   Anticommunist Leaflet: "Paid Russian Stooges, PPR [Polish Workers' Party]"

The bloodiest pogrom in postwar Poland took place in Kielce on July 4, 1946 when a mob plundered, shot, bludgeoned, and thrown out of windows the Holocaust survivors that lived at Planty Street 7. By the end of the day, more than forty people had been killed. This text, published by a Polish anticommunist organization, traffics in the most notorious anti-Jewish tropes: myths of ritual murder and Judeo-Bolshevism.

. . . Here is the last feat of the PPR [Polska Partia Robotnicza or Polish Workers' Party]: the Kielce crime. Living in an apartment building at Planty Street 7 were about 150 Jews (*iwreje*) [Polish spelling of a Russian word for Jews]; a Pole was the janitor of the building. For a long time, little children had been disappearing without a trace in this town. No one knew where and how until July 3 of this year when a nine-year-old little boy miraculously broke free from devilish-communist-Jewish hands; [he was] kidnapped (went missing) on July 1, starved for three days, and was to be murdered on the day of the escape. The janitor of the building, a Pole, knew exactly about the kidnapping and murdering of children; he knew what was going on inside; he knew the number [of children] who had been kidnapped, but did not tell anyone; he kept the secret and joined in the murder. The nine-year-old boy located the niche [*komórka*] where the execution of innocent children is taking place and reported it to the current authorities of the UB [Urząd Bezpieczeństwa, or the office of secret service] and MO [Milicja Obywatelska, or militia]; the reaction was swift, some in the UB and MO went to avenge recently missing and murdered children. In the basement, some mothers recognized the dried corpses of their recently murdered children; please imagine such a scene of such a moment: forty children's skeletons found in that basement—the janitor knew about it [the murder]. Today the PPR is master of life and death and it demands condemnation of those who [went to] avenge the innocent blood of the murdered children; it organized mass meetings and demonstrations with the same aim; it demands signatures from bishops, priests; it demands that the devilish tribe [Jews] be buried in a sacred place. Some in the UB and MO understand now who currently rules Poland; an MO commander from Bliżyn knows about the death of his brother, an UB functionary, who was murdered by his colleagues from the UB because he followed the truth, because he went to avenge the blood of innocent children. [. . .]

O, woe to you, traitor; tears and blood of fathers, mothers, brothers, sisters, and orphans will be avenged. Praise Hitler!! (when it comes to the annihilation of Judeo-communism). [. . .]

We warn all "activists of the PPR," dignitaries in official positions of the UB and MO, and others who harm Poland and Poles, to turn their back from the wrong path while there is still time; to give up serving as the janitor. Death to traitors of Poland!!! Death to agents of the Bolshevik gestapo!!!!!!!!!!!!!

Source: "Płatne Parobki Rosyjskie PPR" [Paid Russian Stooges, PPR], copy, p. 44, Institute of National Memory in Kraków, IPN BU 2207/1. Translated from the Polish by Anna Cichopek-Gajraj.

Further Reading

General Overviews of the History of Pogroms, Coexistence, and Russian and East European Jewish History

Avrutin, Eugene. *Jews and the Imperial State: Identification Politics in Tsarist Russia*. Ithaca, NY: Cornell University Press, 2010.

Avrutin, Eugene M., Jonathan Dekel-Chen, and Robert Weinberg, eds. *Ritual Murder in Russia, Eastern Europe, and Beyond: New Histories of an Old Accusation*. Bloomington: Indiana University Press, 2017.

Bartal, Israel. *The Jews of Eastern Europe, 1772–1881*. Translated by Chaya Naor. Philadelphia: University of Pennsylvania Press, 2005.

Bartov, Omer, and Eric D. Weitz, eds. *Shatterzone of Empires: Coexistence and Violence in the German, Habsburg, Russian, and Ottoman Borderlands*. Bloomington: Indiana University Press, 2013.

Bemporad, Elissa, and Joyce W. Warren, eds. *Women and Genocide: Survivors, Victims, and Perpetrators*. Bloomington: Indiana University Press, 2018.

Bergmann, Werner. *Tumulte – Excesse – Pogrome: Kollektive Gewalt gegen Juden in Europa 1789–1900*. Göttingen: Wallstein, 2020.

Blobaum, Robert E. *Antisemitism and Its Opponents in Modern Poland*. Ithaca, NY: Cornell University Press, 2005.

Brass, Paul R., ed. *Riots and Pogroms*. New York: New York University Press, 1996.

Dekel-Chen, Jonathan, David Gaunt, Natan M. Meir, and Israel Bartal, eds. *Anti-Jewish Violence: Rethinking the Pogrom in East European History*. Bloomington: Indiana University Press, 2011.

Engelstein, Laura. *Russia in Flames: War, Revolution, Civil War 1914–1921*. New York: Oxford University Press, 2018.

Frankel, Jonathan. *Prophecy and Politics. Socialism, Nationalism, and the Russian Jews, 1862–1917*. Cambridge: Cambridge University Press, 1981.

Freeze, ChaeRan Y., and Jay M. Harris, eds. *Everyday Jewish Life in Imperial Russia: Select Documents*. Waltham, MA: Brandeis University Press, 2013.

Hoffmann, Christhard, Werner Bergmann, and Helmut Walser Smith, eds. *Exclusionary Violence: Antisemitic Riots in Modern German History*. Ann Arbor: University of Michigan Press, 2002.

Horowitz, Donald L. *The Deadly Ethnic Riot*. Berkeley: University of California Press, 2001.

Hundert, Gershon D., ed. *The YIVO Encyclopedia of Jews in Eastern Europe*. 2 vols. New Haven, CT: Yale University Press, 2008. https://yivoencyclopedia.org/.

Johnson, Sam. "Uses and Abuses: 'Pogrom' in the Anglo-American Imagination, 1881–1919." In *Jews in the East European Borderlands: Essays in Honor of John D. Klier*, edited by Eugene M. Avrutin and Harriet Murav, 147–66. Boston: Academic Studies Press, 2012.

Judson, Pieter M. *The Habsburg Empire: A New History*. Cambridge, MA: Harvard University Press, 2016.

Klier, John D., and Shlomo Lambroza, eds. *Pogroms: Anti-Jewish Violence in Modern Russian History*. Cambridge: Cambridge University Press, 1992.

Kopstein, Jeffrey S., and Jason Wittenberg. *Intimate Violence: Anti-Jewish Pogroms on the Eve of the Holocaust*. Ithaca, NY: Cornell University Press, 2018.

Meir, Natan M. *Kiev, Jewish Metropolis: A History, 1859–1914*. Bloomington: Indiana University Press, 2010.

Nathans, Benjamin. *Beyond the Pale: The Jewish Encounter with Late Imperial Russia*. Berkeley: University of California Press, 2002.

Nemes, Robert, and Daniel Unowsky, eds. *Sites of European Antisemitism in the Age of Mass Politics, 1880–1918*. Waltham, MA: Brandeis University Press, 2014.

Petersen, Roger D. *Understanding Ethnic Violence: Fear, Hatred, and Resentment in Twentieth-Century Eastern Europe*. Cambridge: Cambridge University Press, 2002.

Polonsky, Antony. *The Jews in Poland and Russia*. 3 vols. Oxford: Littman Library of Jewish Civilization, 2010–2012.

Rogger, Hans. *Jewish Politics and Right-Wing Politics in Imperial Russia*. Berkeley: University of California Press, 1986.

Smith, Helmut Walser. *The Continuities of German History: Nation, Religion, and Race across the Long Nineteenth Century*. Cambridge: Cambridge University Press, 2008.

Weeks, Theodore. *From Assimilation to Antisemitism: The Jewish Question in Poland, 1850–1914*. DeKalb: Northern Illinois University Press, 2006.

Wiese, Stefan. *Pogrome im Zarenreich: Dynamiken kollektiver Gewalt*. Hamburg: Hamburger Edition, 2016.

The Pogroms of 1881–1884

Alroey, Gur. *An Unpromising Land: Jewish Migration to Palestine in the Early Twentieth Century*. Stanford, CA: Stanford University Press, 2014.

Aronson, I. Michael. *Troubled Waters: The Origins of the 1881 Anti-Jewish Pogroms in Russia*. Pittsburgh: University of Pittsburgh Press, 1990.

Boustan, Leah Platt. "Were Jews Political Refugees or Economic Migrants? Assessing the Persecution Theory of Jewish Emigration, 1881–1914." In *The New Comparative Economic History: Essays in Honor of Jeffrey G. Williamson*, edited by Timothy J. Hatton, Kevin H. O'Rourke, and Alan M. Taylor, 267–90. Cambridge, MA: MIT Press, 2007.

Johnson, Sam. *Pogroms, Peasants, Jews: Britain and Eastern Europe's "Jewish Question," 1867–1925*. New York: Palgrave Macmillan, 2011.

Klier, John D. *Russians, Jews, and the Pogroms of 1881–1882*. Cambridge: Cambridge University Press, 2011.

Klier, John D., and Shlomo Lambroza, eds. *Pogroms: Anti-Jewish Violence in Modern Russian History*. Cambridge: Cambridge University Press, 1992.

Staliūnas, Darius. *Enemies for a Day: Antisemitism and Anti-Jewish Violence in Lithuania under the Tsars*. Budapest: Central European Press, 2015.

Weinberg, Sonja. *Pogroms and Riots: German Press Responses to Anti-Jewish Violence in Germany and Russia, 1881–1882*. New York: Peter Lang, 2010.

Wiese, Stefan. "'Spit Back with Bullets!' Emotions in Russia's Jewish Pogroms, 1881–1905." *Geschichte und Gesellschaft* 39, no. 4 (2013): 472–501.

The Kishinev Pogrom

Johnson, Sam. *Pogroms, Peasants, Jews: Britain and Eastern Europe's "Jewish Question," 1867–1925*. New York: Palgrave Macmillan, 2011.

Judge, Edward H. *Easter in Kishinev: Anatomy of a Pogrom*. New York: New York University Press, 1992.

Kopanskii, Ia. M. *Kishinevskii pogrom 1903 goda: Sbornik dokumentov i materialov*. Chişinău: Izdatel'stvo Ruxanda, 2000.

Litvak, Olga. "The Poet in Hell: H. N. Bialik and the Cultural Genealogy of the Kishinev Pogrom." *Jewish Studies Quarterly* 12, no. 1 (2005): 101–28.

Penkower, Monty Noam. "The Kishinev Pogrom of 1903: A Turning Point in Jewish History." *Modern Judaism* 24, no. 3 (2004): 19–43.

Zipperstein, Steven J. *Pogrom: Kishinev and the Tilt of History*. New York: Liverlight, 2018.

The Pogroms of 1905

Ascher, Abraham. *The Revolution of 1905: Russia in Disarray*. Vol. 1. Stanford, CA: Stanford University Press, 1988.

Hamm, Michael. *Kiev: A Portrait, 1800–1917*. Princeton, NJ: Princeton University Press, 1993.

Herlihy, Patricia. *Odessa: A History, 1794–1914*. Cambridge, MA: Harvard University Press, 1986.

Mehlinger, Howard, and John M. Thompson. *Count Witte and the Tsarist Government in the 1905 Revolution*. Bloomington: Indiana University Press, 1972.

Staliūnas, Darius. *Enemies for a Day: Antisemitism and Anti-Jewish Violence in Lithuania under the Tsars*. Budapest: Central European Press, 2015.

Surh, Gerald. "Ekaterinoslav City in 1905: Workers, Jews, and Violence." *International and Labor Working-Class History* 64 (2003): 139–66.

Surh, Gerald. "The Jews of Ekaterinoslav in 1905 as Seen from Town Hall: Ethnic Relations on an Imperial Frontier." *Ab Imperio*, no. 4 (2003): 217–38.

Surh, Gerald. "The Role of Civil and Military Commanders during the 1905 Pogroms in Odessa and Kiev." *Jewish Social Studies* 15, no. 3 (2009): 39–55.

Surh, Gerald. "Russia's 1905 Era Pogroms Reexamined." *Canadian-American Slavic Studies* 44 (2010): 253–95.

Ury, Scott. *Barricades and Barriers: The Revolution of 1905 and the Transformation of Warsaw Jewry*. Stanford, CA: Stanford University Press, 2012.

Weinberg, Robert. *The Revolution of 1905 in Odessa: Blood on the Steps*. Bloomington: Indiana University Press, 1993.

Weinberg, Robert. "The Russian Right Responds to 1905: Visual Depictions of Jews in Postrevolutionary Russia." In *The Revolution of 1905 and Russia's Jews*, edited by Stefani Hoffman and Ezra Mendelsohn, 55–69. Philadelphia: University of Pennsylvania Press, 2008.

Wiese, Stefan. "Jewish Self-Defense and Black Hundreds in Zhitomir: A Case Study on the Pogroms of 1905 in Tsarist Russia." *Quest: Issues in Contemporary Jewish History* 3 (2012): 241–66.

Wiese, Stefan. "'Spit Back with Bullets!' Emotions in Russia's Jewish Pogroms, 1881–1905." *Geschichte und Gesellschaft* 39, no. 4 (2013): 472–501.

World War I

An-sky, S. *The 1915 Diary of S. An-sky: A Russian Jewish Writer at the Eastern Front*. Translated by Polly Zavadivker. Bloomington: Indiana University Press, 2016.

Gatrell, Peter. *A Whole Empire Walking: Refugees in Russia during World War I*. Bloomington: Indiana University Press, 1999.

Gendler, Alexander, ed. *Khurbm 1914–1922: Prelude to the Holocaust: The Beginning*. Skokie, IL: Varda Books, 2019.

Goldin, Semion. "The 'Jewish Question' in the Tsarist Army in the Early Twentieth Century." In *The Revolution of 1905 and Russia's Jews*, edited by Stefani Hoffman and Ezra Mendelsohn, 70–76. Philadelphia: University of Pennsylvania Press, 2008.

Graf, Daniel W. "Military Rule behind the Russian Front, 1914–1917: The Political Ramifications." *Jahrbücher für Geschichte Osteuropas* 22, no. 3 (1974): 390–411.

Lohr, Eric. "The Russian Army and the Jews: Mass Deportations, Hostages, and Violence during World War I." *Russian Review* 60, no. 3 (2001): 404–19.

Löwe, Heinz-Dietrich. *The Tsars and the Jews: Reform, Reaction and Anti-Semitism in Imperial Russia, 1772–1917*. Chur: Harwood Academic, 1993.

Prusin, Alexander Victor. *Nationalizing a Borderland: War, Ethnicity and Anti-Jewish Violence in East Galicia, 1914–1920*. Tuscaloosa: University of Alabama Press, 2005.

Zavadivker, Polly. "Reconstructing a Lost Archive: Simon Dubnow and 'The Black Book of Imperial Russian Jewry.' Materials for a History of the War, 1914–1915." *Simon Dubnow Institute Yearbook* 12 (2013): 419–42.

Zieliński, Konrad. "The Shtetl in Poland, 1914–1918." In *The Shtetl: New Evaluations*, edited by Steven T. Katz, 102–20. New York: New York University Press, 2009.

The Russian Revolution and Civil War

Abramson, Henry. *A Prayer for the Government: Ukrainians and Jews in Revolutionary Times, 1917–1920*. Cambridge, MA: Harvard University Press, 1999.

Astashkevich, Irina. *Gendered Violence: Jewish Women in the Pogroms of 1917 to 1921*. Boston: Academic Studies Press, 2018.

Bemporad, Elissa. *Legacy of Blood: Jews, Pogroms, and Ritual Murder in the Lands of the Soviets*. New York: Oxford University Press, 2019.

Bemporad, Elissa, and Thomas Chopard, eds. "The Pogroms of the Civil War at 100: New Trends, New Sources." Special issue of *Quest: Issues in Contemporary Jewish* 15 (2019): V–195.

Budnitskii, Oleg. *Russian Jews between the Reds and the Whites, 1917–1920*. Translated by Timothy J. Portice. Philadelphia: University of Pennsylvania Press, 2012.

Gusev-Orenburskii, Sergei I. *Bagrovaia kniga: Pogromy 1919–1920 gg. na Ukraine*. Harbin: DEKOPO, 1922.

Heifetz, Elias. *The Slaughter of the Jews in the Ukraine in 1919*. New York: Thomas Seltzer, 1921.

Kalman, Mihaly. "Shtetl Heroes: Jewish Armed Self-Defense from the Pale to Palestine." PhD diss., Harvard University, 2017.

Khiterer, Victoria. *Jewish Pogroms in Kiev during the Russian Civil War, 1918–1920*. Lewiston, NY: Edwin Mellen Press, 2015.

Klier, John D., and Shlomo Lambroza, eds. *Pogroms: Anti-Jewish Violence in Modern Russian History*. Cambridge: Cambridge University Press, 1992.

McGeever, Brendan. *Antisemitism and the Russian Revolution*. Cambridge: Cambridge University Press, 2019.

Miliukova, Lidia B. ed., *Kniga pogromov: Pogromy na Ukraine, v Belorussii i evropeiskoi chasti Rossii v period Grazhdanskoi voiny, 1918–1922 gg. Sbornik dokumentov*. Moscow: ROSSPEN, 2007.

Ostrovskii, Zalman S. *Evreiskie pogromy, 1918–1921*. Moscow: Shkola i kniga, 1926.

Tcherikower, Elias. *Antisemitizm un pogromen in Ukraine, 1917–1918: Tsu der geshikhte fun ukrainish-yidishe batsiungen*. Berlin: Ostjudisches Historisches Archiv, 1923.

Tcherikower, Elias. *Di ukrainer pogromen in yor 1919*. New York: YIVO, 1965.

Veidlinger, Jeffrey. *In the Midst of Civilized Europe: The Pogroms of 1918–1921 and the Onset of the Holocaust*. New York: Metropolitan Books, 2021.

Anti-Jewish Violence in East-Central Europe

Aleksiun, Natalia. "Crossing the Line: Violence against Jewish Women and the New Model of Antisemitism in Poland in the 1930s." *Jewish History* 33, no. 1–2 (2020): 133–62.

Blobaum, Robert, ed. *Antisemitism and Its Opponents in Modern Poland*. Ithaca, NY: Cornell University Press, 2005.

Brykczynski, Paul. *Primed for Violence: Murder, Antisemitism, and Democratic Politics in Interwar Poland*. Madison: University of Wisconsin Press, 2016.

Buchen, Tim. *Antisemitismus in Galizien: Agitation, Gewalt und Politik gegen Juden in der Habsburgermonarchie um 1900*. Berlin: Metropole Verlag, 2012.

Buryła, Sławomir, Kamil Kijek, Artur Markowski, and Konrad Zieliński, eds. *Pogromy Żydów na ziemiach polskich w XIX i XX wieku tom 2: Studia przypadków (do 1939 roku)*. Warsaw: Instytut Historii PAN, 2019.

Cichopek, Anna. "The Cracow Pogrom of August 1945: A Narrative Reconstruction." In *Contested Memories: Poles and Jews during the Holocaust and Its Aftermath*, edited by Joshua D. Zimmerman, 221–38. New Brunswick, NJ: Rutgers University Press, 2003.

Dynner, Glenn. "'I Burn but I Cannot Be Consumed': War, Pogroms, and the Revival of Jewish Religious Life in Vilna." In *Jews during the First World War*, edited by Joshua Karlip. Leiden: Brill, 2022.

Engel, David. "Patterns of Anti-Jewish Violence in Poland, 1944–1946." *Yad Vashem Studies* 26 (1998): 43–85.

Grabski, August, ed. *Pogromy Żydów na ziemiach polskich w XIX i XX wieku tom 4: Holokaust i Powojnie (1939–1946)*. Warsaw: Instytut Historii PAN, 2019.

Gross, Jan T. *Fear: Antisemitism in Poland after Auschwitz: An Essay in Historical Interpretation*. New York: Random House, 2006.

Gutman, Israel, Ezra Mendelsohn, Jehuda Reinharz, and Antony Polonsky, eds. *The Jews of Poland between Two World Wars*. Waltham, MA: Brandeis University Press, 1989.

Hagen, William W. *Anti-Jewish Violence in Poland, 1914–1920*. Cambridge: Cambridge University Press, 2018.

Lewin, Isaac. *A History of Polish Jewry during the Revival of Poland*. New York: Shengold, 1990.

Liekis, Sarunas, Lidia Miliakova, and Antony Polonsky. "Three Documents on Anti-Jewish Violence in the Eastern Kresy during the Polish–Soviet Conflict." *Polin* 14 (2001): 116–49.

Melzer, Emanuel. *No Way Out: The Politics of Polish Jewry, 1935–1939*. Cincinnati: Hebrew Union College Press, 1997.

Michlic, Joanna. *Poland's Threatening Other: The Image of the Jew from 1880 to the Present*. Lincoln: University of Nebraska Press, 2006.

Mick, Christopher Mick. *Lemberg, Lwów, L'viv, 1914–1947: Violence and Ethnicity in a Contested City*. West Lafayette, IN: Purdue University Press, 2015.

Penkalla, Adam. "'The Przytyk Incidents' of 9 March 1936 from Archival Documents." *Polin* 5 (1990): 327–53.

Soboń, Marcin. *Polacy wobec Żydów w Galicji doby autonomicznej w latach 1868–1914*. Kraków: Verso, 2011.

Struve, Kai. *Bauern und Nation in Galizien: Über Zugehörigkeit und soziale Emanzipation im 19. Jahrhundert I*. Göttingen: Vandenhoeck & Ruprecht, 2005.

Tokarska-Bakir, Joanna. *Pod klątwą: społeczny portret pogromu kieleckiego*. 2 vols. Warsaw: Czarna Owca, 2018.

Unowsky, Daniel. *The Plunder: The 1898 Anti-Jewish Riots in Habsburg Galicia*. Stanford, CA: Stanford University Press, 2018.

Żyndul, Jolanta. *Zajścia antyżydowskie w Polsce w latach 1935–1937*. Warsaw: Fundacja im. K. Kelles-Krauza, 1994.

Contributors

Eugene M. Avrutin is the Tobor Family Endowed Professor of Modern European Jewish History at the University of Illinois, Urbana-Champaign. He is the author and coeditor of seven books, including *Jews and the Imperial State: Identification Politics in Tsarist Russia* (2010) and *Ritual Murder in Russia, Eastern Europe, and Beyond: New Histories of an Old Accusation* (2017). *The Velizh Affair: Blood Libel in a Russian Town* was published by Oxford University Press in 2018.

Elissa Bemporad is the Jerry and William Ungar Chair in East European Jewish History and the Holocaust, and a professor of history at Queens College and the Graduate Center–CUNY. She is the author of two award-winning books: *Becoming Soviet Jews: The Bolshevik Experiment in Minsk* (2013, National Jewish Book Award, Fraenkel Prize in Contemporary History, and runner-up Jordan Schnitzer Prize in Modern Jewish History), and *Legacy of Blood: Jews, Pogroms, and Ritual Murder in the Lands of the Soviets* (Oxford University Press, 2019, National Jewish Book Award). She is also the coeditor of *Women and Genocide: Survivors, Victims, Perpetrators* (2018). Her projects in progress include research the biography of Ester Frumkin and the first volume of the six-volume history *A Comprehensive History of the Jews in the Soviet Union*, which will be published by New York University Press. She is the coeditor of *Jewish Social Studies*.

Anna Cichopek-Gajraj is an associate professor of history at Arizona State University. Her research focuses on Polish-Jewish relations, antisemitism, and ethnic violence in Poland and in the Polish-Jewish diaspora after the Holocaust. Her book *Beyond Violence: Jewish Survivors in Poland and Slovakia in 1944–1948* (2014) was a finalist for the 2016 Jordan Schnitzer Book Award and a recipient of the 2015 Barbara Heldt Prize Honorable Mention. Her first book *Pogrom Żydów w Krakowie 11 sierpnia 1945 r*, a case study of the pogrom in Kraków in August 1945 based on her master's thesis, was published by the Jewish Historical Institute in 2000. She is a recipient of the 2016 Shofar Zakhor Award from the Phoenix Holocaust Survivors' Association for "exhibiting and carrying out the work of Holocaust education, Holocaust remembrance, and community interaction."

Glenn Dynner is the chair of the religion department at Sarah Lawrence College and a Guggenheim Fellow. He is author of *"Men of Silk": The Hasidic Conquest of Polish Jewish Society* (Oxford University Press, 2006), and *Yankel's Tavern: Jews, Liquor & Life in the Kingdom of Poland* (Oxford University Press, 2014). He is the editor of *Holy Dissent: Jewish and Christian Mystics in Eastern Europe* (2011); coeditor of the special issue of *Polin* 27 (2015) on Jews in the Kingdom of Poland; and coeditor of *Warsaw. The Jewish Metropolis: Essays in Honor of the 75th Birthday of Professor Antony Polonsky* (2015). He is the coeditor of the journal *Shofar: An Interdisciplinary Journal of Jewish Studies*; and is working on a monograph titled "Godfearers: Hasidism in Interwar & Nazi-Occupied Poland."

Harriet Murav is the Catherine and Bruce Bastian Professor of Global and Transnational Studies in the Department of Slavic Languages and Literatures and in the Program in Comparative and World Literatures at the University of Illinois, Urbana-Champaign, and the editor of *Slavic Review*. She is the author of *Holy Foolishness: Dostoevsky's Novels & the Poetics of Cultural Critique* (1992); *Russia's Legal Fictions* (1998), which was awarded the MLA 1999 Scaglione Prize for Studies in Slavic Languages and Literatures; *Identity Theft: The Jew in Imperial Russia and the Case* of *Avraam Uri Kovner* (2003); *Music from a Speeding Train: Jewish Literature in Post-Revolution Russia* (2011); and *David Bergelson's Strange New World: Untimeliness and Futurity* (2109). She is the co-translator, with Sasha Senderovich, of David Bergelson's *Judgment* (2017). Her new project is "Hefker: The Literature of Abandonment and the Russian Civil War."

Daniel Unowsky is a professor of history at the University of Memphis. His most recent book, *The Plunder: The 1898 Anti-Jewish Riots in Habsburg Galicia*, was published in 2018. His first book, *The Pomp and Politics of Patriotism: Imperial Celebrations in Habsburg Austria, 1848–1918*, was published in 2005. He has also coedited two volumes of essays, one on dynastic patriotism in the Habsburg lands and one on anti-Jewish violence. He is the editor of the *Austrian History Yearbook* and serves on the editorial board of the Purdue University Press book series Central European Studies.

Jeffrey Veidlinger is the Joseph Brodsky Collegiate Professor of History and Judaic Studies and director of the Frankel Center for Judaic Studies at the University of Michigan. He is the author of the award-winning books *The Moscow State Yiddish Theater: Jewish Culture on the Soviet Stage* (2000), *Jewish Public Culture in the Late Russian Empire* (2009), and *In the Shadow of the Shtetl: Small-Town Jewish Life in Soviet Ukraine* (2013), and the editor of *Going to the People: Jews and Ethnographic Impulse* (2016).

Robert Weinberg is the Isaac H. Clothier Professor of History and International Relations at Swarthmore College, where he teaches European, Jewish, and Russian history. Spanning more than thirty years, his research has focused on various aspects of antisemitism and government policies toward Jews in the Russian Empire and the Soviet Union. In particular, he has written about pogroms, ritual murder, and anti-Judaism campaigns as well as the 1905 revolution in Odessa and the Jewish Autonomous Region.

Polly Zavadivker is an assistant professor of history and the director of the Jewish Studies Program at the University of Delaware. She is currently at work on a book manuscript, "A Nation of Refugees: World War I and the End of Russia's Jews," under contract with Oxford University Press. Her previous publications include, as editor and translator, S. An-sky's *1915 Diary: A Russian Jewish Writer at the Eastern Front* (2016); as well as articles in *Quest: Issues in Contemporary Jewish History*, *The Simon Dubnow Institute Yearbook*, and the multivolume series *Russia's Great War and Revolution*.

Steven J. Zipperstein is the Daniel E. Koshland Professor in Jewish Culture and History at Stanford University. He is the author and editor of nine books, most recently *Pogrom: Kishinev and the Tilt of History*. He is currently writing a biography of Philip Roth for Yale University's Jewish Lives series. Zipperstein is a frequent contributor to the *New York Times Sunday Book Review*, *Jewish Review of Books*, and other general as well as scholarly publications.

Index